D0153016

THE ANALYSIS OF
PERFORMANCE ART

Contemporary Theatre Studies

A series of books edited by Franc Chamberlain, Nene College, Northampton, UK

Please see the back of this book for other titles in the Contemporary Theatre Studies series

THE ANALYSIS OF PERFORMANCE ART

A guide to its theory and practice

Anthony Howell

harwood academic publishers
Australia • Canada • China • France • Germany • India
Japan • Luxembourg • Malaysia • The Netherlands
Russia • Singapore • Switzerland

Amsteldijk 166
1st Floor
1079 LH Amsterdam
The Netherlands

British Library Cataloguing in Publication Data
Howell, Anthony, 1945 –
The analysis of performance art : a guide to its theory and practice. –
(Contemporary theatre studies ; v. 32)
1. Performance art – Philosophy
I. Title
700.1

ISBN: 90–5755–085–7 (hard cover)

Cover illustration: Anthony Howell and Esther Rumble in *Objects*. Photograph: Jeni Cooper

CONTENTS

INTRODUCTION TO THE SERIES

Contemporary Theatre Studies is a book series of special interest to everyone involved in theatre. It consists of monographs on influential figures, studies of movements and ideas in theatre, as well as primary material consisting of theatre-related documents, performing editions of plays in English, and English translations of plays from various vital theatre traditions worldwide.

Franc Chamberlain

ACKNOWLEDGEMENTS

For help with research I would like to thank Helen Clifford and Emma Posey; for suggestions, critical responses and encouragement I would like to thank my editors and Chris Short and Miško Šuvaković; while for academic support I owe much to Glyn Jones and the University of Wales Institute, Cardiff. In addition I strongly appreciate the enormous help all the artists and their photographers and agents have given me in the creation of this book.

LIST OF PLATES

PREFACE

I've noticed that there is a term common both to psychoanalysis and to my own theory of performance art. The term is *repetition*. I've identified this in performance art as a primary element (similar to a primary colour in painting in that it cannot be created by a mixture of any other elements). In analysis, repetition is associated with obsession. Jacques Lacan identifies it as one of the fundamental concepts of the field. In the celebrated instance of the "fort–da", Freud noticed that a child whose mother had to go away during the day played with an object attached to a thread. "Fort!" the child would exclaim, throwing the object away from his body: "Da!" he would say, pulling it back by the thread. The game was repeatedly played, suggesting to Freud that the child had sublimated his mother's absence by associating it with his own wilful throwing-away of an object whose return he could control. This observation paved the way for Freud's recognition of the notion of the *transference*.

So what is the notion of transference to performance art? Here, I'm reminded of a useful aesthetic principle which has a bearing on performance: use something you have already used *again*, but in a different way to the way you used it first. We might call this a *transference of use*. Here's an example. In my own "Homage to Raymond Roussel", a girl repeatedly removes her shoes in order to change her stockings. She also employs a hairbrush to brush her hair. Later in the piece, she spills rice on the floor and uses hairbrush and shoe as a sort of dustpan and brush to clear away the rice.

It now seems intriguing to examine certain performance terms in the light of analysis, and to examine certain analytic terms in the light of performance. For instance, what do terms such as "inconsistency" or "stillness" imply in psychoanalysis? What do terms such as "the drive" and "the unconscious" imply in performance?

First we need to get some of the principles of performance straight, since as yet there exists no grammar covering its discipline, a discipline which is nevertheless clearly distinct from that of theatre. Initially I set out to rectify this absence of a grammar, and my book is as much an attempt to identify the components of an action art as it is a psychical interpretation of that art. I took colour theory as my model. Aside from black and white, which are strictly tones rather than colours, painting has three indivisible primaries. Mixing these produces secondary colours. Similarly, performance has three primaries (though one may be considered a ground common to both the others), and these may be mixed to create secondary actions. The primary actions are *stillness*, *repetition* and *inconsistency*.

xiii

It is interesting to note that while repetition is a term much used in psychoanalysis, inconsistency is not used so often, or rather, it is not elevated into a concept, as is repetition. Gilles Deleuze uses the term "difference" (and has enlightening observations to make about this term in his book *Difference and Repetition*). But difference is not inconsistency: it is rather a commodity repetition must rely upon in order to be repetitive. More will be said about what distinguishes inconsistency from difference later, but for now I simply wish to establish that my specific project is to investigate the use of performative terms in a psychoanalytic context and vice versa. My guess is that some surprising insights will become apparent as we examine these disciplines in the light of each other.

As we do so, I shall cite examples, describing performances I have seen, and some which I haven't seen but have read about, and some which I know about only by hearsay. I see no need to apologise to historians over this. Few reviewers were willing to cover performance in its early days. And it is only recently that the live work of these artists has begun to be adequately recorded, and some of it eludes photographic or video-taped documentation. It is in the nature of this transient form that often its news has only been narrated aurally, relayed from one practitioner to another; and if the imagination sometimes supplies what memory lacks, so be it. It is thus that the art has assumed its mantle of legend.

Given its psycho/active interface, the book is designed to be a manual for the performance artist. It follows the stages of a course I have been teaching for several years, and those who would practise this art are advised not to plough through it but to treat each of its chapters methodically, gaining confidence and control in each aspect of the subject before moving on by working through the exercises to be found at the conclusion of each chapter. At a later stage these exercises can be referred to via the index should the performer wish to inquire into some particular component.

The exercises themselves are only examples of the possibilities indicated by the preceding text. Naturally they can be altered, adjusted, made simpler or more complex – and many other exercises inspired by the chapters may be invented. *Free Sessions* – periods of improvisation – should also be held at least once a week, since these provide the best way of digesting the information supplied and turning it into performative material. The clothing worn, the objects used, the items of furniture placed on the space, should all be considered, prior to the free session, together with its lighting. Emphasis should also be placed on the creation of solos, duets and trios, and time allowed to prepare these.

One further consideration. Psychoanalysis has many camps: there's classical theory, ego psychology, Kleinian analysis, personology and process theory – to name but a few of the schisms and developments. Now while I have considerable experience in the field of performance, mine is a lay interest in psychoanalysis, albeit an intense interest, and I wish to make it clear that I find its theorizing stimulating from an artistic, rather than from a therapeutic, point of view. I have some respect for the thoughts of Lacan, who is nevertheless considered an outsider by more orthodox branches of the movement. Suffice it to say that my grasp of this discipline is imaginative rather than comprehensive and that I would unrepentantly claim that mine was a *creative psychoanalysis*, tailored to the use to which I can put it in the field of performance art.

And so, as often as not, I will take those aspects of my enquiry that pertain to action as a point of departure – to lead us away from the analyst's couch and place us on the performance space. I am as intrigued by the divergences which may be revealed as I am by the parallels between the two fields, and shall often be seeking to contrast the psychical concept with its application in an active sphere. And what eventuates is as much a performer's enquiry into psychoanalysis as it is an analysis of the art of performance.

Carolee Schneemann and Robert Morris in a rehearsal for *Site*, a happening by Robert Morris, first performed in New York in 1965. Photograph courtesy of Carolee Schneemann.

Covered in marble dust, Tanja Ostojić stands for two hours in a 5 × 5 metre square of pulverised marble in *Personal Space*, first shown at the 2nd Yugoslav Biennial of Young Artists, Vršac, 1996. Photograph: Saša Gajin.

1

STILLNESS

There's a commonly observed "Zen" content to stillness. This is a stillness gone into itself – a meditative mode. However, there are other ways of being or becoming still. Note these three states:

A   Stillness as arrest
B   Stillness as a state
C   Breaking out of stillness

The *Zen of Stillness* concerns B – a composed state which deepens when one adopts a position which is easy to hold for a long time. The Zen endures, perhaps from the beginning to the end of the piece. Perhaps it begins before the beginning and ends after the audience have gone.

Other notions of stillness emerge. *Arrested Stillness* for instance, when the performer suddenly stops performing, to become engaged in listening or watching. Here the stillness is that of the witness. On stage, in conventional drama, it's common for one person to move or talk while others watch or listen in a position of stasis, their actions arrested or interrupted.

Then there is stillness as *Death or Collapse*. This may often occur after the expenditure of effort. In a dull workshop, this is the commonest, most obvious sort of immobility. One simply lies down on the floor. Limp performers can be dragged into other positions: imagine how the prince may have diverted himself before he actually kissed the Sleeping Beauty. Sleep simulates death, and stillness in a relaxed position performed with the eyes closed will always evoke the dream or the swoon. But there is also the terrifying stillness of *Rigidity*, which may be the tense, static convulsion of madness or the *stiff immobility* of death (as in *Rigor Mortis*).

Death stillness is a non-Zen version of B. But death may suggest or entail rebirth, so another crucial aspect of stillness is C: breaking out of the contained egg of Zen composure, or recovering from or lifting up out of the stillness of death or exhaustion.

Lacan talks about the significance of edges – how sex is not so much the urge to get inside, or the urge to have something within one, so much as the desire to oscillate across the threshold established between inside and outside. Thus the parts which are the landmarks to our entrances are desirable – lips, anus, labia, slit at the tip of the penis, eyelid and ear – but not the liver, not the lungs.

Zen stillness is a continuous drawing-in to the interior, while the stillness of arrest or a stillness which is broken out of are both conditions which lie across the threshold of stillness. *Breaking out of Stillness* implies rebirth.

Note also the difference between "stillness" and "stuckness". For stuckness occurs when arrest is forced or break-out is restrained. Here stillness is imposed on the performer – for example, by ropes or by handcuffs, or by the physical force of other performers. We might call this *Stillness by Restraint*. Such a state of stillness is suffered, as a bird suffers stillness when mesmerized by a snake. This is the stillness of panic, a form of rigidity – the choice of fight or flight stressfully suspended; a state in which one can neither hear nor see, or rather in which one is dazzled or blinded by what one sees, deafened or shocked by what one hears. It's a state akin to hypnosis – a seeing in a frozen state, where some inner vision may be prompted by an outsider or by an outside force.

Physical rigidity, or *rigour*, in performance may read as a catatonic condition; the subject often hiding the hands under the armpits or sitting upon them (poses Breughel uses to depict madness). Here a form of auto-restraint is being practised – the sane part attempting to arrest the unpredictable (and inconsistent) actions of the demented part. Illustrations of patients in lunatic asylums (in Sander Gilman's *Seeing the Insane)* show sufferers from catatonia tying their bodies into knots, or arching to the limit, supported only by head and toes – still perhaps, but very tense indeed in their immobility. Here we have the stillness of the *spasm*, where one muscle is pitted against another as in the performance exercise (and muscle pumping process) referred to as *Dynamic Tension*. This stillness may even start to vibrate (a patina of repetition), which leads to a shuddering, clenching act, probably evoking frustration or rage.

When I was very young, I saw a hypnotist at a fair in France put someone into a rigid, unblinking pose, supposedly a trance. When his arms were lifted away from his sides and released they would slap down tautly against his sides again. The hypnotist was able to write on his subject's eyeballs with a pencil.

The History of Stillness

Performance art emerged out of the "happenings" of the sixties. Stillness was manifest as a key factor in such early experiments since many of these events were devised by visual artists in New York who took the static, two-dimensional image as their starting point. A happening might incorporate a statuesque pose, such as Carolee Schneemann's *Olympia* pose in Robert Morris's *Site,* first performed in 1965. In this piece, the stillness of the pose from Manet's painting provided a contrast to the other artist's active manipulation of the white panels surrounding it.

The notion of becoming a painting, of being a painting incarnate, inspired many of the *tableaux* of previous centuries. Such living images should be part of any history of performance art. In *The Paul Mellon Seminars 1996-7* – organised by Chloe Chard and Helen Langdon – the significance of Emma Hamilton was emphasised in the development of such posed performances – which were popular in the late eighteenth century.

Emma Hamilton in *The Muse of the Dance* – one of her 'attitudes' – etching by Rehberg, courtesy of the British Museum.

Performance art's affinity with visual art rather than theatre can be traced back to the tradition of life-modelling – in which stillness has always been recognised as a skill. Chloe Chard informs us that at the end of the eighteenth century Paolina Borghese, Napoleon's sister, posed in the nude for Canova's sculpture of Venus – and thereafter the Prince, her husband, kept the statue under lock and key! It is Emma Hamilton, however, who turned the art of the model into an art in its own right in the 1790s. In her tableaux, immobility was of short duration, and her attitudes were remarkable for the transitions of mood she was capable of achieving. Chard quotes from the reminiscences of the painter Elisabeth Vigeé-Lebrun:

> "Nothing was more curious than the faculty that Lady Hamilton had acquired of suddenly imparting to all her features the expression of sorrow or joy, and of posing in a wonderful manner in order to represent different characters. Her eye alight with animation, her hair strewn about her, she displayed to you a delicious bacchante, then all at once her face expressed sadness, and you saw an admirable repentant Magdalene.

> *(Spectral Souvenirs,* page 4)

Vigeé-Lebrun describes these attitudes as 'ce talent d'un nouveau genre'. The new genre was performance art. Emma Hamilton used what might be called 'bursts of stillness'. Deducing an understanding of her attitudes from the descriptions of contemporary writers, Chard notes that;

> "Emma dramatically draws attention to the disjunction between the immobility, permanence and aloofness associated with the art of sculpture and the animation of a living human being."

> *(Spectral Souvenirs,* page 18)

Robert Wilson's performance tableaux were celebrated for their employment of stillness and slowness in the seventies. In his fine book on Wilson's theatre, *Conversations with Sheryl Sutton,* Janos Pilinsky talks of *le drame immobile* (see Appendix 2). In such drama the suspension of action has more potency than the conventional unfolding of a plot. The issues raised by this immobility are expanded upon in the book. And we will discuss these issues and Wilson's tableaux in more detail when we come to consider *repetition* and *slowness.*

Gilbert and George also developed motionlessness in *Underneath the Arches,* their seminal "singing sculpture", first shown in 1969, and shown again two decades later – in 1991 at the Sonnabend Gallery – thus confirming the enduring 'sculptural' status of the piece. In it, the rendition of commonplace formal poses prompted by an exchange of glove and stick, poses appropriate to the formality of the suits worn by the two performers, was punctuated by the need for one of them to descend from the table upon which these poses were displayed in order to turn over the sound-cassette in the small recorder placed in front of the table. Stick and glove were exchanged and new poses adopted only when the tape was turned, so the length of the tape dictated the length of the pose. There was a certain 'uncanniness' about their brand of stillness. Freud considered automata uncanny, and noticed an ambiguity about the German word *unheimlich* or 'unhomely', which the standard edition of his works translates as 'uncanny', observing that homeliness itself can also exhibit uneasy, eerie qualities – in the same way as we can talk about a witch's fetish creature as her 'familiar'. About such living statuary there is both familiarity and unfamiliarity. What is familiar is that we are clearly observing living humans in precisely everyday poses: what is unfamiliar is their stillness. And it is the tension between these contradictory qualities which produces the uncanny effect. We shall see that repetition seeks to deny the passage of time, and that inconsistency seeks to establish its passage by creating its markers. Stillness may suggest indifference to time – as a memorial may seem indifferent to the changes of the weather. In his fine essay on *"The Uncanny"*, which accompanied the exhibition he curated for Sonsbeek 93 in the Gemeentemuseum Arnhem, Mike Kelly points out that there is a memorial quality about statues: they stand on tombs, represent the dead. When the dead object proves 'undead' we experience goose-bumps. Consider the voice of the statue of the murdered commendatore in Mozart's *Don Giovanni*. The utterly lifelike statuary created by the neo-classical sculptor Bertel Thorvaldsen constitutes his mausoleum, for he is buried in his own museum in Copenhagen.

Tilda Swinton remains still for longer than the duration of an audio-cassette, sleeping through the day in a glass cabinet. The eccentric William Beckford (1760-1844) maintained that sleeping sculptures were more convincing – sleep supplied a reason for their immobility. Tanja Ostojić stands motionless for hours within a square of marble dust. She's completely shaven, and covered in marble dust herself. With life-like sculpture, we doubt whether the material is really inanimate. With living sculpture we doubt whether the being is really alive. There is, after all, a congealing quality about stillness. We speak of a stilled position as a freeze, and indeed there is an aspect to stillness which suggests coldness – not only the coldness of the lake turning to ice but also the coldness of statues, the coldness of stone. Heat speeds up molecules; while stillness suggests their inertia.

Mention should also be made of a piece by Chris Burden, from California, in which Burden remained in the middle section of a three tier locker for several days. The locker above contained sustenance. The locker below was for excretion. Nothing however was seen but the locker with its three closed compartments. The sounds of bodily functions must have occasionally been heard, but otherwise the piece appears to have been entirely still. One could only contemplate the lockers, knowing that someone was inside.

There is more therefore to stillness than "Zen" depth and physical or psychotic entrapment – more to it than arrest and break-out. The above examples demonstrate the range of this primary action: stillness as a sleep or as a trance, as a painting in corporeal form, as a suspension of the theatrical convention of dialogue and plot development, as indicative of coldness, as an emblem of the enduring quality of sculpture or of the uncanniness of automata – especially after the clockwork movement has ceased or when it suddenly jolts into action – or we can see in stillness a manifestation of sheer physical endurance.

Stillness as a Ground:

It is said that we live in a time / space continuum. In performance art we may consider this a stillness / emptiness continuum. Consider stillness as empty time, into which a performance is to be poured. In the same way, a painter commences with a blank canvas and a composer with a period of silence. These are the grounds upon which their activity occurs. Stretches of blank canvas may remain when the painting is done; just as silence continuously punctuates a musical composition. In a similar manner, the performance emerges out of stillness, stretches of stillness may occur within it, and stillness will punctuate its actions. Before a piece is conceived, a performer starts with an empty space and a durational quantity of stillness within which actions are to occur. Thus stillness may be considered as the ground which persists underneath the other two primaries of action: *repetition* and *inconsistency* (see Figure 1(a)).

During the course of this enquiry we will need to examine each of these primaries in psychoanalytic terms. But let us first tackle an issue raised at this preliminary stage. Does the performer choose to develop the piece in an unfixed durational / spacial amount of still / emptiness by simply *assembling* more and more actions, or does the performer set a limit to the time and a limit to the space and *insert* actions into that defined area?

In general, painters usually insert their painting into a canvas of an already decided size, though of course there are plenty of exceptions to this protocol. Sculptors often assemble. Insertion is a more womblike method, since one's boundaries are already established, while assemblers are akin to the creators of cairns – they can enlarge or diminish their product. In videotape composition, we may note the difference between *assemble* and *insert* editing. Insert editing usually involves separation of sound and vision. Then either the sound-track or the image sequence serves as the spine which is fleshed out by the other element. Such a spine establishes the duration of a video or a performance, just as the canvas defines the size of a painting. Conversely, assemble editing often retains the synchronized unity of sound and image.

Here, though, we need to distinguish between time and stillness. Time is naturally durational, whereas stillness in performative terms is essentially physical. Stillness is *performed,* however immobile it may be. This is why it may be feasible to consider it not as the grounding in time which constitutes the period of the action, but as one of the three primary actions

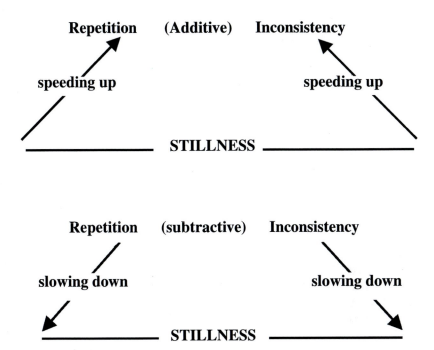

Figure 1(a): Stillness as the ground supporting *repetition* and *inconsistency*

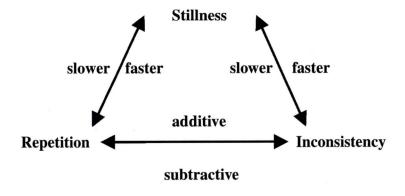

Figure 1(b): *Stillness* as one of the three primary actions

which may be mixed with each other to create secondary actions (see Figure 1(b)). Stillness is hard to perform if it's more than a supine position. Our bodies are like Plasticine – the poses we set them in tend to 'wilt'. The simplest action can become a strain when stilled and sustained. Any life model knows this – it's another factor which contributes to the uncanniness of an extended freeze.

However, if the stilled human being is the obverse of the humanoid automaton, then Freud would have recognised that stillness can be uncanny just as he noted the uncanny effect of 'silence, darkness and solitude'. There is something here about stillness which claims kinship with the 'lost object' spoken of by Lacan, which we will discuss further in the chapter on our 'objects' *(see page* 45). Stillness, like the lost object, can also be 'a lack' – for instance, when a gap in the conversation seems uncanny we speak of an angel 'passing over our grave'. This notion reasserts the case for considering stillness as ground, and perhaps the 'lost object' is literally the ground: the ground the child is set down upon, which is not the mother but which supports and stabilizes him in a motherly way, thus becoming The Mother – and this ground is what gets taken away from him when he tries to stand, suffering a precarious loss of horizontal stability – a stability regained perhaps when the subject is returned to the ground at the conclusion of life.

A Note on the shaping of the Project

This enquiry first developed as a course of workshops, and, during the discourse which the sessions entailed, certain diversions occurred. Issues needed to be raised, and initially the nature of the workshops had to be defined. In order to preserve the integrity of the unfolding of these ideas, I feel that it's best to allow these diversions to be articulated as they happened, so as to remain true to the way the course developed – as if it were some live organism needing to relieve itself of niggling tensions. This should preserve its homeostasis. Such a diversion occurs at this point.

In psychoanalysis, there is *the analyst* (who Lacan refers to as "He who is supposed to know"), and there is *the subject,* and then there is the consulting room and the couch.

I asked the students to consider performance art itself as the subject. I told them, *We are the analysts. Our subject is Performance Art.* And then I said that I accepted that within this metaphorical condition I was "he who is supposed to know" (or "he who is supposed to know most"), coming into the performance space with my own strong projection onto the event.

*   *   *   *

Where are we in this space, prior to our performance? And where are we when we are not performing? Where shall we sit, stand, crouch or perch initially, and perhaps after that as a matter of custom (as if forever)? Where indeed shall we place ourselves to be as forgotten-to-be-there as the analyst?

Since there is no audience other than ourselves in this workshop, and we are also to be performers, we are, in phylogenetic terms, in the position of the chorus in an ancient Greek drama. We are the active witnesses, performing our arrested stillness before the event which may unfold.

While you read this, imagine that we are working in front of a tall white wall with a black curtain hiding us. Suppose that the studio is a larger area than that sectioned off by the curtain. You are one of the performers. Imagine now that the audience will be there if we drop the curtains, and that they will see *us watching* at the same time as they watch the performance.

At present there is only *us watching;* us watching what we are to make out of ourselves. Thus the subject is performance: the analysts are ourselves – positioned in *arrested stillness,* each being both a performer and a place from which to watch what may occur – until we decide to participate in that occurrence (if we are not already doing so by watching it). Here, initially, we define the space by these curtains, and define the performance by where we watch the space from, and define the time it takes by how long we have to watch it in. And in so far as these parameters are defined, the performance will be an insertion within them.

This highlights an obvious problem. Painters begin with a canvas, video-makers with a camera. The performance artist often feels that he or she *begins with a lack,* an absence of what is to occur. One needs to remember though that one's own body is an instrument and that a space and a time is a ground as tangible as any canvas.

How we get to where we wish to perform from our watching place and how we get back again is a matter for consideration. But our *watching* is indeed part of the performance and integral to its making. Certainly the vantage point a painter chooses to observe his painting from will affect the painted result. In our case, our witnessing position is emphatically a "stance" which affects the subject, just as the analyst is indeed part of the analysand. In performance art, one is artist and artwork at the same time. Thus the issue of the 'subject' and its identity is permeated with ambiguity.

Witnessing is a condition of stillness as arrest (and only one of the states of stillness). Moreover, it's a condition that involves listening as well as watching. What, then, do we look like? What, then, do we sound like, in this preliminary stillness in which we look, listen and consider our appearance? In the emptiness of this preliminary stillness there is no performance except us looking, and in this there is already a fullness.

The Reading of Stillness

Stillness enables a reading of the performance piece which is more akin to the way we read a painting than to the way we read a conventional play. When a still tableau is presented, the audience is not required to "follow" the action. They read the scene at their own pace, and the eye travels as it wills, upwards, downwards, across in either direction. When we follow a drama, on the other hand, we are given little time to develop our own thoughts. Instead, we are the receivers of the piece. Our thoughts about it occur in its intervals or after the final curtain. In front of a painting, we develop our own thoughts, and this is an active form of contemplation which the canvas stimulates. We develop our own thoughts also when we look at sculpture. Very often, the emphasis on stillness in a piece of performance art enables this active process to occur in the spectator. If we were to confront the lockers which contained Chris Burden we would have little else to work with other than our own mental observations. Because the spectator is not drawn along like a fish on the end of a hook, performance art retains a kinship with the plastic arts which initially fostered its development. It retains this kinship most specifically perhaps with the art of sculpture. This is why even the most progressive theatre critics have difficulties with performance. They are more used to following a play than to reading a performance. Stillness is probably the key factor which brought about this difference between performance and theatre, between reading the presented text and developing a mental *subtext* during the event.

Stillness enables such a drift of the mind across its surface. It opens up existence to meditation. In conclusion, let us not underestimate this quality of the *Zen* of stillness. Zen of course was mentioned at the outset, but only briefly. Why labour the point, now stillness and the lotus-position have become a cliché? However it is a cliché worth deconstructing. Since time immemorial stillness has been a method for attaining spiritual enlightenment. Stillness is the contemplative being-in-itself of Karl Jaspers, the existentialist; a state opposed to that of being-there, the arena of science, whose repetitive discoveries bring no unity or wholeness, only more accuracy and more detail. Being there is escaped, and being-in-itself arrived at, only through being-oneself. Could a link now be forged between inconsistency and being-oneself?

More recently, in *Anti-Oedipus: capitalism and schizophrenia*, Gilles Deleuze and Felix Guattari have spoken of the body-without-organs, an idealised state of equilibrium relieved from the pressures of the machinery associated with production and demand. Stillness, ultimately, is that body without organs; that carapace: the shell of the turtle; its vehicle, which it moves. To enter its shell, the turtle must pull back its head, withdraw its feet, regress from the world. Perhaps this is why primal psychic repression is like a bump on the nose, a violent inconsistency, like the lightning that changed Saul into Paul. A sudden catastrophe rips us out of the humdrum world into a state of shock, inertia or enlightened meditation. The Zen of stillness is forever balanced by that other stillness which is death.

———

The Stillness Workshop

1. Primary Stillness

After a clap, there is a silence for some fifteen 'internal counts'. Then one performer enters the space and freezes in any position. The stillness of the silence is allowed to deepen. Then a second performer enters the space and freezes in any position. Again the stillness of the silence is allowed to deepen. Subsequent performers enter one at a time, in each case after a deepening interval, and freeze also. When the last performer enters he or she says "I'm the last", before freezing in turn. The stillness is again allowed to deepen, and then the first performer leaves the space, followed, after a deepening interval, by the second performer, and so on, until the last performer is the only one on the space. After another interval of stillness and silence, he or she also quits the space.

2. Stillness Repetitions

Essentially the same exercise as the one above, only this time each performer entering after the first performer has a choice either to repeat a pose already taken up on the performance space or to adopt a fresh one.

3. Sculptures and Armatures

Performers enter the space one at a time. Each becomes frozen, either as sculptural object, or as a support for another performer. Thus performers may adopt stable positions others may utilize or utilize such stable positions as their supports. Last performer to enter says "I'm the last". Stillness prevails until any one performer breaks out of stillness, making some regular noise to signify movement while walking around the still arrangements contemplating his or her next freeze. On freezing again, either as armature or as sculpture supported by an armature, he or she ceases making that regular noise, and then any other performer is free to break out of stillness. However, there should only be one performer moving and making a regular noise at any one time. If two break out of stillness at the same time, both freeze and miss that chance to move.

4. Dynamic Spasms

Each performer claps and throws the body into an unpremeditated position. Dynamic tension – pitting one set of muscles against another set – is then exerted until the entire pose starts to vibrate with the tension. This tension is very gradually relaxed and gradually the performer sinks to the floor, eventually finding the most relaxed position possible. The performer then goes into spasm again on the floor, holds the spasm for as long as possible, relaxes again and then allows the relaxed stillness to deepen.
    Then the performer quietly gets up and repeats the entire exercise.

5. Stuckness

Choose the tallest/strongest member of the group. All the others attempt to restrain his/her movements by any means possible – until the movements of that targeted performer are completely stilled.

6. Stillness Free Session

Improvisation period, utilising only entrances, freezes and exits, though there may be transitions from one freeze to another – after a pose proves impossible to sustain. There may also be preparations for immobility – consider the use of ropes, handcuffs, suspension. Performers should consider the variety of possibilities: figurative poses (friezes), dynamic shapes, spasms, constraints (which might employ methods of binding the performer), repetitions of observed poses, oppositions to observed poses etc.

Stillness should be considered the ground of any subsequent free session. Often a free session is best begun after a minute's silence, a minute's immobility.

Living eyes stare out from a pillow on a hospital bed in Steven Taylor Woodrow's *Going Bye-Byes*, Leeds City Art Gallery, 1991.

2
BEING CLOTHING

Clothing is emblematic, and can be identified as a uniform. Its constituent parts may amount to *mimicry* – helping to create the disguise adopted by the object of the gaze.

Mimicry can be:
Travesty   -   pretending to be what one is not.
Camouflage   -   hiding inside what is already there.
Intimidation -   taking a part of something larger than you.

Clothing can be seen as display. The display may be a *lure* - to attract others. It may be a *defence* – worn in order to protect the body. Helmets, breastplates and shields may be used to this end, also sunshades, gasmasks, bee-keepers' hats and thermal underwear. When the protection required creates a defence against aggression rather than atmospheric extremes, the items worn often project outwards from the body. Given that the best defence can be an aggressive look, defensive clothing may create an aggressive appearance – like Doc Martins and a biker's leathers on a small female. Since aggression may seem attractive, the relationship between lure and defence is ambiguous.

In French, the verb *separare* means to dress and also to arm (to dress for battle). To dress is to prepare, to procure oneself, in Lacan's view, to give birth to oneself. Covering enlarges what it covers, enabling certain parts to be exaggerated for protective *and* sexual reasons: consider the cod-piece and Panurge's reasons for going without it in Rabelais' *Gargantua and Pantagruel*:

"... the Head was made for the Eyes: for Nature might have placed our Heads in our Knees or Elbows; but having beforehand determined that the Eyes should serve to discover things from afar, she, for the better enabling them to execute their designed Office, fixed them in the Head (as on the top of a long Pole) in the most eminent Part of all the Body: no otherwise than we see the Phares, or High Towers, erected in the Mouths of Havens, that navigators may the further off perceive with ease the Lights of the nightly Fires and Lanterns. And because I would gladly, for some short while (a Year at least) take a little Rest and Breathing-time from the toilsom Labour of the Military Profession, that is to say, be marry'd, I have desisted from wearing any more a Codpiece, and, consequently have laid aside my Breeches. For the Codpiece is the principal and most especial Piece of Armour that a Warriour doth carry; and therefore do I maintain even to the

Fire (exclusively, understand you me) that no Turks can properly be said to
be armed Men, in regard that Codpieces are by Law forbidden to be worn.

(Book 3, Chapter VII)

Panurge dilates upon the reasons why the codpiece is held to be the
chief piece of armour amongst warriors in the next chapter which is to be
found at the end of this book *(Appendix I)*. In it, he argues that nature takes
the greatest care to protect the organs concerned with the perpetuity of the
species – "hath most curiously armed and fenced their buds, sprouts, shoots
and seeds, wherein the above-mentioned perpetuity consisteth," - and that
the figleaf was the first article worn for protection because it covered the
organs of generation.

Panurge notices the "curled frisling" of the figleaf, thus admitting
that in such se: .al protection there is already an aspect of display. Certainly
the codpiec ,rew out of all proportion to its purpose during the middle
ages. Clothin.; is *over-determined*. Wearing garments for whatever reason
engages with the issue of how to project oneself as well as how to protect
oneself. Speaking and wearing project what hearing and seeing interpret.

Already clothing has taken on a multiplicity of uses: to simulate,
camouflage or intimidate, in its mimicry mode; to lure or to protect in its
display mode. Thus being erects a screen or a mask, projects how it hopes to
appear through what it looks like. Masks are our very being. As Deleuze
puts it:

"Behind the masks... are further masks, and even the most hidden is still a
hiding place, and so on to infinity. The only illusion is that of unmasking
something or someone....

(Difference and Repetition, page 106)

At the same time there is what Lacan calls the *anamorphosis*
(perspectival distortion) of how the other sees one, i.e. all the meanings *she*
may bring to what *he* looks like or *he* may project onto what *she* appears to
be.

He considers his waistcoat to be the *in* thing: she remembers how
her horny uncle used to finger the buttons of his waistcoat. His associations
differ from hers.

Performance artists do not see themselves as actors - they do not
necessarily take on roles different to their own. However, even if they think
that they are simply "being themselves", they are each still projecting a self
or a persona through posture, through body language and through their
clothing. They are acting being themselves, or, to put it another way,
constructing a *performance self*. The performance self not only projects an
appearance, it also projects a gaze, and it is also gazed upon. In everyday life
(which is a performance), and in performance on some specific, witnessed
space, one attempts to *see oneself seeing* – to imagine what one looks like as

one looks. The complexity of our gaze-lines is quite astonishing. Within a minute of entering a tube train one has surveyed everyone in the carriage, and yet it is only with embarrassment that one notices anyone staring at oneself. The gazes are universally surreptitious: they encompass all, and yet they seldom meet.

Clothing is the playing-field of the gaze.

In performance terms, clothing is often subjugated to use. It might be worth resolving *only to wear what you have a use for.* It's advisable to bring nothing but functional objects into the performance space, and this emphasis on a specific function can also be applied to what is worn. When a performance is led by a concept one only brings into it what is appropriate to that concept, only wears what is appropriate also.

Salome wears seven veils: aboriginal hunters wear bows and arrows. And Bruce McLean once told me about a brick suit. This was a suit covered with pockets, each large enough to contain a brick. When every pocket was filled it was impossible to move in this suit, let alone stand up. We can now see that clothing can be subjected both to psychoanalytic questions and to performative questions.

An ordinary grey suit has several pockets. The psychoanalytic mode asks, What do pockets mean? The performative mode asks, What can be done with pockets? A red dress has no pockets. What does the absence of pockets mean? What can be done without pockets? The answers we might put forward point to some peculiar reversal of sexual roles: the male item covered with apertures, inviting deposits; the female item a sheath, into which the body may be inserted, in order that it may be stripped off later, revealing that erect body's length. Thus the suit lends female sexual characteristics to the male, while the dress enables the female to appropriate male sexual characteristics.

Tongue in cheek answers perhaps, but they point to some compensatory factor akin to the 'aggression' of defensive dressing. It may be that a desire to get away from the ambiguities of these stereotypical ways of attiring ourselves motivates the contemporary trend towards neutrality: the ubiquitous 'uniform' of track-suit-styled trousers and a jumper - this amounts to an ideal of *androgyny*. Performers must ask themselves whether they wish their "performance self" to be as androgynous as their ordinary self.

The two modes of questions (meaning and function) can of course be directed at all sorts of clothing, from formal wear to functional wear: tuxedos and ball-gowns, wedding dresses and nuns' habits, swim-suits and jodhpurs, all have meanings which may be at variance with their functions. Each is a uniform which projects ambiguous messages. The bearded members of the San Francisco "mind-fuck" performance group, "The Angels of Light", favoured beards and tu-tus. Ambiguity may be brought about by the anomalous nature of the body within the clothing. The garments associated with weather conditions - mackintoshes or bikinis - also carry with them meanings which go beyond their function.

Clothing may totemise a fetish, as with rubber, latex or nappy-cloth. The skin itself may constitute clothing, as with the fine filigree of a body-suit tattooed onto torso and limbs.

Some methods of dressing are heavily functional - asbestos suits for walking through fire, divers' suits for descending into the deep. However, even these can be ambiguous if the environment they are supposed to function in is exchanged for some other environment. Consider the meanings which might be constructed around wearing an asbestos suit in a boudoir.

Coming back to those initial modes of dressing: *travesty* can refer to more than the mimicry of the opposite sex: in it there is also a reversal – becoming what one is not. Thus one might dress as an animal – Marcus McLaughlin, for instance, may perform as "April Mule" – or you may assume that your upper part is your lower part and vice versa. Mikhail Bakhtin says of mediaeval "Feasts of Fools":

> "From the wearing of clothes turned inside out and trousers slipped over the head to the election of mock kings and popes the same topographical logic is put to work: shifting from top to bottom, casting the high and the old, the finished and completed, into the material bodily lower stratum for death and rebirth."
>
> (*Rabelais and His World*, page 81)

This touches on the issue of inside-outness, and of interiors becoming externalised – as in the sculptural projects of Rachel Whiteread. In performative terms, to completely turn one's clothing inside out and wear it with outer garments underneath inner ones (perhaps while standing upside-down) could involve a transition through nakedness – but the nakedness might not seem the point. Of course it could *be* the point, and one might simply be seeking to divert the attention from it – to displace that attention, if you like.

Camouflage can concern a part. The Australian artist Mike Parr wears a fake arm for his amputated one, and pretends that his other arm is amputated – he then 'cuts off the fake arm! *(See page 91.)* In Valerian Borowczyk's *La Bête*, made in France in *1975*, the son who is about to be wedded is wearing *his* right hand in a plaster-cast, claiming to have injured it in a riding accident. In the audience, we are convinced that it is really because that hand has become the most terrible paw!

Intimidation is interesting for performers with regard to its possibilities for magnification – wearing something larger than oneself, as in the costumes of carnival. One's *magnified* costume might simply be part of something even larger – i.e. being an enormous foot. Again, one might place oneself inside some larger object which one then uses as one's "shell" – being inside a wardrobe, a coffin or a piano. Such enclosures amount to 'mother-objects'. I have seen Steven Taylor Woodrow inside a table draped with a tablecoth, or with only his eyes showing inside the pillow of a sprucelymade hospital bed – his body concealed in its mattress. In *Table Move 2*, I perform under a wardrobe which has fallen onto the floor with its door open, it then moves across the space as if of its own volition.

The range of possibilities amounts to a performative palette, and so it is possible to mix meanings and effects, to wear a diver's mask and a grey suit, a red dress and stilts, a tuxedo and fishnet tights. One uniform may be worn inside another – like Russian dolls which crack open to reveal smaller dolls inside: toga over grey suit over pyjamas, mackintosh over wedding-dress over swim-suit – mask beneath mask beneath mask. Normal clothing has a construction similar to that of a Russian doll anyway – in that it consists of inner and outer layers. And these may be worn the conventional way or inside out, or one may attempt to wear what is generally worn on one's upper parts on one's lower parts and vice versa. Such inversions and reversals may read as defiance of convention or insanity – just as stripping off one's clothes may imply sexual availability, or read as a metaphor for frankness.

Since many garments restrict movement or dictate function or imply powerful meanings, the issue of what to wear is not a secondary aspect of a performance. One may say that one will begin with neutrality until one has hit upon the concept for the performance. But neutral clothing immediately projects neutrality, and is thus already influencing the outcome. Whether one opts for neutrality or for garments projecting powerful characteristics, what to wear is an issue which requires careful thought at the outset of the performance-making process.

*   *   *   *

Nudity:

The naked body is also a species of costume. And, as with the *breaking out* of stillness, nudity can imply a rebirth. It can be some ultimate reduction (until I find some garment with a function I can utilise, I will wear nothing). This reduction is similar to the philosophical one adopted by Descartes; a necessary stripping away of presumptions and pre-suppositions as one attempts to establish the foundations of being. But then nudity can be used to identify the body as a *lure*. Vulnerability, availability, lack of dignity or obscenity can be read into it, and this will depend on the body language of the performer. It may be that an obscene reading will require the parting of clothing in order to expose a specific organ. Note that to cover only a part will read as modesty or prudery, or even secrecy – but here, as usual, ambiguous games can be played: the performer naked from the neck down who wears a blindfold, or the performer who refuses to allow another a glimpse of a big toe.

Of course it's possible to hide parts of the body with other parts, which may read as shame, and to reveal parts by pulling them apart with other parts – which might read as constipation or toothache.

Nudity allows almost as many readings as does being dressed. And just as stillness may be construed as the basic ground for the twin poles of action (repetition and inconsistency), so nudity may be thought of as constituting the basic ground for dressing and undressing. I'm not saying that nudity has to be still, but that being nude *is* as being still: a basic level of being.

Consider the table below:

Nakedness	Stillness
A: from dressed to nude	Stillness as *arrest*
B: continuous nudity	Stillness as a *state*
C: from nude to dressed	*Breaking out* of stillness

Forcefully being arrested and stripped by another may read as rape: breaking out of stillness and then dressing may suggest getting up in the morning. Our analytical performative axis can lead us now to consider how a child may feel victimised when forcefully undressed and put to bed by an angry parent – a common enough domestic assault. Does the child "ask for it" by drawing attention to itself? Of course, forcefully being dressed may feel just as much of an assault on a grey morning. And being dressed and undressed has geriatric associations as well as infantile ones.

Lacan's notion of desire being linked to the crossing and recrossing of margins or edges rather than to the totality of being inside someone or having someone inside one was discussed in relation to stillness. It applies equally to nudity. Desire is evoked at the moment of revelation, or prior to it, or when what is revealed is snatched away and again hidden from view. Our attention is aroused by the suspense of these threshold experiences more than by the total state of nakedness.

A sense of the uncanny can also be associated with nudity, just as it can be with stillness. There is an uncanniness about the exhibitionist. Imagine a male undressing on a railway platform. His nudity is familiar, but it is framed by an unfamiliar setting. The Freudian notion of the known becoming 'odd' comes into operation here. By exposing oneself physically in a public place perhaps one is calling attention to an internal secret, an inner shame one dare not reveal. And perhaps it is this screened reference to what remains 'unconfessed' that actually causes onlookers embarrassment.

Uncanniness in nudity can be achieved in other ways. By the removal of all customary gender characteristics, for instance. Take Della Grace's photograph, *The Three Graces*. The three women are naked except that they all wear formidable boots. They are all completely shaven – bald heads, bald pubic regions. The central figure stares out at the viewer, confronting the gaze with a hard gaze of her own. The women's heads become knobs, and as such phallic. In her book on psychoanalysis and sexual difference, Parveen Adams considers these women 'beyond recognition. For it is within the space of recognition that the representation of women is played out' – *(The Emptiness of the Image,* page 123). There is an anti-aesthetic quality about the women's positions. A woman's shape often symbolises the aesthetic ideal, but here the arms are not tastefully draped in a rhythmic alternation of waists and shoulders. So there is a recognisable thing here which is now beyond recognition, a thing which gazes out rather than circulating the gaze within its own forms and thus keeping its own perception to itself. But how much of this applies to Tanja Ostojić – who remains motionless in the same position under the same conditions, yet still conveys an intense "femininity" through her image? *(See plate 2, page xvi.)*

For a woman particularly, the removal of clothing leads ultimately to the cliché of striptease, while the removal of everything but underwear or a *cache-sexe* can read as a 'cop-out' – and not only in male eyes. To start undressing but not to complete the act reads as modesty, prudery even. At such a point, one of my students covered herself in cigarette ash and wine and then finally hid herself under her already removed dress. It was as if she were ashamed of her shame, mortified by not being able to remove the final veil – which would expose the fact that her genitals were not ultimately the 'veiled object'. To hide one's sex asserts that sex as an ultimate source of

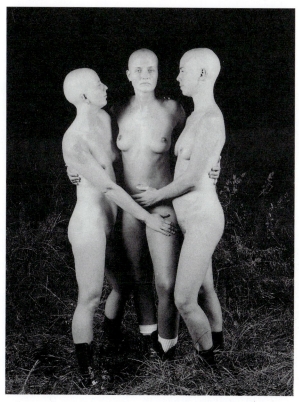

Della Grace's *The Three Graces*. Photograph courtesy of the artist.

unsullied innocence, and with exposure that innocence is revealed as a sham, as a fiction – this is what the modest performance artist does not wish to reveal (to herself or to himself). Nevertheless the strip can easily 'bottom out' into conventional entertainment. It may be more interesting to *begin from nudity,* to dress or to dress someone else.

Orlan, the French performance artist, carries the removal of veils, the peeling away of masks a stage further than the strip by submitting to the scalpel. Her body is first marked where the cuts will be made, and then the skin is peeled away, the shape of the body tightened, altered, as she endeavours to sculpt herself in accordance with models chosen from the history of art or in order to achieve some innovative result such as excessively raised eyebrows. Thus she calls into question the integrity of the naked flesh as the essential object beyond all layers and veils – asking whether our nakedness is really our 'true' image, and pointing out that even this truth can be altered, adjusted, improved or made grotesque. Her work casts doubt on the notion that our naked body is our 'raw' state while our clothed body constitutes our 'cooked' state: the metaphor of innocence versus experience which this implies is thus deconstructed and invalidated. At the same time, cosmetic surgery allows us to command our image and guide it in the direction of some devastating possibilities.

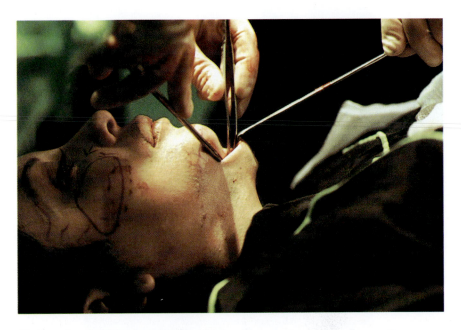

The SecondMouth – Orlan questions the identity of her own image through cosmetic surgery in *Omnipresence,* New York, 1993. Photograph: Vladimir Sichov – Sipa Press.

Conclusion

If a stick is a phallic object, a cloth is vaginal thing. Wrapping and wrapping what has already been wrapped suggests the condensation of thoughts and emotions on the initial object. Silvie Fleurie presents her wrapped purchases, the fruits of her shopping expeditions, as art objects. The wrapping of these purchases becomes something in itself. They are objects presented *as* purchases – to unwrap them will destroy their presentability. The little girls who appear in infant beauty competitions display a similar presentability – as if the exterior surface was the ideal end-product – the flounced dress, the cosmetic look – and as if the object of existence was to be doll-like. There's a strong element of the uncanny here, as there is in the performances created by Vanessa Beecroft – who fills galleries with young women clad in underwear and blond wigs. Here the performers emulate the ideal consumer item: they simply sit or stand around the space, waiting to be purchased or possessed. The arbitrary but obligatory wigs inject a cynicism into this event - these real young women are not real Barbies – for *her* platinum hair grows straight out of her plastic scalp. Their faces are impassive and an atmosphere of charged vacancy prevails.

A live exhibition by Vanessa Beecroft at the C.A.P.C. Musée d'Art Contemporain, 1997.

Finally, bear in mind that clothing is not the only covering. Covering can be viscous. Indian Fakirs cover themselves in dung. And there are pornographic magazines where devotees of excremental eroticism cover themselves in human faeces. André Stitt smears himself with a whole variety of gooey liquids – mayonnaise, swarfega, ketchup. Here the condensation on or about the performer is linked with notions of expiation, of taking on the 'sins' of humanity, of being covered in excrescences, waste products. Then other performers struggle out of baths of clay or plunge into baths of milk; or, like Herman Nietsch, they lie beneath mounds of entrails. They daub themselves in soot – or in paint, like Stuart Brisley. Nylon bags may remind us of membranes, crepe bandages may suggest mummification. So it is not simply a case of asking oneself what to wear. The question is more complex, a case of why to wear what, and a case of what to do with what one wears.

———

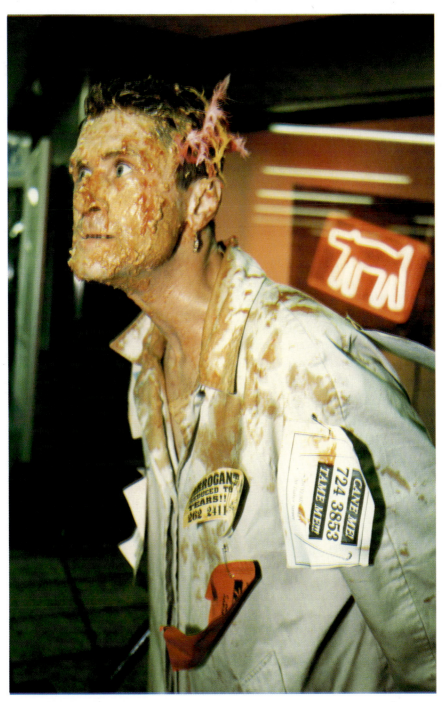

André Stitt covered in viscous fluids while performing as 'The Geek' in *Geek Shop*, the Woodworks Show, Vauxhall, London, 1993. Photograph: Mark Thompson.

The Clothing Workshop

1. Travesty, Camouflage, Intimidation

A day or so before the Clothing Workshop, performers are asked to start collecting/ preparing the clothing they are thinking of using during their performance. On the day of the workshop, they dress in these clothes. Three of them are then asked to utilise their own clothes and the items worn by the others for the purpose of travesty. When this is achieved, a further three performers are asked to utilise their own clothes and those worn by others for the purpose of camouflage. When this is achieved a further three performers are asked to utilise their own clothes and those worn by others for the purpose of intimidation.

The characteristics of the space may come into play during camouflage. Other performers may be used to enhance intimidation.

2. Functional Clothing

Each performer begins by being dressed in whatever way they wish. Then they are asked to perform by utilising every single item of clothing worn in some functional manner, and during this process they should employ as much stillness as they employ action. Eventually each performer should return to the condition of dress which obtained at the beginning of the exercise.

3. Nude Free Session

Performers improvise for some forty minutes in the nude. No objects may be utilised in the first instance. This free session can be tried later though with objects being incorporated into it.

Participation in such nude sessions should always be voluntary.

Note that Exercise 3 in the Stillness Workshop (Page 11) – Sculptures and Armatures – is visually very effective performed in the nude.

4. Covering, not Clothing

A day or so before this workshop, the performers are asked to devise a covering for themslves which is not in any way constructed out of conventional clothing. On the day of the workshop, the performers cover themselves in whatever way they have devised for themselves under these conditions. It's best if this covering is not made in advance of the workshop taking place. The making of the covering, or the pouring of it over oneself or any other preparatory or executive actions necessitated by the chosen covering, should be as much part of the workshop as the final image itself.

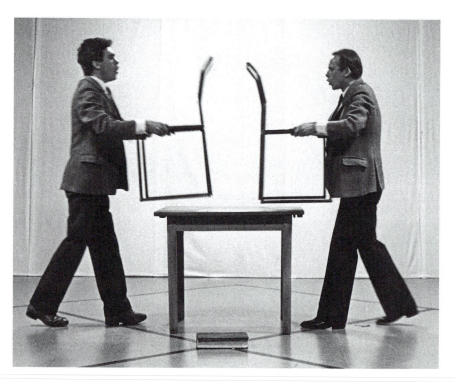

The Theatre of Mistakes: Anthony Howell and Peter Stickland perform *Table Move Duet* at the Künstlerhaus Bethanien, Berlin, 1980. Photograph: Christiane Hartmann.

3
MIMICRY AND REPETITION

"To repeat is to behave in a certain manner, but in relation to something unique or singular which has no equal or equivalent. And perhaps this repetition at the level of external conduct echoes, for its own part, a more secret vibration which animates it, a more profound, internal repetition within the singular. This is the apparent paradox of festivals: they repeat an 'unrepeatable'. They do not add a second and a third time to the first, but carry the first time to the 'nth' power. With respect to this power, repetition interiorises and thereby reverses itself: as Péguy says, it is not Federation Day which commemorates or represents the fall of the Bastille, but the fall of the Bastille which celebrates and repeats in advance all the Federation Days; or Monet's first water lily which repeats all the others."

(Gilles Deleuze, *Difference and Repetition*, page 1.)

Psychoanalysis identifies three sorts of mimicry – travesty, camouflage and repetition. Note that the first two terms have also been examined at the start of the previous chapter (on clothing) – our layers of clothing also *repeat* us even as they alter, camouflage or enlarge us.

Everything we learn comes from outside ourselves. We learn by repeating it, copying it. To learn something by heart, we repeat it until it becomes familiar. We may also repeat something until we *get it right*.

Mimicry can amount to 'kitchen sink' drama when it attempts to represent what has happened in 'real' life – and this is the mainstay of conventional plays. However, the performance artist may turn away from what Janos Pilinsky allows Sheryl Sutton (a performer with Robert Wilson) to call *'mimicry theatre'* in his imaginary chats with her (see *Appendix 2):*

"It's in this that Robert Wilson excelled all his twentieth-century predecessors. Apparently simply by slowing down many times the movement of his characters. It wasn't either mime or slow-motion cinema. I would say it was a frank confession of clumsiness, all kinds of human clumsiness. A step five-times slow is also more beautiful, but much more ungainly and more perishable than the normal. The spell of slowed-down motion lay not in this, though, but in the revolutionary revaluation of time, of normal time. For, consciously or subconsciously, normal plays demonstrated just the opposite. At the usual speed of movement, they compressed the story of a whole life into three hours. Wilson managed to prove that with the help of movement slowed five times, he could present a much more condensed whole than the normal. So how and why, then? Because quality's time differs fundamentally from that of the alarm clock.

Holderlin told his whole life in four lines – and he had time enough for it. In so-called mimicry drama the telephone rings, people knock, sit down, light a cigarette for exactly as long as in life. They too have time for it. For compressing commonplaces, even two hours are in fact a devalued eternity. Wilson's slow play, however, started such a process rolling as only the Greek tragedies were able, with their diction slowed to the utmost and their openness which from the outset destroyed action, to 'utter'."

(Conversations with Sheryl Sutton, page 26)

But mimicry has a wider application than representational theatre. We may learn the meaning of words by mimicking expressions at the appropriate moment. And of course repetition in itself is more than mimicry. We may take something unknown from the outside and by repeating it to ourselves turn it into the familiar. But repetition is more than a process of familiarisation. Repetition causes us to continue – through our breathing and our heartbeats for example. And repetition can strengthen our motivation or weaken it. We can be repeatedly on time, or repeatedly miss appointments.

In analysis, repetition identifies sublimation, or the transference of one's feelings about one object onto another. Thus it is associated with obsession. Obsession is a method of salvaging comfort from a painful situation – as in the "fort-da". Obsession can be identified when the subject imposes a number pattern on chaotic, unpredictable amounts: separating one's chips into groups of four, say. This is a repetitious action imposed on an inconsistent state of affairs.

Meanwhile it is by alternating (left/right/arm/leg) repetitions that we learn coordination. Certain manic depressives may not have learnt to coordinate thoroughly enough, so what is supposed to be a conditioned reflex – walking, for example – remains something a part of the brain may be coping with purposefully: this taxes the brain and may lead to periodic collapse, for our brains can become fatigued as surely as our muscles. Crawl therapy may strengthen the reflex.

Repetition as copying not only mimics it also multiplies the original. This can alter the object, just as cutting out a simple shape on a many times folded piece of paper can create a lamp-shade. And while you can copy a person or his gestures, you can also copy an object, camouflaging yourself in the process. Then, with intimidation, you may copy a thing far larger than you, making its threats your own form of protection. A related tendency to exaggerate may betray our disguises: indeed travesty is often identified by gestures and mannerisms which are larger than those of its subject. The drag-queen becomes a species of super-woman, aggrandised, we might say – her ample threats becoming a form of protection. Does she thus manage to disavow her actual masculinity – or does she remind us of it by hamming things up?

Either way, travesty magnifies representation. But let us look further into the difference between representation and repetition. Representation is a conscious repetition, motivated by desire (i.e. we want to perform this repetition). It is carried out with a conscious purpose: perhaps to disguise ourselves as our enemy, perhaps to depict something we wish to retain and examine. Representational theatre is a theatre of the conscious mind: it uses imitation to reflect the social will. Repetition, on the other hand, is often unconscious, motivated perhaps by what may be referred to as the *death instinct*. Think of a ripple oscillating around a disturbance until it dies away – and the water returns to the state it was in *before* the disturbance occurred. Repetition refers back to the painful – and yet it is a comfort.

And so we repress why we repeat – or so it seems. In its non-representational, repetitive mode, *performance art is an art of the unconscious*. When André Stitt methodically and repeatedly chips away the enamel of a bath, we find ourselves witnessing an action which neither articulates a conscious message nor encapsulates a social metaphor. It is difficult to say what the action is. It represents nothing. It is simply a visually powerful, violently noisy repetition. Deleuze considers repetition to be the unconscious of representation. He speaks of 'an inverse relation between repetition and consciousness, repetition and remembering, repetition and recognition...' The *less* one remembers one's past, the more one repeats it.

André Stitt repetitively chips the enamel off a bath in *Second Skin,* performed at the ASA European Performance Conference, 1996. Photograph: Pietro Pellini.

Repetition in Performance:

Repetition mirrors its own actions. Walking repeatedly mimics the initial pace. Let us consider repetition in performance terms:

1. Even in stillness, there are repetitions. Our very existence requires them. Meditation might be described as listening to our internal repetitions.

2. Consider next the natural repetitions of the gaits (methods of movement): crawling, walking, running etc.

In addition, there are cleansing or evacuating or recovering repetitions. Repeatedly we drink, eat, piss, shit, sleep.

3. After that there are the cultural repetitions attendant on the repetitions imposed upon us by nature: the intricacies of dressing and undressing, the protocols of lifting the seat, pulling the chain etc.

4. In the performance space, we may talk about *simple repetitions* – a series of scissor-jumps, say, or rapping on the floor or on a door – as opposed to *complex repetitions*, i.e. a sequence of initially inconsistent actions which subsequently gets repeated in its entirety.

5. Within repetition falls *copying* and *mirroring*. Thus we can copy someone else's position of stillness or mirror their actions. In one exercise, performers stand next to each other and turn their heads so that one is in the other's line of sight. Moving so slowly no one can see the movement, the performer who can see no other performer takes the lead and the one who can see the leader mirrors the ensuing slow actions. The lead can be transferred by the leader turning his head until that leader has the other in his line of sight, while the follower, who can now see no one ahead, continues the head turn away from the other and thus becomes the leader.

Copying can take place at a later time, i.e. after one has watched a performer doing the actions. This method is often enjoyed – by adults as much as by children. Repetition is the basis of countless games. In its mimicry mode, it is comfortingly familiar to us. It enables us to divest ourselves of autonomous motivation and it forms the basis of our identifications. If we "run out" of actions to copy (having completed our repetition of all the actions we initially watched), then "arrest" ensues: a stillness demanding more watching and listening.

This simple idea formed the basis of *Going* by the Theatre of Mistakes, performed at The Paris Biennale in 1977. The elaborate structure which resulted from its staggered passages of copying and intervals of arrest gave rise to the form of the piece which was very similar to that of a fugue. Thus contrapuntal musical form has its origins in this simple process of copying. The structure of *Going* can be found in Appendix 3.

6. Finally there is the ennui of repetition. Büchner makes his hero Danton say:
"...It is so wearisome. First you put on your shirt, then your trousers; you drag yourself into bed at night and in the morning drag yourself out again; and always you put one foot in front of the other. There is little hope that it will ever change. Millions have always done it like that and millions will do so after us. Moreover, since we're made up of two halves which both do the same thing, everything's done twice. It's all very boring, and very, very sad..."

(Danton's Death.)

Repetition in Psychoanalysis:

Emotional aspects come into play here. Lacan considers the relationship between the gaze and *invidia*. I envy the sight you see. To obtain it I must become you. Repetition must now be divided into self-dependent repetitions and those dependent on another. Often the transferential phenomenon of sublimation occurs when a repetition dependent on another is transformed into a self-dependent repetition. Sublimation comes into play when some repetitive pain or repetition which causes pain has substituted for it a repetition which causes no pain.

Then there is the phenomenon of a *screen memory* – this is an image which we can recall (and do allow to repeatedly appear) which stands in for, or in front of, a painful image we have repressed (forbidding its repeated appearance) – screening the prohibition.

When we apply our performative terms to these conditions observed by ànalysis, we begin to be able to interpret abstract conditions of action in a way which has some bearing upon our emotional life. For instance, repetition with stillness added would cause the repetition to decelerate, suggesting either fatigue or torpor, the torpor amounting to resistance, just as walking slowly can read as unwillingness – as with Shakespeare's schoolboy – while walking increasingly fast may evoke eagerness. Here observe how the amount of stillness added plays an adverbial role and "qualifies" the walk. We may not *wish* to copy or to learn by copying – and this will slow the pace of our repetition. Repetiton with stillness reduced would cause an acceleration, implying haste or impatience.

In childhood, we may copy the actions of more than one person – while watching our mother and our sister, or while observing our father or our teacher. A performance exercise might reflect this. We might listen to one person's language while watching another person's actions, and then try to fuse actions and speech in our own subsequent performance. This exercise would constitute a performance model for *assimilation*.

According to Lacan, the body is the sum of the effects of action upon a subject, at the level at which the subject constitutes himself or herself out of the effects of the move. The move may be 'against one' - as when the stalking animal *imitates* the stillness of the prey

Positive and Negative Reversals:

A reversal is an inverted repetition. Consider some of the basic factors of action: we breathe in and out, we open and shut our eyes and our mouths Other repetitions involve alternation, as in walking, running etc. it is these naturally alternating repetitions which allow us to travel.

Most of our basic repetitions exhibit positive and negative reversals as do a number of other repetitions. You cannot repeatedly pull a dress over your head unless you are wearing more than one dress or unless you first put it back on again before repeating the action. Note also, standing and sitting, opening and closing our hands, jumping up and down. Many of the common objects utilised by humanity are ineluctably fashioned to accommodate reversals, or rather they have reversibility as a characteristic of their use. Hercules died when he put on a contaminated jacket, a jacket which could not be taken off.

It's interesting to consider how walking makes continuous progress only by a sacrifice of the exactitude of the repetition: the movement of the right foot is *transferred* to the left, and this allows progress. If this did not occur, the repetition would involve a reversal but the action would get nowhere – you would simply be moving the right foot forward and back.

The only continuous repetition is cyclic – stirring for instance. This requires neither reversal nor alternation. In her article on *Gesture and Psychoanalysis,* Luce Irigaray suggests that a cyclic repetition might be a more likely action for a girl than the forward/backward (penile) motion of the fort-da – initially observed being carried out by a boy. Seeing herself as a miniature mirror of her mother, a girl would never associate her mother with a cotton reel. Thus, if not traumatised into inertia by the mother's absence, she might cope with it by spinning – creating a comforting spherical space around herself. Cyclic repetition is charged with musicality: the musicality of 'galloping horses', the lulling rhythm of the wheels of a train. Dances often involve whirling the partner round and round. Most children are obsessed by spinning. Such repetition is centred on the self. In classical depiction, the arms of the three graces create a closed circle of continuity - a circle disrupted by the anti-graceful photograph of Della Grace and her two companions. Continual spinning makes you the centre of the universe, since the universe spins with you. At the same time it must induce vertigo, and eventually you collapse.

A complex sequence of inconsistent actions can be turned into a repetitive cycle only if it either a) involves no actions requiring reversal prior to repetition or b) incorporates the reversal of such actions into the sequence or c) incorporates the reversal of such action into alternations of the sequence. In analytical terms, such sequences, by requiring constant reversals or alternating reversals, might imply *hesitance or frustration*.

Ambivalence can also be expressed through this tendency in repetition to require reversals in order to continue repeating. Here we enter into the realm of *obsession*. Consider the "ratman's" obsession with the stone in Freud's celebrated case-history. The subject stubs his foot on a stone in the road, and considers that his girl may stub her foot on it later, since she will be coming along the road. He moves the stone to the side of the road. But then, having progressed a little further down the road, he judges this an absurd action and, hurrying back to the stone, picks it up and places it back where it was in the road when he stubbed his foot on it.

Freud argues that it's not the absurdity of his action which prompts him to replace the stone but his *ambivalence* towards the girl: one moment he feels protective towards her; the next he wants to harm her. Had the subject merely moved stones out of the road, the repetition would have read simply as a tendency towards over-protection of the loved object. We can now see the psychic difference between continuous repetition and reversal repetition - but what of taking one sip from twenty cups of coffee? The aberrance we read into the act depends more on its deviance from the norm than on whether it continues or reverses.

The replacing of the stone in the middle of the road is obviously a repetition characterised by reversal, and *vacillation* may be read into the repetitive reversal of any action such as this. One is reminded of Penelope, coming at night to her loom to unravel the work of her daylight hours. She has promised the suitors that she will marry one of them when the tapestry is completed but wishes to be faithful to Odysseus.

Performing a walk with the right leg only, thus remaining on the same spot, will certainly read as futility. But note the task of Sisyphus. There are innumerable examples of repetitions involving reversals which get nowhere - whereas most repetitions involving alternation make some progress. Then, if we've managed to get walking sorted out, we can then either follow a lead or stroll independently. We can walk towards something or away from it. Doggedly following can be identified as fixation.

Even breathing is a repetition we can modulate or alter in ways which may have neurotic implications. Freud's "wolfman" had to breathe out noisily when he saw people he felt sorry for, by reason of their poverty or their disability, so as not to become like them. And under certain other conditions he had to draw in his breath vigorously - 'drinking in' attractive sights through his nose. This is repetition interfered with - subjected to pressure from inconsistency: the natural rhythm of breathing is impaired by the emotional requirement.

For further thoughts on reversal see *pages 135–148.*

Repetition and Time:

Repetition may seem to annul the progress of time by constantly returning us to the scene of some previous experience, as if one trod water in the river of life. In a novel by Italo Svevo, the main character never manages to maintain his resolve to quit smoking. About making resolutions, he remarks:

> "You strike a noble attitude and say 'Never again!' But what becomes of the attitude if you keep your word? You can only preserve it if you keep on renewing your resolution. And then Time, for me, is not that unimaginable thing that never stops. For me, but only for me, it comes again."
>
> *(The Confessions of Zeno,* page 11)

Anthony Wilden devotes an entire essay to a commentary on this novel. The essay is entitled "Death, Desire and Repetition". Wilden describes the double bind which debilitates the alcoholic:

> "He stops drinking. But his sobriety necessarily and inevitably destroys the very challenge which generated his state of sobriety in the first place. He has no way of continuing to prove himself for the challenge to stop drinking is gone. As Bateson puts it: 'the CONTEXTUAL STRUCTURE of sobriety changes with its achievement' (my emphasis). Pride in performing AGAINST the other self represented by the bottle can now be achieved ONLY by taking 'one little drink', for symmetrical effort requires continual opposition from the opponent."
>
> *(System and Structure,* page 73)

This suggests that there's a species of mental 'reversal' attendant upon repetitions – perhaps implanted by the palpable reversibility of so many of our repetitive actions. The mirror is our twin *and* our rival. Lacan has commented on the crucial importance of the *"mirror-stage"* in our early search for identity. To perceive that, when one experiences the sensation of moving one's arm, one's arm actually moves, teaches one to take the initiative concerning one's own actions. From then on, one can identify oneself with the subject who leads his image into the fray. However, we can imagine a recalcitrant image, an image which did the opposite of what we asked. The mirror image is after all a reversal.

Wilden quotes Kierkegaard:

> "The dialectic of repetition is easy; for what is repeated has been, otherwise it could not be repeated, but precisely the fact that it has been gives to repetition the character of novelty."
>
> (Kierkegaard 1843:52)

Not all obsessions are harmful, however. And repetition can confer value by maintaining that some particular act is noble enough to merit being repeated. Consider the still lives of Giorgio Morandi, who constantly utilized the same bottles, tins and boxes. Kenneth Baker has this to say in his essay on Morandi, *Redemption through Painting:*

> "Morandi's art is proof that a man gave his time to painting. It reiterates his choice of painting, practised as a discipline, to fill his days."

A Note on Motivation

Repetition may supply a performance with a motive. In my table-moves, shifting the furniture through ninety degrees repeatedly gives me *something to do,* an important factor in non-representational work. But perhaps we should try to examine the motive for repetition more deeply. It's been asserted earlier that the death instinct supplies it. Why?

Ultimately dissatisfied with the negative schema posited by the idea that we repeat because we repress, Freud showed, in *Beyond the Pleasure Principle,* that the death instinct, that psychic equivalent to the power of gravity, was intimately connected with repetition phenomena. As Deleuze puts it:

> "Strangely the death instinct serves as a positive, originary principle for repetition; this is its domain and its meaning. It plays the role of a transcendental principle, whereas the pleasure principle is only psychological. For this reason, it is above all silent, whereas the pleasure principle is noisy...
>
> *(Difference and Repetition,* page 16)

By 'noisy', I presume Deleuze to mean that the pleasure principle – which seeks to restore our equilibrium by expelling surplus stress from our system - is continuously making us conscious of its presence, making itself 'felt' – as we feel the need to urinate in order to relieve tension in our bladders. The death instinct, however, runs under deeper water. It is essentially regressive, but can also be seen as an impulsion towards disintegration, a drive towards inertia – as if gravity promoted a desire to fall in the apple hanging on the bough. Perhaps, from the compost that we become, new growth emerges and the cycle repeats. But if repetition is motivated by this instinct, then all repetition is a downwards spiral or else an acceleration which can only explode and disperse. Either way, in these Freudian terms – which contemporary theory might contest – dying supplies the reason for being, supplies it repeatedly and motivates its repetitions.

Because of this dark, deeply-running motive, we may feel the need to disguise our repetitions. Freud was aware of this when he sought for a more profound reason for repetition than that of repression, even though he thought of the death instinct as a sort of repression, *a primary repression.* Deleuze sums it up neatly, "...We do not repeat because we repress, we repress because we repeat..." *(D and R, page 105).*

Difference within Repetition

Repetitions are often disguised. Let us suppose that because I used to steal from my mother's handbag (in order to go shopping) I now shop obsessively. Why did I steal in the first place? Perhaps because I felt she had stolen my comfort blanket (a shred of material which smelt of her and me) which she had replaced with a dull rabbit purchased in a shop. I shop now, but cannot replace the stolen object. I shop to repeat my guilt at stealing from her bag (the guilt I repress). The themes of shopping and stealing repeat themselves in a variety of guises.

Difference is inscribed on repetition. Without difference we would not be able to distinguish between A and its repetition. The gap between repetitions constitutes that difference. Night divides the state of day into repetitions, day does the same for the state of night. Without difference there is no cycle.

Where difference is disguise, the mask is repeatedly peeled away to reveal another mask as in Michael Powell's marvellous film, *The Tales of Hoffmann.* Conversely, Gary Stevens and his co-performer put on more and more items of clothing, repeatedly covering the disguise in a disguise. Equally actions can screen other actions – I get angry with my computer to hide the fact that I am angry with my child, but then, perhaps I am only angry with my child because my boss was angry with me. The repeated anger manifests itself in various forms. It may even be turned inside out, changed into an excessive love, to camouflage the anger actually felt.

Difference operates within repetition in other ways. The uncanniness sometimes associated with twins or triplets may be attributed to our knowledge of their difference and how it seems to *masquerade* as repetition. Our own bodies exhibit symmetry, and yet the left side is fundamentally different to the right side. Then the repetitive frames of a comic-strip may each be filled with a different picture. Repetition can be the uniform envelope which encloses difference. In their 'Singing Sculpture', Gilbert & George's audio cassette generates freezes of repetitive length, while the exchange of glove and stick brings about a difference in their poses. Wedekind, in his play *Spring Awakening,* uses a series of uniformly short scenes to develop the action, just as a sequence of slides may appear projected from a carousel-projector, each dropping down in front of the beam in the same manner though each slide is of a different subject. Here difference in repetition may be similar to a consistent inconsistency. This will be discussed later.

Deleuze tells us that:

"Elements of dissymmetry serve as both genetic principle and principle of reflection for symmetrical figures.... Cadence-repetition is a regular division of time, an isochronic recurrence of identical elements. However, a period exists only in so far as it is determined by a tonic accent, commanded by intensities. Yet we would be mistaken about the function of accents if we said that they were reproduced at equal intervals. On the contrary, tonic and intensive values act by creating inequalities or incommensurabilities between metrically equivalent periods or spaces."

(Difference and Repetition, page 21.)

Hegel, however, maintained that difference was *implicitly* contradiction; that what begins as modification, i.e. the antithesis of any particular thesis, must eventually *oppose* that thesis prior to any synthesis being achieved: "Only when the manifold terms have been driven to the point of contradiction do they become active and lively towards one another." *(Hegel's Science of Logic,* page 431). This assertion might be explored in performance by the *Opposites Exercise:*

One performer creates an action and then another performer 'contradicts' that action by attempting to create its opposite. After that, the second performer instigates an action which the first counters with an action opposite to this new action.

The sequence A, anti-A, B, anti-B, C, anti-C develops; but the exercise hardly evades repetition since each pair of actions becomes bracketed with each other. The definition of what is opposite to what is purely subjective and the result is a repetitive sequence of paired actions, the actions probably more similar to each other within each pair than to the actions made manifest by adjacent pairs. This would confirm the notion that only that which is alike differs (we can only say that we can 'tell a pair of twins apart' by dint of the fact that they are twins).

Opposition may involve acrimony or it may be a simple matter of geometry. In *Elements of Performance Art;* Contradiction *within repetition* is well expressed in performance terms by the *First Conversation Piece* (devised by The Theatre of Mistakes):

"Each performer chooses one verb each.

Make sentences employing the verb you have chosen and/or the verbs chosen by other performers plus any or all the pronouns and auxiliaries.

Sentences may be:
> *A command*
> *A statement*

A query
A negative command
A negative statement
A negative query

You may also employ phrases or single word ejaculations (i.e. fragmented forms of the above). In addition to the verb chosen, the auxiliaries and the pronouns, you may use any other parts of speech bar nouns, adjectives and adverbs..."

It is fairly common for performers to share *a single main verb* at the start of this exercise, together with the auxiliary verbs and the pronouns; and thus they respond to each other in statements, negations, commands and questions. This creates apparently violent expressions of difference: "You rang her." "I did not ring her." "Yes, you did!" "I did not!" "Why did you ring her?" etc. But the contradictions expressed are still dependent on an 'alikeness' about the phrases while the performers share that single verb.

Because repetitions differ from each other, we may note that a certain threefold compulsion governs repetition in plot construction, and is often to be found also in the construction of performance sequences. There is a beginning, then a repetition of certain elements of that beginning in the middle, and a further development of those elements at the end of the piece. There is one event, its echo, and the repercussion entailed by that echo being heard. We can see this structure operating in Hamlet. Event, travesty, tragedy, or event, tragedy, farce: both options show repetition 'distorted' by difference and then 'distorted' yet again.

But difference differs from inconsistency by dint of its normality, its necessity. For without difference being inscribed within it repetition cannot define itself. Inconsistent sequences may resemble difference in repetition; however, in its most refined form, inconsistency is a rarer occurrence. It constitutes the event in itself, the actual death of the father (at least in Hamlet's case). Catastrophe is more than a difference. For if difference rotates with repetition as day follows night, then difference and repetition are symmetrical sides of each other, as repetition and reversal are, irreversibly, fixed to each other – reversal is after all difference. Inconsistency, on the other hand, is in all likelihood an intrusion from a repetition on some other orbit, an orbit which is not on the regular agenda, which interferes, more or less drastically, with the predictability of that agenda. Difference is erotic, and if it is annulled by merger the result amounts to inertia, just as a uniform greyness would transpire if night were to merge with day. The path of inconsistency on the other hand is in essence erratic rather than erotic. Impending inconsistency is fate.

———

The Repetition Workshop

1. Simple Repetition Analysis

Performers stand in a circle. Everyone is asked to perform a simple repetition. Each action performed is then analysed in turn, going round the circle. In most cases it will be discovered that the simple repetition has incorporated its own reversal, though one or two of the performers may have adopted a repetition which involves alternation or a cyclic repetition.

2. Four Action Repetition

Performers are asked to devise a complex repetition involving four actions: one of these actions should incorporate reversal, one should cause the performer to travel, one should be cyclic and one should be an action copied from another performer – the last action can either incorporate reversal or cause the performer to travel or be cyclic.

Once these actions are established, each performer should add language to the actions until each of the four actions chosen is accompanied by a word or a phrase.

3. Repeated Repetitions

After a clap, there is a silence for some fifteen 'internal counts'. Then one performer enters the space and repeats any action. This action is allowed to deepen. Then a second performer enters the space and may either instigate a new action – which he or she then repeats – or repeat the action already being performed by the first performer Again the action is allowed to deepen. Subsequent performers enter one at a time, in each case after a deepening interval. Each may either instigate a new action – which he or she then repeats – or repeat an action already being performed. When the last performer enters, he or she says "I'm the last", before repeating a new action or repeating an action already being performed. This action is allowed to deepen, and then the first performer leaves the space, followed after a deepening interval, by the second performer, and so on, until the last performer is the only one on the space. After another interval, he or she also quits the space.

4. Large and Small Repetitions

Perform a complex (three or four action) repetition in the smallest possible way. Gradually expand this repetition in terms of scale, size, noise etc. Then as gradually diminish the repetition and finally stop performing.

5. The Metronome

Performers stand in a fairly tight circle. One performer moves into the circle, performs an action and moves out again. He or she repeats this, while the other performers also try to perform repetitive actions in the circle which are synchronised with the initial action of the first performer. Thus a sort of combined repetitive 'mechanism' should develop.

6. Mirroring

Performers stand in pairs, preferably with someone of equal height. They should stand about a yard apart from each other and look towards the right. The performer standing on the right now begins to move so slowly no one can see the movement. This movement is copied as simultaneously as possible by the performer on the left. The leading performer should consider that the following performer can only see actions which fall within his or her line of sight and which are not obscured by the body of the leader. The lead may be transferred by a turn of the leader's head towards the following performer. The follower imitates this head turn, and, when he or she can no longer see the leader, continues the head-turn towards the left, thus becoming the leader of the action. This exercise can also be performed in a line, with several performers – though only the performers at the beginning or at the end of the line will be able to transfer the lead.

7. Time-Delayed Repetition

All performers must be able to see each other. The first performer performs an action, then stands still and watches the others. The second performer copies the action executed by the first performer, then adds an action of his own. The third performer copies the action executed by the first performer, then copies the action executed by the second performer, then adds an action of his own. This process continues until all the performers have completed two or three rounds of accumulated actions.

White Wall

---

language (*o*)

language (*o*)P (*o*)

P (*o*)

object (*o*)

P/W (*o*)

P/W (*o*)

Curtain

------------ **Audience (O) Other** -------------

Language (O) Other

Figure 2: The Large Other and the local other (object)

4

THE OTHER AND THE OTHER

Figure 2 is a diagram of the space we are in, hidden by a curtain. This serves as a model for the psychoanalytic distinction between the (capital **O**) OTHER and the (lower case *o)* other – which Lacan might call the *objet petit a* (autre). The Large OTHER expresses general "Otherness" – the notion of "society" or of the language as a whole. The lower case *other* expresses the particularity of objects directly in the locality of the subject / performer. We will signify the Large Other by a large **O** and the local other by a small *o*.

Within the space closed by the curtain, we can be witnesses (W) as well as performers (P). Outside the curtain is the *Unknown:* that which is outside our specific frame of reference. At a later stage we may draw the curtain and discover the audience out there – a conglomerate of beings and language under whose gaze we exist both as witnesses of the performance (our role similar to that of the *chorus* in Attic drama), and as performers. This notion of some presence outside the curtain can be considered as the Large Other (**O**). Our mediating role as performer / witnesses enables the Large Other to experience the performance through our eyes – that is through the eyes of witnesses who have entered into some complicity with the event – as in classical tragedy.

That Large Other could be *God* (who can probably see us even when the curtain is closed). That Other is the culture at large, the *Language* in its entirety – a general presence which gives us our context, and which exerts pressure on us (a pressure to conform perhaps). The Large Other encourages us to do what It expects us to do, or so we feel. *It* may even urge us to defy *It,* if we think *It* expects us to defy *It.* Should we praise this Other or abuse it? Our ambivalence towards it stems partly from the fact that we do not know who the Other is. Rabelais used a grotesque language which addressed both the future and the past. As Bakhtin puts it, speaking of the Other in terms of the audience for such a language:

> "At close range, this many-faced person is the crowd which surrounds the barker's booth, and also the many-faced reader. Praise and abuse are showered onto this person, for some in the audience may be the representatives of the old, dying world and ideology – agelasts, that is, men who do not know how to laugh, hypocrites, slanderers who live in darkness; others are the representatives of a new world, a world of light, laughter and truth. Together they form one people, dying and renewed."
>
> *(Rabelais and his World,* page 165)

Action/Mark No. 13. Bobby Baker balances on a cake-stand. She is adorned with object mementoes of previous actions in *Kitchen Show* for Lift '91, London, 1991. Photograph: Andrew Whittuck.

So much for the Other (**O**) outside our performative world. Within our curtained space however there is also *an other (o)*, and this local other is, in the first instance, anything separate from the performer who is the subject. So it can be an item of equipment, or a prop, or it can be a statement – or any sound or shred of language used in the performance space. It can also be anything which is conceived of as separate (a part of the body, a concept). And of course this local other can be another performer. Considered more deeply, it becomes apparent that the local other can even be the performer who is the subject. For the subject can see himself (or herself) as an object separate from the self. Rimbaud says, "I is another."

That performer who is the subject may be witnessing the performance of others. In which case, the whole performance is *o*, the local other – and even if that witness then starts to perform, everything in the performance space remains *o*: its objects, its performers, their actions and their witnesses (for whom the subject performer is *o*), *and* what is said by anyone in the space. And then, as Rimbaud knew, the subject can perceive himself or herself as an object *(o)*, an it, or a part of himself or herself as an it, or what he says or she says as an it – by seeing or hearing himself or herself seeing, doing or saying.

Melanie Klein explored the notion of *part objects:* those parts, not always separate from the mother or from the father, which arouse privileged interest in the child – the breast, the penis, the mouth, the faeces. Performance has its own part objects. in 1976, Julia Heyward isolated her arm and described its biography as separate to her own – the arm became an it: a *part object,* practically removed from herself (see Rosalee Goldberg's *Performance*, page 112–3). Gary Stevens "objectifies" his face, its expressions and its parts. He once showed his audience how he could push his ear through an imaginary wall.

Part objects, in the performative sense, may also be identified by their passivity. It was common among hysterics for a limb to appear to all intents and purposes inactive – as if paralysed. A psychical inhibition prohibiting masturbation might be the cause of that inability to use the arm. If this prohibition was dredged up from the unconscious the subject might regain use of the recalcitrant limb. Performers have experimented with imposing prohibitions on their movements. Not being able to use the arms at all might cause one to attempt everyday tasks with one's teeth.

Psychoanalysis maintains that, as the subject, you are the sum of the effects of action on you – both by the Large Other and by the local others – though much of what you can ultimately gather about that abstract Other "outside the curtain" will be learned through the objects to hand.

Lacan defined as the *objet petit a* a lost object. This object is a leftover from pre-verbal need. Perhaps it was once the satisfactory womb, or the nipple's satisfaction. It is a 'leftover' in the sense that *now,* now that we are not without language, that object which first aroused our sense of a lack by its removal leaves a need that nothing can satisfy, not even the original source of satisfaction. Our sense of that lack has evolved, grown beyond its origin, grown out of proportion to its cause. This *lost object* is the cause, not the object, of our desire. It leaves us in the position of being creatures with a hole in their being. Objects can occupy the channel of our desire to fill that void – fetish objects, the temporary and persistent lusts we may have for things – but the lack itself always goes beyond the object which hides it. The object is thus like a permeable plug – our desire leaks through it.

What is this lost object in performance terms? Perhaps it is a certain vacuity of meaning. In *Going*, the five performers of the Theatre of Mistakes are perpetually saying goodbye to each other. The way they say goodbye is copied from performer to performer. Nobody says where they are, nobody says where they are going. The piece was constructed around the principle of being each other, of copying each others' actions – as in Exercise 7 of *The Repetition Workshop* – see also Appendix 3. It refined itself around those actions which proved most suitable for copying. As with Samuel Beckett's *Waiting for Godot*, or Alain Robbe-Grillet's *L'Année Derniére à Marienbad*, there is a certain nothingness around which the performance circulates, a void. See also my remarks on André Stitt's bath-chipping performance at Cardiff Art in Time *(page 31)*.

We have pointed out earlier that *stillness*, like the lost object, can also be 'a lack'. There can be a gap between actions, a gap which can be increased or minimised; just as when the other speaks we tend to fall silent, and this may feel like a gap in our own continuity. This gap can be filled, by fidgeting, say, but underneath it is an emptiness, an emptiness which perhaps constitutes the ground of action. The ground itself is of it too. In performance terms, to be still and to lie on the ground is a sort of succumbing to the force of emptiness, a negative energy which may pull the audience's attention to it, as nature is drawn to fill a vacuum. Stillness is being an object therefore, and in sleep we become our own lost object, though equally, moving someone limp around the space might signify the manipulation of one's own loss.

There are also *virtual objects;* objects with no tangible reality. These may be conceptual, imaginary; the projections we place upon our fetishes, fetishes which always feel like parts, rather than entire objects, since they are substitutes for losses and the sense of loss or of something lacking always remains attached to them. However, some of these objects are real enough for all their virtuality. The gaze of the performer is such an object, and so is the hearing. Indeed all the senses, or rather their specific ranges of perception, are objects which may be utilised by the performer. A blindfolded performer might start whispering as soon as he was near enough to smell another performer. One who could see might stop talking as soon as another performer disappeared from view, or remain immobile when contact was lost with an object such as a table. Obviously the voice is more than virtual, even if invisible, since it produces a real sound. The use of our sensory impressions as triggers will be discussed in more detail when we come to examine cathexis.

In Freudian terms, there are *good objects* and *bad objects*. A good object is one the subject loves, a bad object is one the subject hates or fears. Such objects may be internal or external. What's interesting here is that a good object or a bad object has a different meaning in performance terms. A good object might be a sturdy table, or something with a multiplicity of uses. A bad object might be the lid of margarine punnet – fragile and of limited use to the performer. Note that Melanie Klein stresses the ambivalence of these terms – the breast may be good when available and bad when access to it is denied (See "The Psychogenesis of Manic-Depressive States" in *The Selected Melanie Klein).*

Note also the ambivalence of the floor in our diagram. It is both **O** and *o* – because common to both areas. The floor is ubiquitous and unthought of: and I would reiterate that it may also be *a lost object,* lost in the sense of overlooked. A raised stage would establish a difference between performance area and audience area – signifying that the Other and the other inhabit separate worlds.

The curtain is a special case, since it presents one side to us, another to the Large Other. It has a similar function to that of the iconostasis of the Orthodox church – a screen erected between church and altar to preserve the mystery, the holiness, of that altar. We are using the curtain for workshop purposes, but in fact the curtain is rarely put to use in performance art since the artist is often engaged in a demystification of the action by a denial of theatrical "difference". Some establish a difference in other ways. When Gilbert and George stand on their table, as if it were a raised stage, they become aggrandised by the foreshortened perspective utilised by Mantegna in his portrait of the Gonzaga family. They are very present to their audience, but at the same time they are raised above that audience, standing on the table/altar (of art) like sculptures on a plinth. This contributes to the general uncanniness of their showing of themselves and separates them from life. Further remarks concerning objects can be found in *Drives and the Primaries (pages 99–116).*

Overleaf: Elevated objects: Gilbert and George pose for the length of an audio cassette, then turn over the tape, exchange stick and glove and pose again in *The Singing Sculpture,* Sonnabend Gallery, New York, 1991.

Otherness: objects and separation

Objectification depends on separation. To comprehend objects we must first understand the divisions which destroy our original wholeness.

All language (including body language) is acquired from outside ourselves. We come into the world unable to walk, and if we grow up among wolves we will learn to move on all fours. Learning to walk teaches us how to learn. Because walking has taught us how to learn (by imitation) we rapidly acquire language afterwards. Our ability to learn is dependent on our being helpless. It is the human condition that we are born naked, immobile, speechless, and that our survival depends upon our learning to put right these deficiencies, whereas a foal is born with a nice glossy coat on and can stagger to its feet and canter around the paddock within minutes. However, the foal has no reason to learn, and this is why there are no talking horses.

Naked, immobile speechlessness epitomizes your being. You come into the world in a state of raw being. The more language (meaning) you take on from the outside, the more your original sense of yourself seems to fade. People who have used heroin describe the infantile helplessness that the drug induces as the purest bliss: a return to the primal state, experienced in all its intensity.

Comprehension is fading of being. This is the dilemma of learning. For learning will change you and changing is dying, just as a "character" dies when an actor changes roles. The first thing we learn is a rupture, after all, which occurs at the moment of our birth.

We erect shields before our being. We resist being named by the other *(o)*. For knowledge is *No* – a restriction imposed on our primarily free being, an edge given to that which is without edges. There is no "No" in the unconsciousness. All the restrictions are introduced by the other. "Don't do that" is the burden or refrain of knowledge.

From our conception onwards, a series of separations occurs. At first we are a unity with the Mother (there is no other); then we are born, and later we learn to perceive ourselves as separate from the mother. Later still, we learn to distinguish the mother from other objects, and we also begin to comprehend our separation from other presences. Each of these separations feels like a rupture of our being. Each rupture is a catastrophic event at variance with our previous state and its comparative security. From feeling at one with the whole world of the Mother we progress to feeling small and separate from the entirety of the Large Other, and separate from most local others as well. Our progress from single, world-encompassing subject to mere object in a world of objects is made into a personal history by a series of devastating inconsistencies which are the ruptures and painful partings we must suffer in order to learn our identity.

To cope with such painful partings we employ *transference:* a repetition, like the *fort da*, which fictitiously restores to us the comfort we have been deprived of by the most recent separation – a separation resonating with all the previous separations suffered. The transference is the enactment of the reality of the unconscious. Our fetishes are its objects.

As unborn beings we exist in the womb in a state of sublime gratification. When the waters break, and we lose our security in the womb, need is born. Each separation creates a lack, a lack of the previous unity, and each lack is in turn filled by a need. Need is desire – and this is ultimately expressed through sexuality. Repetitive and fetishistic, sexuality is the reality of the unconscious. *Desidero* is the Freudian *Cogito* (according to Lacan) – I need therefore I am.

Because the Large Other (**O**) is originally the Mother – first source of the gratification of desire – we strongly wish to oblige the Other through its impinging form (the form of the others at hand) in order that our desires may be gratified.

You are, therefore, *what the other wants you to be*. And when you doubt something about yourself you attempt to confirm it (to yourself) by convincing others of it. This leads to the hysteria of conversion, which surely signals a dubious faith; for, after all, if you are truly convinced of something, you have little need to convince others of it.

Objects in Performance terms:

The Large Other (**O**) is behind the curtain which may be drawn. Meanwhile the object at hand is the local *other (o)*, whether that object be a person, thing or phrase. First let us think about the Large Other.

In *voyeurism* what one looks at is what cannot be seen. When I was young I used to imagine the girl I loved listening to records alone in her room. This is a perfect subject for the voyeur. For the voyeur would observe what the other does when the other is alone – a contradiction in terms. Thus the voyeur's longing is for an impossibility, perhaps for Lacan's lost object. In our diagram, the Other outside the curtain is about to become our voyeur, and, could it achieve the impossible and see through the curtain, it would observe what cannot be seen – as distinct from the performers as witnesses, who can be seen and are objects *(o)* to the performers. The convention of traditional theatre is that an invisible audience sees what cannot be seen.

This opens up the debate touched on when we discussed the curtain – as well as the table used by Gilbert and George. It concerns our separation from our spectators.

Is the notion of the invisible audience only an attribute of theatre – or does it also apply to performance? In theatre it amounts to the "doll's house" effect, with one wall removed from the residence of the characters. Performance artists, however, may take on the "frankness" of disingenuous reality – recognising that the audience is there, and that the sound of a gale has actually been created by a tape-recorder. Are they obliged to respond to that audience?

Consider this issue in a roundabout way. From where do we get the notion of an audience *visible* to the performers? From circus perhaps, from vaudeville or the concert. But these days the medium which most commonly uses the notion of the visible audience is the medium for whom the audience is, in fact, entirely invisible (except in terms of ratings and correspondence). Television makes a fetish of participation. Compères and announcers address us as if we were actually there. Thus the notion of the visible audience can be as illusory as that of the invisible audience.

Rose English addresses her audience. However, unless this audience is composed entirely of her acquaintances, she does not actually know this epitome of the Large Other which has come to observe her performance. Her intimacy with the audience is as much a fiction as unawareness of the audience is a fiction to the actors in "A Doll's House".

Inanimate art objects – paintings, sculptures, poems, compositions – have no awareness, therefore they cannot be aware of their audience. The difficulty impinges upon performance art because the art object is made of a sentient being. When the audience is considered visible there is a pressure upon the performer to acknowledge it (see the *Note on Interaction* at the end of this section); but to acknowledge the audience may fundamentally interfere with the essential homeostasis of the artwork.

The audience has a transcendent reality for the performer – a form of unreality, even if this is only a convention. To acknowledge the audience destroys the performer, since it dissolves the difference between them. As Wittgenstein said at the end of his Tractatus: "What we cannot speak about we must pass over in silence." He is speaking about transcendental deliberations. It is pointless to hypothesise about a 'Being' outside our world (or our experience), for instance, since we can prove nothing about what lies beyond our experience. The conventional fiction of the theatre is that the audience constitutes such a 'Being', and that it exists in such a 'beyond'.

But what is 'the essential homeostasis of the artwork'? What is homeostasis?

Homeostasis: the maintenance of metabolic equilibrium within an organism by a tendency to compensate for disrupting changes.

Homeostasis: a universal tendency in all living matter to maintain constancy in the face of internal and external pressures.

The arts concern making, bringing something to life. As such, they are more aligned to growth than communication. The wonder is that an inanimate creation can resemble an organism. Thus the "integrity" of an artwork, including a performance, suggests this condition of homeostasis that Freud identifies with the living being.

Deleuze maintains that in addition to an 'aesthetic' there is an 'analytic' *(D and R,* page 109). Now the analytic examines the 'integrity' of the work – its wholeness, its soundness – rather than its beauty, which concerns its aesthetic, though one might argue that our contemporary aesthetic is the analytic (as Wittgenstein argued that 'ethics is aesthetics').

An artwork holding itself together. Bodies as sculptural objects in Carolee Schneemann's *Water Light/Water Needle*, performed in 1995. Photograph: Herbert Migdoll.

If this is the case, the notion of homeostasis has replaced the notion of beauty, or we could say that the ideal homeostasis of a piece constitutes its beauty. In art, therefore, homeostasis, or something very similar to the homeostasis of an organism, is achieved by creating a situation where each element or action is under as much tension as any other, and where no element or action is subservient to another or merely there as a support, and where each part is essential to the whole. An artwork "holds itself together".

Joel Fisher is a sculptor who draws his inspiration from filaments discovered in paper which he has made himself. Paper is made by lifting the pulp fibres out of the water where they float in dispersion, using a filter mesh, in order to deposit them onto some base where the fibres may dry out. Fisher has observed that "the tiny cellulose fibres interlock, fibre upon fibre, each holding in place and in turn being held by others. There is no glue for it is unnecessary; it is a self–structuring surface maintaining itself."

Acknowledgment of the audience/Other can interfere with art's self-structuring ability to maintain itself. Instead it becomes structured via the audience and can only maintain itself in the audience's presence. By acknowledging the audience, performance can become a parasite. Conversely, it might be argued that all organisms enjoy an intimate relationship with their niche in the environment, and that the environment conditions their homeostasis. Thus the integrity of site-related sculpture is affected by the nature of the site, while the performance is affected by the nature of the audience *and* by how it is sited (situated/seated).

Balance is the key. If a performer talks too quietly he will not be heard, if his actions are obstructed they may not be seen. If individual participation is demanded, the audience's unity may be destroyed, and it may fragment into a collection of self-conscious others; or, if the audience goes along with some inducement to participate as a group, it may transform itself into a herd of asses braying the chorus conducted by the performer.

In the more traditional terms associated with the theatre, acknowledgement of the audience can be a transgression – as children know it is in pantomime. It can bring about a debasement of the rules of acting – which in many cases will lead to weak entertainment pandering to the audience (pop-music, game shows, stand-up comics with catch-phrases but no jokes); while performance artists who use the audience successfully often do so by compensating for their art-transgression by also breaking the unwritten rules concerning how the audience should be treated. Thus André Stitt pelts the audience with oranges and fire-crackers (in a piece which contains references to Northern Ireland), and by these violent acts he refuses to acknowledge the audience for what it is (dissidently inclined art-students): instead he projects onto the audience the notion that they are a brigade of police horses.

Homeostasis calls for relief from tension (pain) when abnormal pressure is exerted on any part of the surface. For instance, the excitation (tension) produced by pressure on the bladder causes pain and is terminated by the emptying of the bladder.

The Large Other (**O**) exerts an overall pressure on the performance. The performer is the victim within the amphitheatre of the audience's gaze. If this is understood, then transgression may be a way of reversing the roles – so that the performer ceases to be victim but instead becomes the aggressor; his or her victim being the audience.

Very natural acts become transgressive by being performed in front of the average audience: nudity, pissing, masturbation, shitting, fucking, etc. when such transgressions occur, the audience, while necessarily present, is nevertheless forced back into the role of (hidden) voyeur, because it is obliged to observe "what cannot (or should not) be seen".

Nowadays the killing of animals, even the simulated killing of animals, is considered transgressive by many of the audience. However, in *The Joyful Wisdom*, Friedrich Nietzsche anticipates Freud when he says of Richard Wagner:

> "The attempt of Wagner to construe Christianity as a seed blown away from Buddhism, and his endeavour to initiate a Buddhistic era in Europe, under a temporary approximation to Catholic-Christian formulas and sentiments, are both Schopenhauerian. Wagner's preaching in favour of pity in dealing with animals is Schopenhauerian; Schopenhauer's predecessor here, as is well known, was Voltaire, who already perhaps, like his successors, *knew how to disguise his hatred of certain men and things as pity towards animals...*"(My italics.)
>
> (*The Joyful Wisdom*, Book II, page 136.)

Thus sentimentality masquerades as enlightenment. The ancients were not so pathetic. The final scenes of the Greek tragedy, *Ajax,* by Sophocles, reveal a holocaust of animal sacrifices.

Innocuous acts can become transgressive by repetition, since the audience is gathered in the auditorium or viewing area in order to witness something, and the implication is that this something will be out of the ordinary. That protracted repetition can make something extraordinary may not appease their malevolence towards the piece.

Having thought about the Large Other, let us now consider the local other: that which resides within the space.

1. The other as a person:

You shield your eyes against this other – for acknowledgement incorporates defence. To ignore this other's presence is a fiction, albeit one favoured by a variety of performers. Mostly, you "keep your eye" on him or her, for this other may intimidate you, and you in turn may wish to simulate the other or be camouflaged by the person the other is – taking on their colours – or you may intimidate this other, so that the other perhaps takes on your colours. This other may protect or rape you, you may protect or rape it, or it may lure you or you may lure it. It perceives its notion of what you are projecting as your identity, a notion influenced by its projection on you. But what you project may be influenced by what it is wearing – and what you use for clothing may be used against you, *is* used against you indeed.

These notions come alive if we vary the pronouns: I may simulate you, you may simulate me, he may simulate her. You may intimidate me, I may protect you. She may lure you, I may lure him, he may lure them. The local other is not just an "it" – "it" can be any of the pronouns. And while to *ignore* this other is a fiction, such fiction often comprises the dynamic heart of a performance. This deliberate lack of acknowledgement will be discussed later.

Naturally, our relation to the other can be active or passive. And naturally our perception is affected by those virtual objects, our senses. Imagine seeing a fuzzy person. Would you believe your eyes?

2. The other as a phrase:

The large concept of the Language itself resides with the audience, outside the curtain. Inside our space, there are words dislocated from context, phrases we can repeat, deny or alter, as in the First Conversation Piece (*see page* 39), sentences we can string together or dismantle. If we can think of words, phrases or sentences as objects, then we can kick them around like furniture!

Dialogues similar to those in R.D. Laing's "Knots" can be constructed around similar principles to that of the First Conversation Piece. We can treat the other's phrase as a thing to transform, play with, deny or question. We can repeat what the other says *ad nauseam*, or turn it into gobbledegook.

Equally we can turn our own phrases into objects and put them through similar transformations, or we can learn a speech by heart, and that speech then becomes an object subject to our interpretations of its meaning.

Tape-recorders can be employed to enmesh our words with language previously recorded, or to record what we say in order that this may be played back, or to provide an undercurrent of sounds. Here, again, we must be aware that a pre-recorded tape may interfere with the natural growth of the performance in the accumulating moments of its own presence. Spontaneity may be annulled, and certain unrehearsed events may no longer occur, since the performance cannot evolve in whatsoever direction seems most fruitful. A pre-recorded tape is similar to a backdrop in that its pre-existence may incline the performance towards a static, theatrical repetition of rehearsed matter. Such a tendency is less evident when the recording device is visible in the space and simply used by the performer as an object among others.

3. The other as physical object:

In performance terms, the objects in or on the space are considered in terms of their functional value: chairs can be sat upon, smashed, stacked or arranged in rows. Newspapers can be folded, opened, made into hats or torn to shreds. Alternately, in psychoanalytical terms, the objects may be considered as symbolic instruments: a chair when sat upon might represent a (wished for) victory over an older sister; when smashed represent the destruction of a regime; when stacked represent the number of orgasms achieved in a single night; and when arranged in rows, they might represent our children. The newspaper might symbolize a wife: someone to fold or open, display or discard.

Both the functional nature of an object and its symbolic implication will alter with its state of course. Actions possible with a lump of ice will not be possible once that ice has melted, and in analytical terms the meaning of the object will have changed, and the meaning of "melting" will have to be taken into account as well. The merging of fluids, and their contourlessness, may suggest the inchoate condition of infancy. The clear shape of a brick may suggest the formed nature of adulthood.

The internal world is after all conditioned by the material one, since that remains the only world we know. Again and again we will see that physical actions have their echo in psychic processes. Perhaps it's for this reason that the performance artist so often sticks to the functional aspects of a set of objects when constructing a sequence.

The psychological implications of the sequence will look after themselves.

*   *   *   *

But is this performance a solo, or does it involve other performers? The question demands that the performer decide upon the local other *(o)*. Let us consider duets and solos.

If the performance is a duet, then the second performer is the other (whether acknowledged or not), together with the objects, the language employed, and the clothing worn by the subject and by the other. Now the question of acknowledgement becomes urgent. For note, Gilbert and George seldom acknowledge each other; they are simply both there in the work, as the gods Gog and Magog would stand on either side of a map of London, or as the lion and the unicorn may hold up the heraldic shield of Britain.

In another scenario, one performer might acknowledge, the other ignore, the existence of the other.

Both performers blithely acknowledging each other is contributive to the cliché which Pilinsky's Sheryl Sutton identifies as "mimicry" theatre. Mimicry theatre simply attempts to trace life as it appears to be lived. It is horizontalist. The signifying finger of its representations moves along the outline of reality. Its language also travels horizontally, from mouth to ear, and elicits a horizontal response. The art of rendering daily life has become paramount. It makes its fiction convincing by the removal of inconsistency, but that the actuality thus described is ultimately so normal as to be dull is never taken into account. The dilemmas of mimicry theatre are indeed too ordinary to engage the attention of any persons other than those so doubtful of their own reality that they require a stable diet of the mundane in order to be convinced that it offers them an accurate reflection of themselves.

Denial of acknowledgement is also a form of acknowledgement. But it enables accidents to cause relationships, it defeats predictability, it allows presence to become sculptural. Two performers who come into contact not because of recognition but because one is playing blind man's buff while the other is counting to a hundred with closed eyes – that is a qualitatively different contact to that of the performer who takes crisps from the other's offered bag.

Whether they acknowledge each other or not, in the end the subject *and* the other become the local other, the piece – together with any language used in it and any items of clothing or equipment needed to perform it. For the performer must ultimately be able to contemplate this duet as an object hopefully imbued with homeostasis, maintaining equilibrium under both external and internal pressures, where each element or action is subject to no more tension than any other, i.e. where the tension is spread and maintained over the entire structure.

If the performance is a solo, then the local other *(o)* is the 'route through time' described by the soloist's actions, as well as the body which performs those actions – taken as a whole or in its parts – together with the clothing worn or used, the furniture employed, the objects and the language. Ultimately the performer will need to put the performance outside himself including his role in it, so as to perceive it as a self-structuring system.

In a solo, the performer is the sole motivator, supplying the dynamic to the piece; and this is the case even when the performance places the motivator in some passive position, as in the work of Claire Pritchard – who endeavours to tie herself up in a way she cannot undo, or hang herself in chains in a position from which she cannot extricate herself. Chris Burden gets shot, in one of his performances, in order to be rushed to an intensive care unit. Everything happens *to him,* and yet he remains the motivator of the piece, seeing himself as the other: some passive object to whom things happen. Thus the performer is prime mover, or 'God', in the microcosm which is the performance, but, in this performance, Burden becomes a God sacrificed to his world.

The ironic nature of contemporary art necessitates the contrariety of such reversal. 'God', therefore, often disappears into his creation – fading into it by fashioning it. In the early eighties I performed a series of "table moves" in which I repeatedly shifted furniture through ninety degrees, a sort of 'performance cubism'. There was a necessity for these pieces to undergo some transition, and, in the second half of "Table Move 2", I began hiding behind the furniture while moving it. Finally only the furniture could be seen moving.

The Consciousness of Being an Object

The process of devising a piece requires that one works towards putting the performance outside oneself – in order to regard it as a self-structuring system maintaining itself (a homeostatic whole), whether one is in it or not, and regardless of whether it is being performed. One finishes making one's performance, and by so doing makes it the other, a local whole enclosing its ingredients; thus, on completion, its maker can contemplate this piece as if he or she were the Large Other outside the curtain.

Now the solo particularly is very often the manifestation of "what cannot be seen", stimulating the heightened perception of the voyeur. It often feels ridiculous to rehearse; and horribly embarrassing, especially if people peek in on you while you are doing it.

This is because they are witnessing you in the act of "doing something which should be done alone" – such as pissing behind a bush or masturbating – for when you create a solo you are playing with yourself. Many writers cannot work when someone is peering over their shoulder. Even a group requires privacy while creating a piece. This is why our present space is curtained off.

The "ratman" (in Freud's case-history) believes that he sometimes speaks aloud without hearing himself do so.

A similar sensation may be experienced while constructing a solo. This is because, before completion, you have fallen outside your work, which is a form of play, into the condition of looking at yourself from the Large Other's view, which is the audience's view and "society's" view – and you sense that you are behaving in a way which suggests that you are "unhinged", or in some unviewable condition of disarray –as if you were barged in upon before you *had finished* on the lavatory. It is important to reconcile yourself with this "unhingedness" – since phylogenetically it is akin to the disarray associated with the divine madness of antiquity, the trance of the skald or the shaman inspired by a god.

All new art has a vulnerability about it. It is open to criticism precisely because it has decided to abandon some time-honoured cliché of construction. Much good art seems ridiculous when it first appears – Picasso's cubist women, Carl André's bricks, Joseph Beuys living with a jackal or the performances of Annie Sprinkle. When constructing a performance solo, there is no need to steer clear of an action because it appears ludicrous. That's probably a sign that you are working in some original way.

If your work embarrasses you to such an extent that you feel constrained to stop working, consider that Lacan might advise you to speak 'à la Cantonade' – as children do who speak without addressing anyone in particular. Here, the language rises vertically, instead of moving horizontally across to the other (which is the cliché of dialogue in horizontal "mimicry" theatre). Sheryl, in Pilinsky's *Conversations,* remarks that speech in Robert Wilson's theatre is mostly like "speaking to oneself". And just as one can speak 'à la Cantonade', or 'to oneself', so one can move, perform or play to oneself.

Some of the best group performances are solos performed by the subjects in an ensemble condition. Each performs his solo 'to himself', but in the presence of the others. There is no need to acknowledge each other in a group performance, and sometimes the audience will perceive a significance in the conjunction of solo actions which was in no way intended by the performers. This is not a fault but a felicity.

*   *   *   *

To create a performance, the performer must decide where to be when not performing, and where to watch the space from, and must ask, "What should I wear and Why?"

Then the performer should put the Large Other (**O**) out of the sphere of consideration and identify the local other(s) – (*o*)s – the objects (including other performers, if any), the parts of his body employed, the language used, if any, the senses relied on.

Next the performer should begin to work "playfully" at the performance; acknowledging, even expecting, that any of the characteristics or objects initially chosen may change as the performance moves towards homeostasis, and therefore discarding items (or others) which exert some particular, over-privileged pressure on any one part of the structure only – thus creating a tension which cannot be dispersed throughout the piece.

Objects and Transport

One factor which is crucial to consider where objects are concerned is the effort required to transport them. A mirror here is not a mirror *there.* You may wish to work with the generic image of an object – in conceptual terms – and risk being obliged to use what you happen to find when you arrive in a foreign city without your own mirror. However, there may be very specific advantages to using the particular mirror you have worked with in rehearsal, or to employing the precise chair. Such advantages may concern some specific action only possible with that mirror or chair – in which sense, it is a *good object* for you. It may concern the notion of bringing the 'outlandish' to the foreign part. The tradition of performance is bound up with that of wanderers, exotics, and the conveyance of what may read as exotica out of its natural habitat. When Raymond Roussel's mother asked him to send her something outlandish from Australia he sent her an electric fire – that seemed to him outlandish in the outback. The simple transference of an object can demand a supreme effort – or a tiny one. The cost of transporting props, equipment etc. from one country to another can sink the entire enterprise. It's a lucky company that can afford to remain resident in one performance space. The priest occupies this situation in a church or temple, and a procession of effigies around community boundaries is common to many religions.

To expend such effort as may be required to transport one's objects to a distant space touches on another interpretation of the Lacanian object. Here the lost object he describes can be construed as the object of one's drive, the virtual object which constitutes a goal. This goal requiring the transportation of all other objects is in itself an object like the perspectival vanishing-point, in that it moves with us.

Objects and Supports

In theatre, there is a traditional difference between 'a prop' and 'the set'. Thus a free-standing table may be merely part of the set, since it is not specifically employed by the actors. Performance artists, however, are liable to question this demarcation between utilised objects and objects in the background. The sculptural tradition of performance may demand that every object in the space be assigned a specific function in the development of the action: it is there to be used, not there to provide some adjectival commentary on the piece. Thus it is often the case that if a performance artist employs a chair, that chair will be manipulated, stood upon, perhaps broken, during the course of the performance.

Still, there are times when an object will be used as a support – when the chair employed is for sitting on but has no other role. A table might be considered as a stage – it often was just that for the street-performers of eighteenth-century Venice – as we see in the paintings of Pietro Longhi. Performances may take place in baths or in wardrobes.

The supportive object constitutes a home. It might be thought of as a 'mother-object'.

Mother-objects can give birth to other objects. One is reminded of Breughel's woodcut of a huge fish which has been cut open to reveal the smaller fish it has swallowed, which in turn have smaller fishes in their mouths. Stuart Sherman may carry all the objects he needs for a performance onto the space in a suitcase – the performance may begin by him removing a collapsed camp-table from the suitcase and erecting it. Subsequent objects removed from the suitcase are manipulated by the artist on the surface of this table.

A Note on Interaction

Today many performers are intrigued by the notion of interactive art. In technological terms, this is art which calls into question the assumption that inanimate objects have no awareness and therefore cannot be aware of their audience. Whether 'aware' or not, video cameras installed within artworks can register the presence of a spectator and trigger responses in the artwork itself. Electronically wired pressure-pads can react to the footstep and cause sounds to occur, lights to flash etc. Often, however, the participatory element depresses cognition in the spectator. Its invitation beguiles him into the enactment of obedience. Instead of actively thinking about what is going on (i.e. creating a subtext to the action), the spectator passively performs the action, such as clicking on a mouse or accepting a sweet, simply because it is demanded by the apparatus or by the performer. The danger is that while a certain liveliness has been conferred to the artwork, the spectator has been reduced to an automaton.

But interaction need not be banal. As well as questioning the requirement that an artwork remain static in its object-hood, it can call into question assumptions about the nature of the audience/performer relationship. In doing this it will also question the relationship between the subject and the Large Other, and may throw doubt on the unity of that Large Other – which is after all only a fiction convention is complicit in maintaining. Today the Large Other has been fractured by cultural diversity. The audience incorporates a plurality of views. The analysand lies on a couch surrounded by a diversity of analysts. When the entire audience claps there is a brief semblance of unity, but the intention of the interactive performer may be to dissolve any such unity. Such a unity may be seen as coercive, signifying some vested interest in a previous cultural identity.

Thus the interactive performer may question the conventional siting of performances. Why should the performance occur on a stage or in front of rows of raked seating? Those of Claire Hayes occur on the escalators of shopping malls. She travels up and down these for hours, usually devising a repetitive route around the mall that takes in several escalator flights. Prior to the performance she will have been manicured, made up and given a haircut perhaps by shops renting space in that mall.

The performance artist, Claire Shillito, performs in a hotel bedroom. Members of her audience make appointments to see her and enter the room one by one. She removes the shoes of each person who enters and then invites that person to get into bed with her. In the dark next to her audience, she performs an intimate action or one which might be construed as intimate. Then she leans over the body of the audience in order to pull out a matchbox from under the mattress. Striking a match under the covers, and therefore lit only by this, she invites the audience to tell her something intimate or personally embarrassing. As soon as the match goes out the confession of the audience is terminated. Shillito gets swiftly out of bed and tells her audience in a brusque voice to put on their things. She then shows that audience into the en-suite bathroom, revealing that the previous single-person audience has been in the bathroom, possibly overhearing everything that has occurred during the performance. At this moment, the construction of the piece reveals itself to be a trail which loops back on itself.

HI, I'M CLAIRE

COME UP AND SEE ME
AT THE DOM HOTEL
ON SATURDAY, 10TH MAY 1997.
I'LL BE WAITING...

**NOTICE: TO VIEW THE PERFORMANCE AN APPOINTMENT WILL
HAVE TO BE MADE. AN APPOINTMENT TO SUIT YOU CAN BE
MADE ON FRIDAY, 9TH MAY, AT 13.00-17.00H, DOM HOTEL**

Poster for Claire Shillito's interactive hotel-room performance, *Hi, I'm Claire,* Osnabrück
Media Art Festival, 1997.

A similiar trail looping back on itself may be recognised in another interactive piece – *You: The City* by Fiona Templeton. In this piece, performers take members of the audience one at a time through a city, passing each member of the audience on to a new performer at the end of their passage in the piece. Two thirds of the way through the performance, the audience member is led back to a site previously visited in the company of an earlier performer, and thus witnesses a scene very similar to that of their own interaction with that earlier performer a while before, at the same time as they realise their own interaction was also observed by a member of the audience and by another performer.

In such performances, the issue of acknowledgement is again crucial. This time it is not a question of performer acknowledging performer but a question of the performer acknowledging every single member of his or her audience. However, it is probably important that such acknowledgement should remain a mask. What is at issue is the control which informs the experiment. When Shillito's audience gather together later, in order to compare notes, an ironic unification overturns their separateness. As far as she possibly can, Shillito repeats herself. The performance one audience member experiences is identical to the performance the next audience member experiences – except in one respect: between each performance in the series in any particular hotel-room, she changes her clothes – can be heard, even seen changing, since she neglects to close the bathroom door after the previous audience member has left, only closing it prior to admitting the new audience member waiting outside the hotel-room. So, though the clothes change (actually two outfits alternate), the action of changing her clothes remains a repeated part of each performance.

In a sense, it is important that she should perform as an automaton, a charming one, one that encourages intimacy; an automaton masked in acknowledgement. Only thus can she ensure that each performance stays identical to the previous one and to the one that follows. That each performance is the same for all members of her audience, so far as her actions are concerned, contributes greatly to the intrigue of this interactive work. Without such a discipline of repetition there would be no discourse. It is thus, also, that she maintains the essential homeostasis of the piece.

———————

The Object Workshop

1. Good and Bad Object Exercise

Prior to the workshop, performers are asked to bring in what they consider a good object and what they consider a bad object. The objects thus gathered together form a collection which can be used for a variety of object-orientated exercises. Initially, each performer is asked to show the good object brought in and then the bad object. Each is asked to say what is good about their good object – and whether its seems good to them in psychical terms or in performative terms, and then asked to say what is bad about their bad object – and in which terms they perceive it as bad.

2. Object Exchange

Each performer works with one object, trying to find functional uses for it, and accumulating actions normally associated with that object. Then performers exchange objects and attempt to put the object they have received to the uses found for their initial object, performing with it the actions previously performed with that initial object.

3. Stillness/Repetition Objects

Entering the space one at a time, performers freeze or perform repetitions with their objects. Later they may use triggers (See Cathexes and Chaos*) in order to switch from repetition to stillness or from stillness to repetition.*

4. Part Object Exercise

Each performer should treat one part of their anatomy as a privileged object while considering the rest of their body-movements as the background to the movements of that privileged part. They may address that privileged part of themselves. Then they may treat one part of another performer's anatomy as a privileged object and address or make contact with that part of the other performer.

5. Enlarging Objects Exercise

One performer brings a small object onto the space, then exits. A second performer brings a larger object onto the space, then exits. The presence of the two objects is allowed to deepen. Then the first performer, or a third performer, removes the first object and replaces it with an object larger than the second object. The presence of these two objects is allowed to deepen. Then the second performer, or a fourth performer, removes the second object and replaces it with an object larger than the third object. This continues until the objects are so large that it requires more than one person to lift them.

Another way to perform this exercise is to start it off as described above – but at any time a performer or a pair of performers not involved in the placing of the objects may shout, Stop! Then this performer or pair of performers enter the performance space and work with the two objects occupying that space.

6. Interactive Performance

Performers devise audience-interactive solos, duets or trios.

7. Hidden Other Exercise

Each performer devises a performance which demands the help of a hidden other – i.e. a performance which cannot be done alone, which in some way requires a helper.

8. Object Stages Exercise

Each performer works with an object, or with several objects, while utilising another object as their stage or performance space.

9. Performance Elsewhere

It is suggested to the performers that at least three times a year they should arrange for their performances to be mounted at venues other than their regular performance space, coping both with securing that venue and with the problems of transportation incurred by performing elsewhere.

Inconsistency as a sequence of isolated, unrepeated actions: Fiona Templeton and Michael Greenall of the Theatre of Mistakes performing in Stuart Sherman's *Duet* for *Conceptual Double Portrait* at the Mickery Theatre, Amsterdam, 1980. Photograph: Bob Van Dantzig.

5

INCONSISTENCY, CATASTROPHE AND SURPRISE

In a mental hospital, I have seen a man obsessively ironing a pile of shirts. I didn't watch him for very long. I was visiting another patient. He was still ironing these shirts as I left the ward. When the pile was finished did he turn it over and start again? *Was he trying to get the ironing right?*

Freud sees repetition as the sign of the transference: he identifies it with some compensatory action which reconciles the subject with his trauma. And when we considered mimicry and repetition we touched upon ambivalence, and how some compulsive repetitions might exemplify a state of vacillation between the positive and negative (on/off) aspects of a reversible action. "Shall I keep my jacket on, or shall I take it off?"

But what happens when one does *not* repeat, or feels that one must not, cannot repeat?

The patient I was visiting was a brilliant poet who had become blocked. He could no longer write because he only wanted to write something original, and he felt utterly oppressed by his belief that everything had been written before.

In a sense, everything *has* been written before, even if one's writing is original – since all the words have been used before – otherwise they would not be words, i.e. collections of letters of agreed shape, pronounced in an agreed fashion and signifying agreed things. But if you have a phobia about avoiding clichés, and you carry it to an extreme, you might consider words as clichés in themselves. Thus, as a method of signifying a table, the word "table" might be dismissed as a cliché. And now it is easy to see how pursuing this line of thought could lead you into silence. And if you extended your loathing of clichés into the sphere of action, you might end up trapped in a "stuck" condition of stillness.

The clinical term for such a state is *catatonia* – often an extreme stage of schizophrenia. Certain schizophrenics refuse to use a generic term such as "table", because they have no faith in the generic image this evokes. After all, every table is different: some are circular, some are rectangular, others have four legs, some have a single stem. Even among the circular ones, there are circular tops of different sizes, and even if two with circular tops *were* of the same size, they might be made of different sorts of wood, or one might have a formica surface, and even if made of the same sort of wood, one might have a scratch on its top, which the other didn't have – so how can all these wildly different objects all be called by the same name?

In the example given above, the chain of "reasoning" used to prove that the word table is inadequate appropriates a regressive series to establish its logical cadences – and even if, and even if, and even if... Obviously any such series indulges in repetitions – repetitions which delineate an ever-diminishing set of options, which may not cease diminishing until infinity is "reached", for each repetition of "even if" reveals a fresh difference. A subject refusing to use the word table by dint of the above process would be exhibiting a hypersensitivity to difference. But earlier we observed that difference is normal, that there can be no repetition without it. Carried to an extreme, difference becomes abnormal, turns into *inconsistency*, the third primary of action.

Inconsistency is not a term used with much frequency in psychoanalysis. It does not appear to be considered a fundamental concept, as is repetition. Yet, in my theory of performance art, inconsistency is a primary action, one of the fundamental poles of action. For action emerges out of inaction either in a repetitive way or in an inconsistent way.

Of course, anomalies can be found within any inconsistent string of actions, and it can be argued that *pure inconsistency* is impossible. However, this is as true of repetition. No repetition is exactly the same as that action which it copies – if only by the fact of it being a repetition rather than the initial act, or of being the third repetition rather than the second. Conversely, it has to be recognised that even when behaving inconsistently we continue to breathe – a repetition, even if irregular – and of course our hearts continue to beat and our blood continues to circulate. Repetition underpins our inconsistencies.

Suicide might be defined as a loathing of repetition: a loathing of the dawn returning and of the heart's unending beat. And this brings us to the notion that inconsistency is often a singular act – a "once and for all" occurrence – a surprise or a catastrophe. Note here the irony of the phrase "repeated suicide attempts".

Repetition is by nature multiple, whereas inconsistency implies a singular event – it may be a chain of singular events – but then we are being repeatedly (or consistently) inconsistent, which is a different state to that of suddenly becoming repetitive.

Inconsistency in Performance:

Inconsistency is problematic in performance. At first one may attempt simply to perform in some inconsistent way – no structure, no repetitions. But this often leads to inertia – all too rapidly one runs out of ideas. So here are several strategies which have been devised for the generation of strings of inconsistencies:

1.   *Generation of inconsistent actions by suggestion:*

   a.   Take the letters of your name. For each letter perform an action suggested by that letter.

For example: H–O–W–E–L–L. H – howl like a dog; O – open your shirt; W – wipe your nose; E – exaggerate your stomach; L – laugh; L – laugh again.

(Since certain letters are repeated in my name, I choose to repeat the action associated with the repeated letter: this goes a way towards ensuring that the string of inconsistencies is not consistently inconsistent.)

b. Choose an emotive word, or a word which is of significance to you. For each letter perform an action suggested by that letter. You could choose a word which meant nothing to you, or a sentence instead of a word, and you could establish some consistency about the suggestions – that they prompt words rather than actions for instance. Thus the word "Horrible" might generate "How openly Robert Redford is blessed like eternity. " Inconsistent sentences can be generated this way in improvisation sessions.

c. Choose an object. Think of the verbs associated with that object. Perform these verbs as actions.

For example: BOOK. Open, read, quote, throw away. The object does not necessarily have to be present. And, as a variation, you could subject some other object to the actions suggested by verbs associated with the initial object: open the chair, read the chair, quote the chair, throw away the chair.

Now this way, however inconsistent your actions, you are still repeatedly using the chair. So instead you might try subjecting a number of different objects to the string of actions: open the banana, read the wardrobe, quote the stock-market, throw away the skin.

Note that the objects need not be material. Neither need they be inanimate: open the shirt, read the tattoo, quote the motto, throw away the man.

2.   *Generation of inconsistent actions by task:*

a) Many everyday tasks call for a string of inconsistent actions, even if all these actions consistent with the goal of accomplishing the task. Consider having a bath, or changing a plug, or taking books to the library. Inside each task there are local repetitions – turning taps, unscrewing and screwing, walking etc. – but the string of actions each task constitutes is not in itself repetitive.

Further inconsistency can be achieved if the goal remains unaccomplished, and this may be possible simply by varying the order of the procedure: if the first action of having a bath is to put the plug in, a different result occurs if one makes this first action the last action one performs.

b. Now consider assembling a group of incongruous objects. Next, perform some sort of task-orientated operation on or with each of them. For instance, with a can of paint, a cup of tea, pencil and paper and a bucket of sand. Several performances by Stuart Sherman seem to have been developed along these lines, though his objects may originally have been assembled through some ideational connection more apparent to the artist than to his audience. Nor is his manipulation of certain small objects entirely task-orientated. One senses that he arranges sequences of things as others might arrange words into sentences. Often his actions seek to establish a relationship between divergent meanings of the same word. He is therefore concerned with the inconsistencies inherent in the *epos* of speech and in language.

Inconsistent strings of action can lead, as life so often does, to performing several tasks "at once" (or perhaps in alternating stages): setting the computer to print out your text while making a cup of tea and in the meantime doing a spot of gardening. Bobbie Baker, a performance artist who specializes in food and cookery pieces talks about "roaming" from task to task in the kitchen.

*   *   *   *

However attractive these performance exercises may be, inconsistency still seems to have slipped through our fingers; for all the methods for generating it appear tinged with consistency, which is obviously allied to repetition. The suggestion string runs the risk of being consistently inconsistent. The task tends towards a consistent goal.

This, it must be said, is an observation rather than a value judgement. From a performer's point-of-view, all the above methods are capable of generating fertile and provocative sequences of actions. Perhaps they should be referred to in some later section of this analysis, along with other mixtures of the primary actions – such as additives, subtractives, accelerations and decelerations: the secondary colours of performance art.

Consistent inconsistencies are employed by some fine performance artists. Sherman, for instance, creates such action-strings out of an array of objects when presenting his vignettes: these purport to be portraits of places or people, or sequences devoted to concepts such as "time" or "the erotic". He calls these collections of vignettes "Spectacles". The 'consistency' of an inconsistent string of actions, such as he uses, may be diversified by varying the specific types of action chosen. These can be a medley of fixed, transportive, supported, supportive, gestural and functional actions incorporating exchanges, creations, destructions and miscellaneous local repetitions such as scratchings, chewings etc (*more about these on pages 187– 188*). Here is how I described the first performance I ever saw by Sherman, back in 1972. It provides us with a fine example of a string of inconsistencies:

"*Portraits of places,* a work by the performance artist Stuart Sherman, is being presented in a tiny loft in downtown SoHo, New York. On either side of the stage is a heap of tat – plastic roses, artificial grass remnants, plastic macs, bits of card. My programme tells me that I'm about to witness approximately 30 vignettes of places – Amsterdam, Cairo, Coconut Grove, Copenhagen, so the list goes on through the alphabet.

A little man, casually dressed, comes on to the stage, chooses various items from the heaps, sets up a camper's table, touches something, scrubs this with that, holds both in front of his nose, puts away his table, exchanges the objects for fresh ones, glances at a list he removes from his breast pocket – presumably to see which country comes next – opens an umbrella, sticks a plastic rose through a hole in the umbrella, answers the telephone, searches in his pockets, throws away the telephone and the rose, picks up another object, spins it, blows on it, unties a package, allows some rubber balls to roll out on the floor, places patent leather shoes under the legs of the newly erected table, turns on a tape, turns off a tape, dismantles everything, runs a film, does something else, does something else.

At the end of the performance I am nonplussed. I have never seen so much happen in so short a time, but I am unsure of what I have seen. I can't say I recognised any of the places from the events which took place. Anyway, I go to a nearby bar to mull over what I remember. I have to make a phone call. I go to the phone, put down my drink on the ledge, pick up the phone, put it down while I unzip my jacket, search for my address book, my dime, my specs, pick up the phone, insert the dime, dial, pick up my drink – and there I am perceiving myself doing this, coping with the myriad procedures of living. Could these actions in a phone booth be my vignette of New York? When the work of an artist enables me to glimpse some new aspect of myself I know I have seen something original..."

(*Five Finger Exercise*)

Shades of difference divide consistent inconsistencies from inconsistent repetitions: repeatedly touching another performer, but never in the same place – or consistently using the same object, but never in the same way.

Goal bending must be mentioned here, for by drifting away from the inconsistent string generated by a task, there is the possibility of altering the goal before completing that task, which naturally increases the inconsistency of the string: an artist is making a cup of tea, but then, in a moment of abstraction, he chooses to paint a watercolour with the tea before pouring it out of the teapot, perhaps adding milk to the tea in the pot in order to alter the colour. Chaplain understood this, and Station House Opera have employed similar devices (threatening to punch someone, for example, then turning the drawn back fist into a fist which rubs the back of the head).

There's still a readable logic though, so we haven't yet identified a pure form of inconsistency. *Charades* is yet another way of generating a string of apparently inconsistent actions. Again, there's a consistent logic, even if the charade is so complicated that it remains unreadable. If we turn to psychoanalysis, perhaps we will get a bit further.

Inconsistency in Psychoanalysis

Inconsistency is not a term employed to any great degree in psychoanalysis, but from what we have already learned about repetition, what can we say about its axiomatic opposite? If repetition is a comfort, inconsistency is not. It is rather a pushing-out into the unknown. Where repetition denies the passage of time, by eternally returning to the same, inconsistency creates an event, punctuating time. In a sense, it makes time by making a memorable event. There's an elite loneliness about inconsistency. It connects with the sin of pride: a delusion of grandeur or genius. "I AM NOT LIKE THE OTHERS. I am not a clone." Inconsistency elevates the unique.

We have mentioned the schizophrenic's unwillingness to accept the generic image for a thing (no two tables are alike so why should they be called by the same name?). This notion informs Magritte's painting, *La Trahison des Images*. The painting shows a very bland image of an average pipe exhibiting no specific characteristics. Beneath the pipe is written: "Ceci n'est pas une pipe." A host of commentators, including Foucault have developed theories concerning this work. I like to think that it constitutes *a painting of a generic image rather than of a pipe*. It was apparently painted in 1926. A later version, *Les Deux Mystéres*, painted in 1966, depicts this painting and an even blander generic image as its subject. In *An Experiment with Time*, first published in 1927, J.W. Dunne had this to say about 'Generic Images'.

> "When a number of partly similar impressions have been attended to at different times, there is observable, besides the several memory images pertaining to those several impressions, a vague, general image, comprising nothing beyond the key elements which are common to all those separate images. For example, the images of the hundreds of tobacco pipes which I have seen, smoked and handled, all contain a common element which is now apparent to me as an ill-defined image of 'pipe' in general. It presents all the essential characteristics which serve to distinguish a pipe from any other article such as, say, an umbrella. Such characteristics are: hollow bowl, tubular stem – in short an appearance of utility for the purpose of smoking. But this indefinite image does not exhibit any indication of specific colour or precise dimensions. It seems, however, to be the nucleus of all the definite images of *particular* pipes to be found in my mental equipment; for, if attention be directed to it, there will quickly become observable the image of sometimes one and sometimes another of such particular pipes.
>
> These vague, almost formless general images are called *'Generic Images'*. and they appear to be analogous to a central knot to which the specific definite images are in the relation of radiating threads."

(*An Experiment with Time*, page 34)

It's hard to believe that Magritte had not read precisely this definition of 'Generic Images' prior to executing his painting, since the pipe is chosen as an example and the concept so powerfully expressed through it. All Magritte's images are generalized – all are generic images – which means that the man looking at the back of his own head in the mirror in another of Magritte's works is no more a man than the pipe is a pipe in the painting under discussion. What is the generic image of a painting? In those days of idealistic abstraction, a figurative painting might have seemed merely a generic image to modernists – a picture like all the others that had gone before. The implication is that *La Trahison des Images* is not a painting, simply the generic image of what a painting is supposed to be – something rectangular, depicting something like a pipe. Only the phrase below it is inconsistent with the generic image of what a painting should be, or, according to modernists, should *not* be. Interpreted thus, the painting reads as a satire on the modernists' oversimplified criticisms of figurative pictures.

Is the verbal statement an inconsistency, or is it simply a painted title, reinforcing the naivety of the generic stereotype? As it functions, below the object, it makes the painting unique. Magritte was only ironically interested in creating a painting "like all the others". His particular inconsistency resides in the negation of the actuality of the object – for in a stereotypical painting of a pipe the caption would surely read "This is a Pipe". It is this anomaly which distances the work from the generic daubs exhibited in Montparnasse or on the railings of Hyde Park.

A hypersensitivity to inconsistency would admit of no generic images and no similarities. Inconsistency in gait would constitute a refusal of coordination – or as in the 'funny walks' of John Cleese, a refusal to walk the same way twice. To repeat nothing, to demand a total absence of familiarity, to shun every cliché like the plague: these are the attributes of deliberate inconsistency.

Inconsistency could be viewed as a *rite of passage* out of the familiar into the unknown – just as most initiation ceremonies demand a period beyond the safety of the walls of a familiar village with its comforting repetitive daily round. The inconsistent act is one which is out of the ordinary, and therefore inconsistency informs 'coming of age' – some ceremony which is a unique event, and which, unlike most repetitions, cannot be reversed. In many cultures, 'coming of age' is achieved via circumcision, an irreversible act: phylogenetically, it is the symbol of the castration of the son by the father, which was a savage deed "civilized" by the diverted sacrifice of Isaac.

This irreversibility of the inconsistent act reinforces the notion that it is often not part of a string of actions but a 'one-off' – not a multiple but an incident: just as the cause of a trauma may be a single, out-of-the-usual event – in other words, a surprise. It is like being given a fright – if it happens too often one gets used to it, comes to expect it, and then it is no longer a surprise (instead it becomes consistent with our expectations). Here I would come back to the idea that a *repetition kills time* by reduplicating the past, whereas an *inconsistency creates time* by providing the unique, memorable (traumatic) incident which enables us to map out the past. Inconsistency as suicide denies the possibility of transference.

Another way of looking at it is to consider the poet Laura Riding's differentiation between lethargy and boredom. Boredom occurs when what we are trying to read is so familiar to us that we lose interest in continuing. Lethargy occurs when what we are trying to read is so unfamiliar to us that we cannot summon up the strength to plough through it. The two experiences "feel" similar – but one confronts repetition (in the form of cliché), while the other contends with inconsistency (in the form of innovation).

Loathing of repetition implies the suicidal, but it is also a defiance of the repetitive urge of the death instinct with its regressive spiral into the loam of time. Repetition accepts the drudgery of dying everyday. Suicidal inconsistency deals with death once and for all, consciously defeats it by willing it and by causing it to happen in life. There's a positive aspect to this as well as a tragic one, for irritation with the humdrum comforts of the daily round might spur one on to achieve something unique, dangerous and unusual – the ascent of Mount Everest, for instance, while the sadness of some constant reminder of loss (as in repetitiously mourning for someone) might strengthen the desire to "end it all"; to terminate repetition by the single abrupt act which removes one from it.

In the 'fort-da', repetition unifies loss and return by incorporating both into a naturally alternating activity. Inconsistency, on the other hand, is rupture. Where repetition envelops the event, swathes it in replication, inconsistency tears it open and pierces the skin of it. In 1995, during the recent wars in the Balkans, the Serbian artist Bálint Szombathy lay bleeding on the Yugoslav constitution until he passed out. A powerful comment, conceived as an action, here was a single inconsistent act extended over the entirety of the performance.

In June, 1985, Stelarc, the Australian performance artist pierced his body in order to hang suspended by eighteen hooks, dangling from a crane, high above the roofs of Copenhagen. The suspension in Copenhagen was one of twenty such performances created around the world. Today, Franko B cuts his body and allows the blood to drain out of it. In the early days of performance art, a Berlin actionist castrated himself. These are events, not enactments. But Franko B is accustomed to donating his blood, and Stelarc would deny that his suspensions were traumatic, even though they were painful. Such performances involve bodily incisions, but in Franko B's case, as well as in Stelarc's, repetition annuls the shock of the piercing, the trauma of the cut. Nevertheless, Stelarc hangs separated from the earth. And inconsistency epitomizes separation. The repetition of the breath is held as the incision is made, and the heart skips a beat. In its purest manifestation, inconsistency comes as an abrupt surprise – not as part of a string of actions but as a *singular event*.

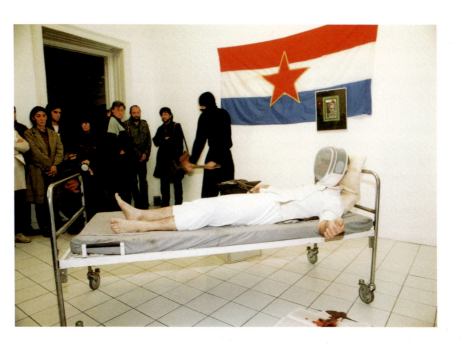

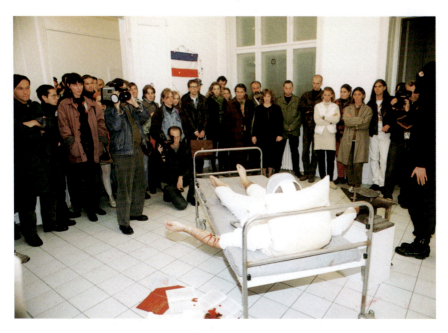

Bálint Szombathy bleeding onto the Yugoslav constitution in *Flags II,* at Novi Sad in 1995.
Photographs: Branislav Lućić.

In the unconscious, this singular act of inconsistency (or act which is inconsistent with the subject's view of things) may well *reverberate*, that is, it may create transferential repetitions of itself for a long while after. In other words, the act which becomes repeated is, in its first instance, an inconsistency. In a similar way, a single stone thrown into a pool creates a multiplicity of ripples. As Deleuze puts it, it is the fall of the Bastille which celebrates and repeats in advance all the Federation days which commemorate it.

Often the inconsistent incident has the characteristics of a positive/negative diode. It could be a surprising revelation of pleasure rapidly followed by some punishment catastrophe. Shitting is primarily a pleasure, while shitting in one's nappies is one of life's first catastrophes. The gift one would release from the body remains uncomfortably close, indeed it still cleaves to the aperture from which it came. Inconsistency is making a mess by accident, or messing oneself. A loathing of repetition expressed by a child sequestered with its mother might imply rejection of the mother, just as kittens complain when the mother cat subjects them to yet another gruelling bout of washing. In itself, this rejection might be the outcome of its reverse, a sudden feeling that one has been abandoned, which leads to a distrust of the comforts afforded by the mother. For when a parent leaves us to cope on the toilet for the first time we experience a confrontation with the unknown; the unknown being that of whose consistency we cannot be assured.

Thus an inconsistent incident occurs when the known is ruptured by the unknown.

Returning to inconsistency in performance:

Inconsistency can now be identified as *surprise*: it is the key ingredient which lifts the performance out of the predictable into the unpredictable. With repetition and stillness, but lacking surprise, we can only build field performances – "all-over" events, with no emphasis on development or incident. The two-dimensional art of the abstract expressionist painters utilized the notion of "field painting" to create meditative surfaces undisturbed by any one incident; and although Jackson Pollock's paintings are full of incident, they are not full of inconsistencies, since, in his case, the incidents *become* the field. Field paintings contain few surprises, but to make surprise effective, some predictability must first have been set up by the use of repetition, and this predictability will constitute a field. Surprise is the defeat of our expectations, rather than an incident in a chaotic world. In chaos we expect nothing but the unpredictable, therefore, within it, there can be few surprises. Surprises are ruptures – they signify the ends of chapters, they herald new stages of development. Surprises are often unique events or diodes (the latter being unique events with practically instantaneous repercussions). More needs to be said about predictability and the creation of expectation prior to surprise when we deal with mixtures and compounds of our fundamental principles, our primaries, and consider doing "two things at once".

We've already noted that a chain of inconsistencies must entail some repetitive input into the inconsistency (one is being repeatedly inconsistent), and this may reduce inconsistency to mere difference. Bear in mind though that a series of very large inconsistencies is often used in comedy or farce. Slapstick humour is regularly created by generating a *chain of catastrophes* (Buster Keaton was a major exponent of this sort of chain); or take the scene, in the film *Foul Play*, when Goldie Hawn, terrified by a bible-toting dwarf who she takes for a hit-man, sweeps him out of her third-storey window: the dwarf lands in a dustbin, the bin rolls down a hill, via a series of steps, and when it comes to a halt the dwarf spills out of it to plunge straight down the lidless shaft of a manhole. A certain so-that-was-what-it-was-for enhancement of the surprise is set us by having seen some men working around the manhole in an innocuous previous shot (the dwarf arriving with his suitcase). Here note the balance that must always be struck between predictability and surprise in art – for the manhole cannot just "appear". In genuine performance-surprise there is always the possibility that *one could have guessed what would happen.*

Inconsistency as accident is of course crucial to humour. It also plays a considerable role in the nature of grotesque. The chimera is an inconsistent creature. Bakhtin has shown how the mediaeval carnival which nurtured the grotesque turned the world upside down, exemplifying a reversal inconsistent with the serious view of established church and state. The Roman mime was, as a performance artist, given permission to make obscene gestures under certain imperial regimes, and suppressed by others. His role evolved into that of the fool of the middle ages. This character embodied licence – or authorised inconsistency – at the court of the ruler. The fool performed a psychical role by expressing what Bakhtin calls the language of the lower stratum of the body – articulating the doubles-entendres and 'Freudian' slips ineluctably attendant on pious pronouncement and the reading of weighty documents. Recent performances by André Stitt have paid homage to "The Geek", a character once common to Irish fairs. The Geek would perform in a hole dug in the ground – and there he would carry out shockingly inconsistent acts of outrage and abuse. Further below ground, the devil himself is a character inconsistent with divine creation. But though the devil may be at the bottom of all evil, the 'holy fool' can allow an outlet for suppressed thought by mimicking Satan and articulating his perceptions of mankind's inconsistencies – products of the chimerical rift between upper and lower body – and thus the fool performs a valuable act of homeostasis for society.

An inconsistent string in language could produce a secret language (employing "words" which have never been heard before – suggesting signifiers whose signifieds have yet to be assigned to them). In formal, more analytical terms, language is, in its normal occurrence, obviously an inconsistent string, just as everyday tasks are often inconsistent strings, since words are not articulated in repetitive patterns except perhaps in poetry or in chanting. Any repetitive aspect that may accrue to language must reside more in its structural consistencies than in the nature of any specific utterance. Therefore, when we talk about using inconsistency in language to generate surprise or create some expression at variance with consistent narrative usage, we are suggesting methods of inconsistent usage overlaid on the basic inconsistency of any ordinary string of words, i.e. a form of interference such as the secret language mentioned above.

Alternatively, a paragraph of text might be constructed 'atomically' – in the manner favoured by the 'L–A–N–G–U–A–G–E' poets. Then no (consistent) continuity would bind the sentences together: each would be sufficient unto itself while establishing only tenuous links with sentences contiguous to it. The texts used by Fiona Templeton often exhibit such atomic independence from each other – see Ron Silliman's *The New Sentence*.

Another method might be to generate a *transgressional language* – such as a string of abusive terms with no appropriate relation to each other or, if the language was a language of signs and actions, a charade which spelt out insults or obscenities. Obscenities can be considered as parts of a dark, transgressional language in themselves, but they can also be used inconsistently, as endearments – proofs of complicit and devoted intimacies. Rabelais understood both these aspects of transgressional speech. The custom of using 'billingsgate' – a language of comic exaggeration, slang and abuse – was a rich source of inspiration for Elizabethan theatre – particularly in the work of John Marston – whose devilish, picaresque character, Cocledemoy, has a marvellous line in the scurrilous and the scatological:

> "The fox grows fat when he is cursed. I'll shave ye smoother yet! Turd on a tile-stone! My lips have a kind of rheum at this bowl – I'll hav't. I'll gargalise my throat with this vintner; and when I have done with him, spit him out. I'll shark. Conscience does not repine. Were I to bite an honest gentleman, a poor grogarian poet, or a penurious parson that had but ten pigs' tails in a twelvemonth, and for want of learning but one good stool in a fortnight, I were damn'd beyond the works of supererogation..."
>
> (*The Dutch Courtesan*)

Then, again, we should consider persons suffering from *Tourette's Syndrome* who are subject to uncontrollable bursts of loud obscenities. These rupture their discourse in a surprising way, but, of course, if the syndrome has been identified as their affliction, we can predict that the outburst will happen.

Still, the best surprise, as we've noted, is born out of the predictable, just as our worst traumas are caused by the known behaving unpredictably. The relationship between prediction and surprise is well expressed by Baltasar Gracián, the seventeenth century Jesuit philosopher of Huesca in Spain, who was much admired by Lacan. The world of repetition is that of the daily round, of the compulsive habit and the obligatory natural function. We can trust its predictability. Gracián understood that the inconsistency of betrayal was a skill required by the courtier – in the unreliable game of diplomatic chess, of bluff and counter-bluff. In para. 13 of his manual, he says:

> *Behave sometimes disingenuously, sometimes with candour.* Man's life is a manoeuvre against the malice of men; crafty schemes are the weapons of the shrewd. Cunning never behaves as appearances would suggest: it takes its aim, indeed, in order to provoke confusion: it skilfully contrives to keep its threats indefinite and carries them out in an unforeseen way, intent always upon dissimulation. It affords a glimpse of its purpose in order to ensure the attention of a rival, and then does the very opposite, triumphing by means of the unexpected. But keen intelligence shrewdly foresees this and lies in thoughtful ambush; it always comes to a conclusion contrary to the one it is intended to reach and at once recognizes any attempt at deception: it ignores every first and obvious aim and waits for the second, and even the third. Dissimulation is intensified when its trick has been detected and then endeavours to deceive by means of the truth itself. It alters its play by some new feint, and turns simplicity into guile, basing its astuteness upon a show of extreme candour. Observation comes along and, its perspicacity seeing through the trick, unmasks the wolf in sheep's clothing; it detects the purpose and sees it as the craftier the more straightforward it appears. In this way, the cunning of the Python combats the candour of the searching beams of Apollo."

> > (*The Oracle*, page 59)

Inconsistency may set the field in situations of intrigue. More often than not though, in quotidian terms, it is repetition which sets the field, whereas inconsistency may be the single event which disturbs or fundamentally alters that entire field, just as a single drop of chemical falling onto a semi-saturated solution can instantaneously turn the liquid crystalline. A thought-provoking theory concerning what might be called the friction between repetitions was advanced by Norman Walter in *The Sexual Cycle of Human Warfare*, published in 1950. On the simplest cellular level, the repetitive division which creates daughter-cells from a single original mother-cell may be followed by the 'inconsistent' onset of a sexual phase – where the daughter cells require partners from other cell-families. In a cellular aggregate, where the cells remain connected, this will entail the disruption and dispersal of the aggregate, a sort of sexual bursting. In the human male, ejaculation amounts to an inconsistent bursting forth of sperm – an ejection as much as an ejaculation. On the family level, Oedipal stress may force the son, who is increasingly disrupting the repetitive homeostatic state of the parents, to be ejected from the home. In society, the threatened repetitions of peacetime are suspended by the inconsistent 'solution' of war – when the disruptive sons, mere carriers of our genetic gametes, are ejaculated from the nation as a conscripted group, to die conveniently on the battlefield or mate with the females of a defeated aggregate – thus forming a new aggregate which may eventually rupture or explode; if it does not ejaculate its own young men in order to regain its homeostasis.

As a rupture, the inconsistent event is fundamental to the construction of tragedy: Oedipus discovers two inconsistencies – one, that he has murdered his own father; two, that he has married his own mother. These cause a third inconsistent event when he puts out his own eyes. Paradoxically, these three inconsistencies amount to the threefold repetition we have already observed in the plot of *Hamlet*. In the structuralist terms of Claude Lévi–Strauss, it is the end of the myth folded back on the middle of the myth folded back on the beginning of the myth. Opposites become as much a part of the pattern as similarities. For Oedipus, death is a crime, then love is a crime – and he puts out *both* his eyes – signifying how blind he was to the facts in *both* instances. Here inconsistency is catastrophe, an absolute breach of the hero's expectancy as well as the termination of his notion of his own history. As catastrophe, inconsistency is even more pronounced in the tragedy of *Hercules Furens* by Euripides. In this great play, Hercules returns from the underworld to rescue his wife and children from imminent destruction by a despot. However, no sooner has he slain the despot than he is sent mad by Hera and proceeds to murder his wife and his children himself. This action is so inconsistent as almost to read as a flaw in the homeostasis of the play. However, nothing could better express the unpredictability of events and actions.

As we have seen, the inconsistent occurrence is also fundamental to surprise and to humour. It turns matters upside down, introduces chaos into situations and causes frights with the ensuing release of tension which is laughter. In its more serious vein, a similar release constitutes the purgative of tragedy. In both farce and tragedy, it is inconsistency which triggers that release; and therefore, by that specific easing of the tension, it *brings about* the homeostasis of the drama. It is both catastrophe and catharsis. It may constitute the rising moment within the play, as well as the *deus ex machina* which ensures that its endgame will not amount to a stalemate. Inconsistency should perhaps be considered the dramatic antithesis to the repetitive unconscious of performance. But just as the drama has been much influenced by this contemporary art form, influenced by the integrity of actions repeated for their own sake, actions which may shun an illustrational significance, I maintain that performance would be advised to incorporate inconsistency into its repetitions, however dramatic their import. For otherwise Thanatos may triumph, at least in the guise of his brother Somnus, and the artist may find that his watchers have fallen asleep. Inconsistency, surely, will keep them awake, for it punctuates time, creates chapters and ends, and often reads as a shock.

———

The Workshop in Inconsistency

1.   Improvised Inconsistency

Performers are simply asked to improvise inconsistently. Afterwards the experience is analysed. How easy is it simply to be inconsistent in performance without recourse to any system or structure?

2.   Suggestion Strings

Performers work through the methods for creating strings of inconsistent actions described on page 72 – Generation of inconsistent actions by suggestion. Later they may be asked to utilise an entire sentence as a suggestion string.

3.   Facial Suggestions

Performers, again work through the methods for creating strings of inconsistent actions described on page 72, this time performing only with the face.

4.   Object Exchange

See Objects Workshop, Exercise 2, page 67

5.   Continuous Verbal Exercise

Performers are reminded that speech is an inconsistent string. They are asked to speak continuously, all at the same time – without considering what they are saying.

6.   Single Inconsistencies

Performers freeze or perform repetitions. Whenever each wishes, he or she may perform a single inconsistent act. If a performer has been in a freeze up until this action, he or she then starts performing a repetition. If a performer has been carrying out a repetition up until this action, he or she then freezes.

7.   Catastrophes

Devise a chain of catastrophes – each fresh catastrophe dependent on the catastrophe before it. Next consider the site of these catastrophes and devise a chain of catastrophes for a dining-room, a bathroom, a kitchen etcetera.

8.   Disastrous Repetitions

Perform a repetition which must inevitably lead to collapse, spillage or disaster.

9. Sabotage Piece – from "Elements of Performance Art"

One person enters a limited space and performs any action. A second performer joins in after the first performer has had sufficient time to establish the initial action. The second person may also perform any action.

A third performer watches the "drama" that the first two have created between them – they may or may not be consciously performing in relation to each other. When this drama seems to have established itself the third performer enters the limited space and deliberately "sabotages" their performance.

After a period of resistance, having attempted to continue activity despite the presence of the saboteur, the first performer quits the performance space.

A fourth person watches the new "drama" that the second performer and the saboteur have created between them. When this seems to have established itself the fourth person enters the space and performs a fresh act of sabotage.

This is sabotaged in turn by the first performer, and so on.

Before the performance everybody should state how much physical violence they are prepared to put up with.

As each performer quits the space that performer should be blindfolded and given a whistle. Detecting an apt moment by audible clues alone, the blindfolded performer blows the whistle once. At the blast on the whistle all the other performers freeze. At a second blast everybody may start moving again. The blindfold is then removed and tied over the eyes of the next performer to quit the space.

An image from *The Brig* by the Living Theatre. Photograph: Living Theatre Archives.

6

CATHEXES AND CHAOS

Having discussed the three primaries of action, *stillness, repetition* and *inconsistency*, our next concern will be to consider methods of manoeuvring between these primaries. Freud's term, *cathexis*, can be brought in here. Cathexis is analogous to an electrical charge or a switch: it signifies choice or appropriation. There is *object-cathexis* – an object choice occurring at an early stage of a child's development, and then there is *ego-cathexis* – where a choice is made with some degree of decision by the subject at a later stage of development. And then there is also *anti-cathexis* – which refers to the suppression of choice.

Now in workshops concentrating on inconsistency, there's a tendency for the performance to disintegrate into chaos. Chaos can be interesting of course, however, in performance, it often extends too long, flattening out into normality: daily life itself being mildly chaotic – a matter of loosely inconsistent strings and accidents.

If the entertainment of the Large Other (**O**), outside the curtain, is not a pressing issue, then a chaotic performance workshop can help its participants to lose their inhibitions, to "let go" behind the closed curtain, without caring whether anyone will ever watch what transpires. This may enable the performers to discover actions whose extremity might not have been attainable during exercises calling for some degree of control. Of course these extremities may be made manifest in front of a public. It was the liberating aspect of chaos which inspired the early work of Carolee Schneemann in USA in the sixties. Participants in *Meat Joy* and *Water Light/ Water Needle:*

> "...did not interact so much as they entangled each other in one another's bodies, becoming part of a collective activity in which touching or otherwise crossing the threshold of physical distance was fundamental to the process of communication. Seen in this light, one of the unique features of this stage of Schneemann's work is the extent to which performance enabled her to blow up a previously intimist aesthetic to public scale."
>
> (*In the Flesh*, essay by Dan Cameron in
> *Carolee Schneemann: up to and including her limits*, page 11)

But shifts between primary states of action need not be chaotic. Experienced performers will have developed the ability to switch on or switch off such extreme activity at will – to "turn on a button" from one state to some state diametrically opposed to the first. These states may be induced through behavioural changes while seeming to present an emotional content. We now need to examine the cathexes which enable the subject to switch from one such state to another.

For cathexis, or its equivalent in performance, let us employ the performance term "trigger". A performer chooses a trigger to signify when to start or when to stop an action or a series of actions. Triggers are described at greater length on page 37 of *Elements of Performance Art* (see also Appendix 4). Start-triggers are cathexes; stop-triggers are anti-cathexes.

A trigger might be chosen for when to break out of stillness into repetition; another might be chosen for when to stop repeating an action or for when to insert some sudden, inconsistent event into the repetition. There is, of course, a considerable variety to the possibilities which the triggers might entail. Starting from stillness, there are, if we stick to the primaries, two choices; and, after a choice has been made between them, two further choices can again be triggered:

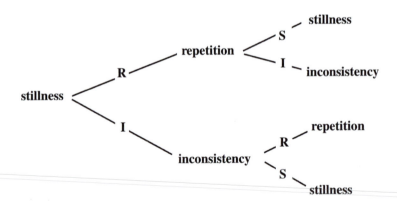

There is no need for a stop-trigger (anti-cathexis), since any stop is the start of another action primary. Perhaps all suppression of choice is triggered by the switch to a new choice rather than a deliberate arrest of the previous mode (of behaviour). Thus, in the action model above, only three triggers are required – an R-trigger, to set off repetition; an I-trigger, to set off inconsistency; and an S-trigger, to bring about stillness.

As a model, this works well enough for an interplay of stillness, repetition and inconsistency, but it does not take into account any secondary actions, and also it might be taken to imply that its inconsistency will be a string of actions. If we try to stick more closely to the essential nature of the primaries, the following diagram might be a better guide:

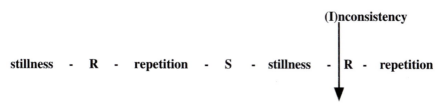

(I)nconsistency

stillness - **R** - repetition - **S** - stillness - **R** - repetition

Here, the singular, surprising act of inconsistency now occurs but once, punctuating the ongoing action. Such a surprise might also bring about a change in the primary, as in the following diagram:

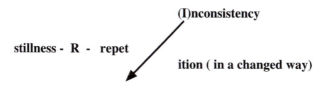

(I)nconsistency

stillness - R - repet

ition (in a changed way)

Or it might lead to a change *of* the primary, as in:

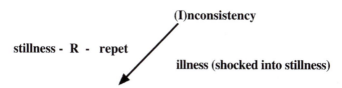

(I)nconsistency

stillness - R - repet

illness (shocked into stillness)

The inconsistency which interrupts repetition may be the outcome of the friction entailed by that repetition, in which case inconsistency is *jouissance*, orgasm, the release which facilitates homeostasis. This is a reversal of the traumatic scenario in which an inconsistency, in the form of a shock, causes compulsive repetition or the illness of catatonic stillness as in the diagram above. Lacan noted an ambivalence about the cause of a trauma and its effect since a cause could generate an effect more traumatic than the initial incident – which would then lead the initial incident to be remembered with far more apprehension than was initially the case. He likened this perpetual reinforcement of the cause by its effect to a Moebius strip, where the twist in the looped ribbon of paper turns side A into side B, or effect into cause, or cause into effect. In farcical terms, one might develop a psychosomatic symptom – a tingling in the thumb, say – and then grow so irritated by it that one cuts off that thumb with an axe – anxiety about this loss then causing a whole multitude of tinglings. Something along these lines is going on in Mike Parr's performance, shown at the 1977 Paris Biennale. Wearing his fake arm in place of his missing one, while hiding his existing arm, he berates his father in a taped interview – as if his father had caused his amputation. But he seems to accumulate guilt by so doing since eventually he 'cuts off' that fake arm, 'amputating' himself – as if this event was occurring for a second time.

Cathexis versus Simplicity

Systems triggering responses and alterations of response have an obvious utility. It should be born in mind, however, that a performer need not respond. He or she may simply sustain. By this I mean that the performer may choose to remain in the state adopted at the start of the performance for the entire duration of that performance. Truly effective stillness is often such a constant. The paintings of Elsworth Kelly, Yves Klein and Ad Reinhardt have shown us how powerful a single primary colour can be in painting. A continuous freeze, a single action continually repeated or an endless string of inconsistencies can be just as effective in performance.

Too great a reliance on triggers may dissolve the primacy of the actions utilised. A switch to a brief repetition may make that repetition seem merely an illustration of repetition – there is something illustrational about actions used as 'examples'. Trigger-responses can resemble acknowledgement – and therefore a reliance on these can 'horizontalise' the performance, aligning it too closely with the responsive representations of conventional theatre.

An exception to this is *The Brig*, performed by the Living Theatre back in the sixties. Based on the reminiscences of a man incarcerated in a US military prison-ship off the coast of Japan, *The Brig* demonstrates the daily routine that the prisoners were forced to undergo: being woken before dawn triggering an immediate tidying of the cell, the crossing of any white line in any corridor triggering the shout, "Permission to cross the white line, Sir," and failure to shout loud enough triggering a beating. Performed at breakneck pace, this utilised triggers to make manifest a coercive environment. Really excessive use of spatial rules, masking tape, barriers etc, coupled with enforced cathexis must generate this condition of a regime. Here response is repression. Just as the pyschotic must respond to the stimuli which trigger his psychosis, so the citizen must respond to the strictures of psychotic government. A performance with too many rules conveys a sense of the constraints of totalitarianism. We are caged in by the demand that we respond.

Normality's responses may be exaggerated until a condition of paranoia is attained, or they may simply be removed, allowing another arena of action to emerge, an uncanniness perhaps, a ceremonial, an expiation or a meditation. The integrity of any primary which establishes this will require that the primary be allowed to 'deepen in the space'. Certainly, in a free session, a strong emphasis on stillness helps to establish the 'otherness' of performance time, the time 'five-times slowed' which Pilinsky's Sheryl Sutton describes in his imaginary conversations with her (*see page 29–30*).

Equally it is the continuous nature of the repetition which makes the Finnish artist Teemu Maki's work so frightening when he bangs his shaven head repeatedly against a metal locker until he slides to the floor unconscious in his videotaped performance *The Good Friday*. And again it is the continuous nature of Stuart Sherman's inconsistent actions which transforms them into what can only be described as a different kind of stuff to anything one may have watched before.

I have heard about a performer who sat using percussive wire brushes on a small cube of marble. With these he beat out a repetitive rhythm for eight or nine hours. At the end of the performance there was a shallow spherical hollow on the top of the cube.

Chaos and others (and others' objects):

In the chaos of an *inconsistent* workshop, it may be assumed that inconsistency gives one licence to trespass on the objects of others, and to impose upon their bodies. Turmoil may prevail, and many acknowledgements may occur; often acknowledgements which are forced out of the performer who is being trespassed upon. The performers may steal objects from each other, to use them for their own ends; but then, as performer/witnesses, they can no longer identify which objects are the (*o*) objects of others, nor can they claim to possess their own objects. All distinctions are now swamped in the anarchy of the perceived licence of inconsistency. This leads to a situation similar to a general mixing of all colours. Nothing can be distinguished. And though children sometimes assume that the more they mix their colours the brighter their results will be, this proves not to be the case. An indeterminate khaki-grey is the result.

When a performer trespasses indiscriminately and imposes indiscriminately on all the other performers in the workshop, he or she has ceased to separate the Large Other (**O**) from the local other (*o*). The general is confused with the particular, and the chosen group of specific bodies, objects or words – which is practically an extension of the subject – becomes submerged in a generalised notion of what is outside the subject. In other words, the other performers simply become a sort of audience, against which one transgresses, demonstrates rebellion and so on. If everyone is engaged in a similar rebellion, very few distinct identities emerge. The performance disintegrates into a rowdy but normal shambles.

Perhaps a single performer could take on this transgressive role while the others attempted to stick to their proper objects. But this implies that some agreement ought to be reached, and at first sight, this seems to be the case. Performers need to identify their own particular objects, and whether any of those objects constitute other performers. They need to decide on what is a trespass and what is a permissible act. They need to agree on whether certain items of furniture may be moved, or on whether they must remain where they are, and also agree on who may move what. If some of these decisions are to be left to chance, that has to be agreed. It is therefore inconsistency which inevitably introduces legislation. However, legislation creates too rigid a system of prohibitions: too much design and not enough laughter! The rules adopted may mitigate against the occurrence of the most effective catastrophes. Legislative decisions are made with conscious minds

– and the laws thus generated may obstruct the materialization of events prompted by the unconscious.

Instead of legislation, the performers might bear in mind that in traditional theatre only one person speaks at a time. If such a rule is democratised, then a performer's domination of the action might be divided by the number of performers, i.e. each of three performers might dominate the action for a third of the time.

Total inconsistency, simultaneous inconsistency, destroys suspense. And when preparing some inconsistent act you need to *choose your moment*, if you wish to maximize your effect.

There is a latent, *méchant* quality in all of us, which may very well project sadism, lust, jealousy, avarice etc into the performance. These are just the qualities which make the performance interesting to watch. Performance, after all, must compete with the violence of Sophocles and Shakespeare, with the mental cruelty of Ibsen and the blood-lust of Abel Ferrara. However, if you are going to (wickedly) sabotage another performer's action, *wait* until that action has developed sufficiently to cause that performer rage or disappointment when it's wrecked. Children know that it is more effective to destroy someone's tower of bricks *just before its completion*, rather than immediately after one brick has been put on top of another.

To ensure suspense, or to preserve the object-extensions of others, I advocate, instead of legislation, "listening with the third ear", as stressed by Freud's follower, Theodor Reik:

> "Young analysts should be encouraged to rely on a series of most delicate communications when they collect their impressions; to extend their feelers, to seize the secret messages that go from one unconscious to another. To trust these messages, to be ready to participate in all flights and flings of one's imagination, not to be afraid of one's own sensitivities, is necessary not only in the beginnings of analysis; it remains necessary and important throughout. The task of the analyst is to observe and to record in his memory thousands of little signs and to remain aware of their delicate effects upon him. At the present stage of our science it is not so necessary, it seems to me, to caution the student against over-evaluation of these little signs or to warn him not to take them as evidence. These unconscious feelers are not there to master a problem, but to search for it. They are not there to grasp, but to touch.

> We need not fear that this approach will lead to hasty judgements. The greater danger (and the one favoured by our present way of training students) is that these seemingly insignificant signs will be missed, neglected, brushed aside. The student is often taught to observe sharply and accurately what is presented to this conscious perception, but conscious perception is much too restricted and narrow. The student often analyses the material without considering that it is so much richer, subtler, finer than what can be caught in the net of conscious observation. The small fish that escapes through the mesh is often the most precious. Receiving,

recording and decoding these "asides", which are whispered between sentences and without sentences, is, in reality, not teachable. It is, however, to a certain degree demonstrable. It can be demonstrated that the analyst, like his patient, knows things without knowing that he knows them. The voice that speaks in him speaks low, but he who listens with a third ear hears also what is expressed almost noiselessly, what is said *pianissimo*. There are instances in which things a person has said in psychoanalysis are consciously not even heard by the analyst, but none the less understood or interpreted. There are others about which one can say: in one ear, out the other, and in the third. The psychoanalyst who must look at all things immediately, scrutinize them, and subject them to logical examination has often lost the psychological moment for seizing the fleeting, elusive material."

(*Listening with the Third Ear*, pages 144–5)

Like analysis, performance is a "fleeting, elusive material". Robert Wilson has employed stillness and slowness to create performances where the third ear prevails as the architect of the action and even the audience's perception of what has occurred is more like touching than grasping. Remember, we, the performer / witnesses, are the analysts of the performance. We are listening watchers, who often watch without direct or deliberate acknowledgement of the others who perform with us, and therefore we may not scrutinize with our gaze. To look around one reads as just that. It is better simply to trust to one's sense of timing. Then, as often as not, chance will aid and abet one's action, causing marvellous coincidences to occur – simply because one trusted to chance and 'the feel' of the piece instead of attempting consciously to assess the situation by some surreptitious survey of the action. There is no overall view from within the performance. Often, indeed, the gaze gets hidden by the pose adopted. Instead of our gaze, we may use "the third eye" as much as "the third ear" – getting our sense of the entire performance from within ourselves.

———————

The Cathexis Workshop

1.   Sensory Cathexes

Employ a trigger for a change of action. The trigger might be: a touch, a sound, a smell, a taste or a sight.

2.   Cathexis Exercise for the Primary Actions

Each performer chooses a trigger for stillness, a trigger for repetition and a trigger for inconsistency. Each also decides upon a still pose, a simple or a complex repetition and on a method of performing inconsistently. They then perform in the space chosen, utilising these primary actions and the triggers they have adopted for switching between them.

Problems are bound to develop. Several performers may have chosen triggers which fail to occur. Does this matter, or does it imbue the performance with a shape dictated by chance? Would it be sensible to consider adopting triggers after the performance has begun – triggers based on the possibilities observed once it has started? Could one trigger do the work of three?

3.   Triggered Alterations

a) One performer is chosen to create one single major inconsistency during the performance. The others perform stillness or repetition until the occurrence of that inconsistency, then switch from stillness to repetition or vice versa.
b) Again, one performer is chosen to create one single major inconsistency during the performance. The others alternate stillness with repetition, adopting a single trigger to switch between these two primary actions. When the inconsistency occurs, they alter the primary action they happen to be performing instead of switching to the other primary.

4.   Trigger Possibilities

Performers study the exercise reproduced in Appendix 4. They then perform a free session which explores the possibilities outlined in that exercise.

5.   Sustained Primary Actions

Each performer is asked to create a performance based on a single freeze, or a sustained repetition or a continuous inconsistent string. There are no triggers and no changes.

The primary action chosen lasts for the duration of the performance. This exercise can be performed as a group event, or as a number of solo performances. Performers are asked to consider the quality and the impact of the primary action chosen. For how long is it possible to perform the freeze adopted? What is it that makes the repetition interesting? How will one prevent the inconsistency petering out or turning into repetition?

6. Altered Object Cathexis

Performers choose an object and a trigger. Each performs with their object either in a functional way or in an emotional way. When the trigger occurs, those who have been performing with their object in a functional way start to perform with it in an emotional way instead, while those who have been performing with their object in an emotional way start to perform with it in a functional way instead. When the trigger occurs again, each performer reverts to their original response to their object.

A performer with Station House Opera achieves two aims with one action.
Photograph: Julian Maynard Smith.

7

DRIVES AND THE PRIMARIES

Lacan maintains that all discourse has its effect through the unconscious. Perhaps we should bear this in mind while touching on the psychoanalytic debate as to the nature of our drives and desires, what differentiates them, and how they function. Drives, in the Freudian sense, are not *instincts*, according to Lacan, so much as 'pulsions'. "A drive gives you a kick up the arse." Elsewhere he says that "the drive is the advent of the signifier" – first you get a feeling, then the need to articulate that feeling. On the other hand, since words tend to exist before we do, a word, such as 'love' or 'hate', might be envisaged as a magnet, drawing certain feelings into contact with it. Drives "draw up our lines of fate." These are compulsions without the 'com'– they *are* us, they are not forced upon us.

Drives have a source, an aim, an object and an impetus. The *aim* of the drive is to eliminate the *source* (of pleasure or irritation) which first prompts it (disturbing homeostasis). The source of such tension is eliminated by the removal of the bodily need causing it. This innate activity of tension release is known as the *Pleasure Principle*.

The *object* of the drive is the means by which this aim (of relief) is achieved, and the impetus is the measure of urgency in the aim – so one might suppose that the greater the need, the greater the impetus of the drive. It might be argued though that the impetus of a drive may depend more on some overdetermination of the signifier which has come to represent the object than on the pressure from the source. Do we eat only when hungry, or are there subordinate aims – the need to bring some object to the mouth, or to cease from speaking while we chew? Lacan emphasises these subordinate aims over the source.

Drives as Content

There are of course, in each of us, psychical as well as physical compulsions. But from our performance-orientated viewpoint perhaps we should look first at the natural compulsions which comprise the body's needs and its functions. Our primary drives are those which we cannot resist: eating, sleeping, urination and defecation. Breathing should also be included here. We are also 'driven away' from pain, and our bodies must obey the law of gravity. We are also compelled by exhaustion – to stop doing whatever demands too much of our psychical or physical systems.

Many artists have treated such drives as their primary content. Bruce Gilchrist has experimented with sleep deprivation. Tilda Swinton slept through the daylight hours of the exhibition she shared with Cornelia Parker at the Serpentine Gallery, London, in 1996. Bobby Baker is a food artist, and in a recent piece called *Kitchen Show* she performs certain feats in her kitchen and then attaches an object to her body as a memorial to each feat. Gilbert and George create enormous photographic works concerned with excrement. They are eager to demystify the body's functions, conscious that hiding its operations from ourselves contributes to the spread of infection. Sleeping, eating, defecation. Today's artists take the drives as their subject, but none of it is new. Down the ages, ascetics have experimented with the visions induced by hunger and sleeplessness. Soothsayers have examined the turds of emperors in order to complete their prognostications.

Love is a matter of urgency too, and erotic desire and its vicissitudes might be considered the root of all tragedy. Certainly Freud would have maintained that sexual energy is at the root of everything. But to some thinkers this is debatable. Is the spoon Bobby Baker twists into her hair necessarily a phallic symbol? Must the flapping dish-cloths she attaches to her heels be vaginal emblems?

Can objects resist their Freudian inscriptions? Can there be love without lust? In a somewhat Platonic mode, Lacan asserts that the thirst for love is not based on a demand arising from any need. Perhaps he means by this that we can survive without having sex. Sexual desire is a construct, even if its basis is instinctual. Although we cannot prevent ourselves feeling the urge, we *can* do without act – any animal can. The "sex-drive" is therefore, more precisely, a desire rather than a compulsion like sleep or hunger. In much the same way as we need sex but can do without it, we have a need for light rather than darkness. Nor are we comfortable if our ability to hear is removed from us.

In addition to the obvious compulsions, Freud speaks of a death instinct. But whether this is a drive remains debatable. Certainly we are compelled to die – eventually. Like sex, so far as it affects our life, death, like love, is a construct. Animals are not aware of it – even when they are hunted. Their urge is simply to run away. Only a language animal can envisage death. Both death and sex may be instinctive, but still, they remain constructs with an element of choice about them. Even if we are dying a little each day, we can choose to ignore the fact in a way that we cannot ignore our need for food, sleep, air or evacuation.

Certain performers have played with death – Chris Burden has allowed himself to be shot, and then transported immediately to an intensive care unit. He has also lain close to a high voltage wire passing over a pail of water. A pool of water connected the artist with the pail, tempting the audience, vertiginously, to bring the wire in contact with the water – thus electrocuting the artist. Franko B bleeds till he falls unconscious.

Other artists have experimented with breathing. Performers in the Chicago-based *Goat Island* company are obliged to keep their heads underwater while others perform certain intricate tasks, only yanking the head of their colleague out of the water after the completion of the tasks. A student of mine, Heather Griffiths, performed underwater in 1995, first with a snorkel which she then exchanged for an aqualung, exchanging that for a plastic bag as she emerged from the water, and only removing this to inhale through an amplified harmonica.

In addition to these drives and near-imperative constructs, we possess a need which is phylogenetically rooted, although it has never been adequately acknowledged. This is the impulse to *groom* ourselves. Grooming is almost as urgent an impulse as the desire for sex. While not governed by the absolute necessity which distinguishes the drives, grooming is more than a behaviour pattern acquired through conditioning. It is, rather, an activity we have inherited from the animals. Grooming has a traditional link with Narcissism. The tidying of a place is its extension. It is one of the deficiencies of psychoanalysis that it has never identified grooming as one of our instinctual urgencies. Compulsive grooming is a common neurosis, and can indicate severe mental derangement. "Out, out, damn spot!" sighs Lady Macbeth. Women artists have made much of obsessive scrubbing and ironing, the interminable brushing of hair, bathing, and the repetitive washing of hands. The nagging compulsions of grooming are about as ubiquitous in performance as the urge to bring about a reversal of its excessively neat outcome and create a 'godawful' mess. Gilbert and George promote an air of neatness even when they show their turds. These items have been carefully photographed. You could say that their turds are well-turned out, very well formed – nothing sloppy about them. On the other hand, André Stitt's performances read as expiations. One is reminded of an Indian holy man covered in dirt and dung. By the end of his performance, Stitt may be daubed in mayonnaise and ketchup and coated in feathers, while the space may suggest the aftermath of a tornado.

By grooming itself, an animal comes to know its own body. I think we can assume that our being bathed improves our tangible sense of ourselves. As infants, we are touched all over by the bathing hand of the caring parent. Surely, if the mirror-stage helps a specular image of ourselves to form, our being bathed may also alleviate our infantile sense of a lack of shape – teaching us our contours in a tactile way. Perhaps Lacan places too much emphasis on the visual. It is likely that we become aware of our identity through a combination of the senses: smelling others as different, tasting our own excrescences, feeling our physical boundary, our volume, our weight on the earth, and hearing our own voices as distinct from the voices of others.

*   *   *   *

Suppression

The drive is a fiction you are forced to believe in. Each should convey you towards the homeostatic resting point of the satisfaction that is relief from tension. However, in urges such as sex, an increase of tension may enhance the felt effect of discharge.

Here we can identify an energy generated by denial: the longer the delay, the stronger the eventual tension release, and therefore the greater the pleasure. As a child, I used to delay my peeing so that I could eventually direct it higher up the urinal than anyone else. My 'directing' of the jet of urine suggests that impetus is achieved through temporary *suppression*. In a similar, caterpulting, way, a rider may rein in his horse when the rest of the field gallops off, only to release the grip later, so that the horse will "go like a rocket" in order to catch up with the other horses.

Our social conditioning dictates that suppression is common to all the drives and to most desires. In our minds, the drives and their suppression are intimately connected. Indeed, it's feasible to believe that in art, at least, suppression is just as important as expression. Any build-up of pressure calls for a valve, and, with pressure behind it, matter emerging via that valve will shoot forth with intensity. But there is no call for a valve where there is no build-up of pressure. It could be argued that without censorship there would be no need for the imagination. Wittgenstein's exhortation to us to pass over in silence that about which we cannot speak might be adjusted here to cover more than metaphysics: remain silent about that which you need to speak, so that its message may manifest itself in a sublimated way. Today, though, this projection of taboo issues into the imagination is very much being questioned. War has been declared between fiction and non-fiction. Taking a good hard look at what we "really" are, at what we "really" do, seems to exemplify a justifiable frankness in this age of immune-deficiencies, a frankness for which it is worth jettisoning the intrigue generated by the suppression of intimate facts. The work of Annie Sprinkle seeks to dispel that obfuscation. She bares her vagina, and lets the audience queue up to view her cervix. Then she masturbates as the climax to her show. Her work both demystifies and celebrates sexuality. However, intrigue is a lure in art. Intrigue is what holds our attention. If we are queuing up to peer into it we can all too easily predict that pretty soon we will contemplate the cervix in question.

Today we *can* speak freely about our sexuality. For better or worse, the vagina is no longer a mystery. Erections can be contemplated and the *cache-sexe* traditionally used to hide the pudenda now reads as an unnecessary prudishness. Such honesty is permissible in the twentieth century, and to skirt these matters on aesthetic grounds seems pointless: an unnecessary censorship artificially applied. But the vogue for candour can lead to flat art – since it requires no valve to mediate its content. Mind you, the new sexual frankness is probably still the outcome of suppression, since we now talk endlessly about what we can no longer do.

The Elizabethans employed pastoral settings inhabited by lyrical personages such as shepherds and knights-errant to put across views about the state that might have led to the executioner's block if treated directly. Dissident writing flourished in the Soviet Union so long as it was officially illegal. Recently such adverse legislature has been swept away, and writing or theatre which expresses what were once illegal views is now encouraged by the state. However the writing and the drama have gone flat. Now there is no need to speak in parables, or to find ways of saying the unsayable.

It may be that "dissidence" is always re-creating itself. In our present climate, it is socially permissible to speak about concerns such as housing shortages, the milder forms of sexual aberration and instances of ethnic inequality. But these subjects may now be unsuitable for art, since they require no pastoral mediation and need not be expressed through a parable. Thus it could be argued that an artist should always be looking for what is unsayable in his or her society, for that is the subject matter which most requires the mediation of art and the valve created by it out of intimation, suggestion, allusion and parable. This will be the art with the greatest allure for the age, since it is in this area alone that suppression of the direct facts may still be obligatory. Classical catharsis can only occur where the emotions stirred up by a drama are prohibited. What is innocuous can hardly be a taboo – although of course we are not supposed to be innocuous in the sphere of 'entertainment'.

A vagina may have shocked Ruskin, especially with pubic hair attached to it (being used to polished marble statuary, this was what disturbed him, it is said). But these days, surely, such a sight can hardly be a threat. However, a play describing a happy family of child abusers would probably incur censure today, as would any play in Russia which suggested that Stalin was right after all.

Performance art is a new genre which may often lean towards the presentation of taboos. It is not traditional theatre, and it is the more performative the less it strives to represent. It relies on the reality of a sequence of actions rather than on the illusion of an event. For the suggestive qualities of the imagination it may substitute the inventive qualities of acrobatics or the sensationalism of freak-shows. When Stelarc suspends himself by hooks he is not tying to create the illusion of flight: instead he is presenting us, confronting us, with the reality of his suspension. Stelarc considers that it would possibly be dangerous to employ meditation or drugs to evade the pain incurred in this operation. So here, nothing is alluded to. We are simply presented with a performance fact, or feat. If there is any suppression in this, it remains very much a private concern of the artist's.

The Individual's Drives

To return to the drives behind our suppressions: in each of us the unavoidable functions intermingle with urgent constructs. At the same time, we are each busily adapting to the constraints of our own particular niche in the way that niche requires. Beyond the simplicity of the basic demands which we are compelled to obey, there are individual, psychical components to that which charges us up, and unconscious prejudices which dictate what we suppress. We will now examine the nature of the drives in these more personal terms. Featuring strongly here are the emblems which trigger our sexual

Stelarc suspended by hooks in *City Suspension*, above the Royal Theatre, Copenhagen, 1985. Photograph: Morten Schandorff.

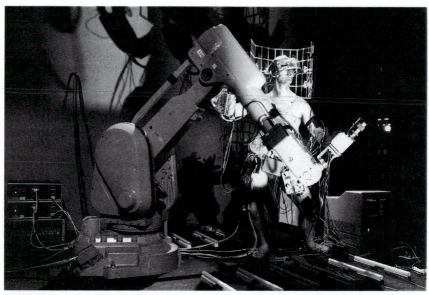

Split Body/Scanning Robot – Stelarc wearing artificial attachments including a robotic video-scanning arm – at Tisea, MCA-Sydney, Australia, 1992. Photograph: Tony Figallo.

responses – whether these be likings or aversions.

It is said that a drive tends to *regress*, to return the organism to an earlier condition prior to tension. In this sense, the drives are considered to be conservative. Drives account for our daily *repetition compulsions*: these are the habits that govern our sleeping and our eating as well as our sex life.

Controversy rages over the precise nature of the origin of our drives, for here we are trying to identify the essence of our *elan vital* – our life force – which is a problem as metaphysical as that of locating the soul. The object of the drive (the means by which its aim is or appears to be accomplished) resembles an onion when one sets out to discern its source: peel away one skin and you encounter another. Or the source may be insignificant – its object a fiction so far as that object concerns the drive successfully discharging its aim – and if the drive is a fiction, then that fiction is a family drama, incorporating parents and siblings.

The Classical Freudian drama is that of the *Oedipus Complex*, and, underlying that, "penis envy" for girls and "castration complexes" for boys. Ernest Jones, Freud's follower, appeased the feminists with a different scenario, which is sometimes simplified into a "to each his own" theory of a child's initial dynamics. According to this, little boys have pricks, sticks, swords and guns; while little girls have bells, shells, nests and bags. Nobody need envy anything or worry about having anything cut off.

Freud's drama takes as its starting point the commonality of the mother. Whichever sex we may be, we wish to become the desire of the mother, to ensure that we get to be suckled. This desire of the mother equals the penis – for that is what the mother desires of the father. Then little girls discover that they are, like their mother, wounded by the removal of the penis – which they are doomed to crave from the father. Why was it removed? Perhaps as a punishment for their becoming the desire of the mother. Meanwhile little boys live in fear that they will have their penises cut off by their father if they become the desire of the mother. Their naughtiness visibly distances them from the mother's love. Thus girls endure a punishment, while boys live under threat; though girls are only made of "loveable" things like sugar and spice, while boys still possess "naughty" things like puppy dogs' tails.

That all life's motivations are constrained by this Mummy/Daddy theatre is a supposition some find offensive. Deleuze and Guattari go some way to easing its grip on the interpretation of our drives by positing a more factory-like scenario in their *Anti-Oedipus*. Any commodity must create a desire for itself, just as any desire must ultimately invent its object. Thus we are desiring engines – forever in the process of producing desire and its objects – constantly spewing and ingesting, linked ourselves to sustenance-giving machines and to waste-removal systems. These engines are harnessed to the vehicle or carapace of the conceptual 'body without organs', an idealistic notion of the body in a state of homeostatic equilibrium. At the same time, the motors of the desiring machines generate another energy, an asexual energy, or language, an energy that tackles the world outside the sphere of need, inscribing it with need and production evaluations. It's a model which can be aptly linked with the performance primaries: stillness being 'the body without organs', repetition being the desiring machines and inconsistency being primal psychic repression, the traumatic avatar.

In recent performances, Stelarc has attached a third hand to his right arm. He is also connected to a robotic eye which is in turn attached to a video screen. Movements of these extensions may be controlled by link-ups to his muscles and their contractions, and these contractions may be involuntary, controlled by electric signals sent through the internet from somewhere else. The body is simply one machine connected to a team of machines – just as a machine generating desire will inevitably attach itself to a machine generating a product. Orlan and Stelarc have pronounced the demise of the body as any sort of absolute, for the body may be artificially enhanced, altered, connected to wider communication systems. Humans may be cloned in the future – the trauma of birth may thus be avoided, and perhaps innovation will liberate us from the domestic tragedy of Oedipus.

Yet Oedipus remains the prevalent theory, a psychical myth which seeks to explain our tensions. Few alternative myths have been offered, but there are variations to it. The analyst Melanie Klein, initially a follower of Freud, suggested modifications to his scenario which have particular bearing on the early development of little girls. They were based on her own direct observation of the behaviour of children rather than on theoretical calculation. According to Freud, there is a stage in a girl-child's development when she turns away from the mother towards the father. This he attributes to her discovery that she lacks a penis. Klein argues, in her paper *Early Stages in the Oedipus Complex* (1927), that the deprivation of the breast, in weaning, is the most fundamental cause of the turning to the father. She believes that the girl has an innate knowledge of her vagina, and therefore she does not have to struggle with the castration complex which causes little boys anxiety. All the same, the little girl initially turns to the father's penis in order to suckle, having been deprived of the nipple, and when this desire is rejected by the father, her hatred of the mother for refusing the nipple is compounded by envy of the mother who is able to suckle the male "nipple" in fellatio. This hatred and envy results in the urge to destroy the contents of her mother's body. But the destructive desire causes her anxiety retroactively, since being without a penis, she identifies with the mother, and having wished to damage her mother's insides, in her unconscious she fears retribution against her own maternal capacity. Thus the girl worries about whether she will be able to have babies, while the boy worries about having his penis cut off.

In general, male analysts of Freud's generation developed theories which depicted the "normal" woman as a passive, submissive type, subdued by her punishment, her penis lack; while female analysts, with the support of Ernest Jones, developed theories which depicted women whose relationships with men were tinged with revenge and disappointment or, as in Klein's theories, driven by ambition through associating with the paternal superego, and reaching fulfilment by fusing this with the capacity for self-sacrifice and the intuitive gifts derived from the mother.

The Oedipus complex, with its interpretive variations, is supposed to bring about rivalries within the family, and to influence our initial sex-drive prior to puberty and our later sex life. The fear it describes, of some loss of some vital part, combines with our first realizations of separation from the mother (the shock of discovering her otherness). However, it is quite obviously a *construct*, a construct which anticipates Lacan's lost object. The multifarious substitutions of that lost object for the phallus comprise an imagery which excludes the equally powerful if two-dimensional "picture" of the vulva. Vulva and penis are balanced by the equality of their failings, for the penis attains a 'phallic' sculptural dimension but only intermittently, thus proving itself an unstable object, while the vulva is only two-dimensional and therefore 'painterly', steeped in illusion. However, like the entrance to Aladdin's cave, the vulva secretes the vagina – which constitutes a whole repository of lost objects.

Lacan was a champion of castration anxiety, perceiving the slit as a cut, and evidence of the lack of the phallus. However he owned a painting that was, for many years, presumed lost – the *Source of Creation* by Gustave Courbet: a very fine rendition of a vulva! Naturally we should be suspicious of biographical details when they are used as intellectual ammunition. Still, I find it difficult to resist drawing certain inferences from the fact that Freud was born an uncle. I can well imagine that he suffered from the infantile realisation that his nephew had a bigger one than he had! His theories are distinctly phallocentric. Ultimately we performers need a bag myth as well as his myth of the stick (and its loss). The story of Alcmene would be suitable.

Plautus tells the story in his play, *Amphitryon*. Alcmene was the wife of a general of that name. While he was away at the wars, Zeus came down from heaven and seduced her in the form of her husband, aided and abetted by his servant, Hermes, who takes the form of Amphitryon's servant, Sosia. She would have known a swan or a shower of coin! Nine months later she lies in the throes of labour – prevented from giving birth by the midwife servants of Hera, the jealous wife of Zeus. These midwives tie their bodies in knots – thus preventing the child's arrival for seven days and nights. Finally Alcmene's handmaid, Galanthis, holds up a veil between the midwives and the vagina of her mistress and cries out, – "Oh, look, he's arrived! There's his little head!" Astonished, the midwives unravel their limbs and Alcmene gives birth to a child the size of a fully-grown wild boar.

The play of doubles at the start of this drama, and the use of the veil at its conclusion make this the archetype of vaginal tales. Doubling as a prelude invokes the labia, and the veil suggests a replacement of the hymen – which is probably what so disconcerts the midwives. This makes the birth of Hercules a virgin birth. He is of course the child in question, and the son of God – the Father.

Of course I see things from a male viewpoint, but many of the apprehensions I would associate with being female appear to come into play here. If God stands for the father, this suggests to me that very young girls may imagine being penetrated by their fathers and think, 'Since my father is larger than me, if he gave me a baby (little girls know about these things now) it might be a "grown-up" baby disproportionate to my own size – the size of a fully-grown boar – a baby which might split me apart.'

This fear might then make little girls act as if they were smaller than they are – to emphasise to their daddies that, while they are very like their mummies in all other respects, they are only *miniature versions* of their mummies – and as such quite impossible to get into. And wouldn't this go some way to explaining a female tendency towards self-belittlement?

The artificial hymen which the veil signifies seems a fairly clear way of expressing a woman's longing to be as she was before she gave birth – an expression of the wish to regain a tight vagina carried to an extreme degree of intactness.

Freud's Oedipus is a phylogenetic interpretation of our impulses which sounds as if it would have been more appropriate coming from the hand of Carl Jung. Perhaps he adopted it as a screen to cover his retreat from his earlier seduction theory which suggested that children were abused more often than his Viennese contemporaries cared to contemplate. It was more convenient to view the notion of such experiences as the mere fantasies of children. The danger here is that we exchange the frying-pan for the fire. If we dismiss the fantasies of children, on a no-smoke-without-fire basis, we may fall into an unfair condemnation of all fathers. That Freud was quite willing to recognise that abuse occurs is evident in the story from *A Case of Obsessional Neurosis* (quoted on *pages 135–136*).

Oedipus and Alcmene are both rather Jungian ways of going about explaining our compulsions. But note the performance implications of these myths. In the first place, they generate a comprehensive symbolism of our objects – (*More about objects in* The Other and the other – *pages 44–66*). There's the staff that comprises the third leg of the Sphinx's riddle, the conjurer's wand, the caduceus, the penis. Tybalt and Mercutio clap their hands to their swords, and it seems that performers are very often swaggering about with their substitute penises. Because of suckling there is much wishing to put these in the mouth, but this urge is suppressed, and we point them at other performers and say "bang" instead. War may begin as play. But only the girls carry their guns around in bags – as we see in Hollywood movies. Note also, among the girls, there is much wearing of bags on heads and calling them hats, and much slipping of feet into similar enclosures and calling these enclosures shoes. We boys will carry our own guns around in cases. Yet obviously the hard-edged case, whether a pistol-case or a suitcase, is simply a *masculation* of the vagina. Men take over feminine objects by making them hard.

Equally, a feminisation of the penis makes it soft: and this is useful too for it gives us rope, the hose, the sleeping snake: an entire other species of object to play with. Perhaps the feminisation continues by making the penis multiple: exemplified by strands of spaghetti and tresses of long hair.

The bag and the veil may epitomise the vagina and the entrance which screens it. Certainly the veil or the cloth is as powerful a symbol as anything phallic. As a generic image, it includes the cloak of invisibility and the shroud. The notion of a screen held up before a mystery is found in the iconostasis of the orthodox church.

If the stick is phallic, what is the cloth? Its namelessness is endemic to the condition of our sexual politics. Should we call it 'cuntal' or 'hymenal'? Nowadays the phallus demands its female counterpart. And so it strikes me that cunt and vulva have as much right to enunciation as penis and phallus. There is a reversal however. Phallus and vulva provide the advertisement, yet one term is ancient and the other technical. Penis and cunt describe the anatomy, yet again one term is technical and the other ancient.

Let us consider the cloth – it wraps and it clothes and it hides. As a child, I would wrap my blanket around my thumb, not only to smell its comforting difference but also to disguise my own identification with my thumb – thus disguised, it was more of a nipple perhaps. And let us consider the bag. Perhaps little boys aggrandise and externalise the bags which stand for their imaginary vaginas – merely to carry them on the arm would make each boy a girl – and so the boys make dens, houses and shelters.

If little boys aggrandise and externalise their imaginary cunts, do little girls internalise and diminish their imaginary phalluses? Lipsticks, eye-pencils and cotton-buds all have a place in the bag which is their nest.

It has been observed that both attributes have their failings. It should also be admitted that the cunt is just as changeable as the penis. Where the penis is hard or soft, the cunt is wet or dry. About both items there is a degree of instability. Man's penis being outside him, he externalises his instability – in compulsions – echoing this external unstable object of his. Woman's vagina being internal, she internalises her instability – in hysteria – the unstable object kept within her.

Oedipus complex or Alcmene syndrome: the psychoanalytical use of these myths provides no narrative answer, but rather a significant encoding of our objects. Lipsticks have a place within this code, and lampshades – indeed, practically the entire gamut of our objects can either be inserted or enclose (note how the passive use of the verb describes the male symbolic act, whereas the female symbolic act is described by an active use). Whether we "buy" Freud or not, our awareness of how our objects might read gets heightened by this, and we sense how Russian doll within Russian doll points not only to the regressive series but also to the labia. Gary Stevens and his partner Caroline Wilkinson put on coat upon coat – they end up "enwombed" in their lapels. Fellatio is the interesting position that two chairs get into when one is stacked upside-down on top of another: this was a position

Caroline Wilkinson and Gary Stevens performing in Stevens's *If the Cap Fits*, ICA, London 1986. Photograph: Georgina Carless.

imitated by two male members of The Theatre of Mistakes – when they 'became' the furniture in *Homage to Morandi*.

And now, since our discussion of these emblems of love and sexuality has brought us into the vicinity of the "palace of excrement", how do our anal drives and suppressions affect our performance? Pissing has become a stagey cliché, but some of us *expel* speech by means of rhapsodic declamation, so we can see immediately that speaking has a natural affinity with excretion – since it just comes out at the other end – while the inability to express feelings is associated with constipation. Equally we can speak of verbal diarrhoea – that hysterical, unstoppable outpouring. Then Freud links dreams of burning with attempts to prevent incontinence during sleep – thus screening the effect of wetness by the invocation of flames; an opposite which nevertheless acknowledges the stinging sensation which a urinary accident may cause.

The diarrhoea of hysterical speech points to the notion of shitting out of fear. But faeces have positive as well as a negative aspects. The child's first gift is a turd. To squat and defecate connects one to the earth. Priests threw dung at the people during the Feast of Fools in the middle ages. As a memorial of a good meal, the good shit is a gift of fertility imbued with a sense of giving, cairn-making – leaving one's mark. Nowadays we may feel ambiguous towards this last attribute, critical of the evidence European civilization has always 'shat out', preferring an invisible passage through time and space as exemplified by the Navajo.

Objects invoke our products as well as our means of production. We produce saliva, vomit, urine and faeces. One might consider orange juice the urine from an orange tree. Some objects – bricks, stones and balls – incorporate an ideal sense of solidity, although the turd can be phallic at times, at other times ductile or shapeless. Our mouth bites off a part of the world and our arse returns it to the world. Eating and shitting engage us in ceremonies of incorporation and exclusion, filling and emptying, address and avoidance, fusion and separation.

Lacan maintains that the parts which arouse us are emblematic of places where parts may have been cut away – the lips and the labia, and indeed the slit at the tip of the glans, resemble seams and sutures. And it is at these sites of our severances that we wish for reunion, longing to be joined up again at the locations where we received our wounds. Such a longing may communicate itself to us when we witness videos of Orlan's performances involving cosmetic surgery, her body sliced apart and then resealed.

The key objects of psychoanalysis are all tokens of separation: the vulva is the sign of the cut, the breasts are withdrawn from the mouth, shit gets ejected from the body, the penis is *there* when erect and then *not there* when limp (as if it had been removed). Urine flows from the body and away. And all these items possess topological characteristics – "alterality" – that is, they can be kneaded into different shapes, they can have form and then appear formless, they can be spread or compact. In particular, the body's waste products have no *specular image* (according to Lacan), no ultimately familiar shape – note how the term 'waste products' balances the good and bad aspects of this 'issue' – and how deeply the digestive system is incorporated into our language. Lacan goes on to assert that, since we look outwards from ourselves, we also have no specular image. We are subjects prone to alterality – stuff topologically alterable. In other words, we feel like shit – when we want to be erect (non-imaginary) phalluses.

Such are the dramas which overdetermine the drives, causing wishes and desires which amount to mental *inconsistencies* which punctuate yet sustain unbreakable loyalties. Lacan observes that "the act of devouring concerns other organs than the mouth. "

And remember, it is not just these anatomical things, these parts, which provoke these dramas. The parts are inseparable from their names, and the words for these parts are with us always, with us and within us, and not simply to be identified on our bodies and on the bodies of others. Equally the names for family members, mother, father, sister, brother, get mythologies built about them over and beyond their personal reality – as do their personal names – the name of the father being particularly important in our society, since, if the mother "gives" life, the father "gives" (or withholds) his name. And therefore our drives condense around a *treasure of words* "which interwreathe like a nest of asps. The bite of these words is both deadly and delicious," says Lacan.

But since the motives here touched upon, which supposedly govern our drives, hark back to an epoch before the advent of language, they appear to me to be beyond the reach of language. Just as issues such as the existence of life after death inflate cloud castles of elaborate conjecture, so the motives governing the behaviour of the pre-linguistic child can be hypothesized with gusto – more to the imagination's entertainment than to any more concrete purpose. If philosophy should abandon metaphysical conjecture, according to Wittgenstein, being at best the handmaid of science, then perhaps psychoanalysis is at best the handmaid of the imagination. One may ask metaphysical questions about the universe around us, and frame further metaphysical posers about the universe within us. Proof is another matter.

One thing is clear, though. The baby's cry is specific speech. Never again can we be so specific about our needs. As Lacan puts it, man is "all the further away from speaking the more he speaks."

The Relation of the Drives to the Primaries

At first sight, in terms of vague analogy, the basic drives might be equated with the performance primaries: sleep being akin to stillness, hunger and evacuation akin to repetition. But we are compelled to stop and sleep again and again just as we are obliged to eat and to defecate again and again. Repetition therefore seems to embrace everything. And sex? Perhaps we may at least approximate that with inconsistency, since it is in all likelihood more occasional than either sleeping or eating, although of course in most animals it re-occurs at a particular time of the year. Even among humans, in fact, the sex-urge makes itself evident as a phase in some repetitive process. Ultimately these analogies' break down, and we must accept that repetition presides over all our drives.

Stillness is our body, our vehicle, the shell: in its Zen mode, it is an ideal, our homeostatic instant, before our balanced needs tip one way or the other once again; an instant in which we imagine ourselves freed from the pressure of their drives. Repetition comprises the drives themselves and our diurnal rhythms, the servicing of our pleasure/production machines. Inconsistency is an outburst, an electrical charge, disturbing and revivifying that quotidian activity. Sometimes its effect is traumatic, but at other times it becomes a string, a language: the threaded series of small incidents which constitute both our intricate tasks and their inscriptions and expressions.

Among our repetitive compulsions, the forces of fatigue and hunger dominate, with punctuation supplied by the sexual urge, albeit at regular intervals, while the first vestiges of a sophistication which might create a bridge between urge and reason is brought about in us by the instinct which prompts us to scratch each others' backs.

While all drives must be repetitive, sex is so much improved by suppression and the tension this causes, that culturally and romantically speaking, sex *amounts* to inconsistency. The arrows of Eros strike unlikely targets, and passion is aroused in subjects whose rank is inconsistent with that of their objects. Regal Venus prefers to make love behind the stairs or over a bale in the stable. Loathing is equally inconsistent with reason, where reason is confused with the approved order of our repetitions. Inconsistency may be aroused by some intrusion into our sleepy and repetitive habitat, either by a possible mate or by a possible enemy. If it is the former, the inconsistency manifests itself as a sexual response. If it is the latter, the inconsistency will be manifested either as fight or flight – pumping adrenalin into our system. If we cannot resolve the situation which has prepared us to be inconsistent we will experience stress – the adrenalin keeps pumping into muscles which cannot expend it – a situation which can seriously interfere with personal well-being.

The Drives in Performance

We have seen that the basic drives often provide the matter for performances. Tilda Swinton reverses the sleep-pattems of day and night. Bruce Gilchrist falls into a deep sleep despite being surrounded by very loud noise – after having deprived himself of sleep for a considerable number of days. From this sleep experiment we learn that suppression of the drive causes behavioural change. Hooked up to a machine which translated typed messages into electrical stimuli, Gilchrist came traumatically awake when a member of the audience kept reiterating the message, I love you, I love you, I love you. A student of mine has experimented with depriving himself of food, with force-feeding another performer and with force-feeding an inanimate apparatus. Interference with natural homeostasis can cause harm, but in performance art it may enable a new homeostasis, that of the action, to occur. Teemu Maki, the Finnish artist, makes disturbing performances where auto-masochism leads to orgasm. In all these cases the performers are concerned with the drives as subject-matter, often in defiance of their coercive power: the power of fatigue, hunger, sexual urge or pain. But aside from the biological drives we should also identify the compulsions which bear on performance and consider'being driven' in dynamic terms.

So what is it that drives a performance? Could it be the need to begin it the need to get through it and the need to end it? "Begin at the beginning, go on to the end and then stop," as the King of Hearts says to the white rabbit. Certainly beginnings, middles and ends inform conventional drama and popular film. Like the novel, as opposed to poetry, these are anticipatory. They are concerned more with becoming than with being. However spectacular, what matters is the conclusion, the outcome; how the story ties up, what happens in the last few moments, what issues get resolved before the credits roll. Thus these forms seek an ending. Poetry however may rely more on being; being simply an image or a rhythm. Performance and avant-garde film may have more in common with poetry than with the novel.

But while the poetry of action may unify beginnings, middles and ends into an extended image – as did the 'living paintings' of Collette and the 'singing sculpture' of Gilbert and George – there is sometimes a lack of dynamic about allowing an image to inspire a performance. Action is a matter of sequence, after all: and performance is not simply a picture. If the inspiration for a performance is an image, however, it may be advisable to consider that instead of simply presenting that image to your audience, you might construct it in front of their eyes. This supplies you with a beginning, at least, which may be enough. If not, destruction, or the dismantling of that image, may well provide an effective conclusion. Bear in mind that if the dismantling of the image is simply a reversal of its construction then you may lose the attention of your audience. Because of this, *The Tower* I built in the Art Gallery of New South Wales in 1984, which was made of tables, had to be brought down in a different manner to the way in which it was put up. Construction was simple, straight-forward; but the dismantling involved 'cartwheeling'connected sets of tables off the edifice and then sliding other tables down the ramps ultimately provided by the cartwheeled tables when they met the floor.

Effort can defy ending. *Goat Island* perform arduous actions for extended periods during performances. One of the main reasons for finishing is that we are forced to do so by fatigue. These performers are dedicated to combatting their exhaustion. Tension mounts in their audience as they continue crawling on their toes and their fingers, their bodies kept low, near the ground without touching it. Intense, extended rehearsal enables them to go on, way beyond ordinary ability. In a similar way, Seiji Shimoda from Japan attempts to crawl under a table while hanging onto it. Again, tension mounts as he clings beneath it, his toes pushed against the legs of the table, inches from the floor. We know that if he fails, a certain magical energy will drain from his performance. Sometimes fatigue and gravity combine to defeat his colossal effort. Knowing that it is possible for him to fail enhances the performance for me. It proves that the action is not just a circus trick.

The need to end and the search for an ending concern another compulsion which merits consideration. Beyond the pleasure principle, there is the compulsion to repeat, and, as Freud believes, to return to the state we were in before we existed. Thus he equates *pre-being* with *death*, since the state is in his view the same. Freud reckons that the death instinct pulls all organisms towards their conclusion by dint of the stress to their systems caused by their repetitions. It need not be thought of as a negative force. Shakespearean tragedy often concerns how to end, and how to confer dignity to one's ending. Religion would see ending as a beginning, and many fine performative endings have something about them which recalls the opening of the piece.

Timothy McCain, Matthew Goulish, Greg McCain and Karen Christopher of Goat Island carry the performance of actions to the point of exhaustion in *It's Shifting, Hank,* directed by Lin Hixson at Wellington Avenue Church, Chicago, USA, 1993. Photograph: Eileen Ryan.

Death hardly impedes us, rather we impede it by inventing delays. Imagine a marble run. These were popular in my school-days, days of lidded desks! One dropped one's marble into the ink-well hole. It would roll down a route created out of books, rulers and pencil cases – the longer the route the better – and finally it would strike a bicycle bell in a bottom corner of the desk. Its momentum depended on gravity. The way the force of gravity is used here is a good analogy for Freud's notion of the death instinct and how we can make use of it.

The Tower was a piece dependent on gravity – first defying it, and then making use of its force. Gravity in itself is a drive which affects space. We're compelled to obey it; and again it is a drive which we may utilise. In *A Waterfall,* created for the Hayward Gallery in the summer of 1977, The Theatre of Mistakes devised a structure made out of tables and chairs stacked on top of each other. Performers poured cups of water into cups held by higher performers, thus transporting water from a bucket at the foot of the structure to one balanced at its top. It took an hour to fill the top bucket. Once filled, the highest performer picked up the top bucket, stood on the top chair and poured all the water back into the bucket below. Several years later, *Station House Opera* devised a structure of tables suspended above other tables. Performers in formal dress sat at these tables, their feet dangling from their perches on suspended chairs, and bottles of drink were sent from table to table by means of pullies. Stelarc's 'defiance' of gravity has already been described. By defying it he creates an awestruck silence in his spectators, very much like an angel 'passing overhead'.

———

The Workshop on the Drives

1.   *Deprivation/Surplus Exercise*

The performers are given three days to prepare a performance concerned either with the deprivation of something essential to existence or concerned with a surplus of something essential to existence: i.e. being deprived of air, the ground (gravity), food, sleep, physical comfort or the ability to urinate or defecate, or being subjected to an excess of air, gravity (burial), food, sleep, pain, urine or faeces.

Alternatively the performance may concern grooming or a lack of grooming, light or the deprivation of light; noise or the suppression of sound.

The deprivation of life itself could also be the subject of this exercise, or whatever might be construed as an excess of life. Equally it might concern being deprived of of sex or excessive sexual activity.

2.   *Sublimation/Suppression Exercise*

Each performer is asked to create a performance about something he or she would prefer not to talk about, or to create a performance which conceals its own subject.

3.   *Easy Taboo Exercise*

Each performer is asked to think very carefully about something he or she would find comparatively easy to do – but which would probably shock others or fill them with consternation. Then they are asked to prepare and perform a solo concerned with the activity thus identified.

4.   *Symbolic Objects, Symbolic Actions*

Each performer gathers objects together, and these may be either hard, penetrative objects or soft, enclosing ones. Now each devises a hard language of actions or a soft language of actions, whichever is appropriate to the objects chosen. Now the performers work in pairs, each pair initially contrasting hard actions and objects with soft actions and objects. Gradually the performer utilising hard objects must find a soft language for dealing with them, at the same time as the performer utilising the soft objects must find a hard language for dealing with them. After this the performers exchange objects and repeat the exercise with the other's objects.

5.   *Verbal Excretion Exercise*

Performers are asked to form pairs. One then utilises verbal diarrhoea while the other suffers from verbal constipation for the duration of the exercise.

6. Product Spiral One

One performer creates a product. This is passed to the next performer who alters that product in such a way that it becomes another product, i.e. one might write a letter, the next might tear that letter into little pieces. The new product is then passed to a third performer who alters it again so that it becomes another product.

Can this performance be formed into a circle, so that eventually the evolved product returns to the initial performer whose alteration to it returns it to its original construction? If it cannot be so formed, allow the performance to 'spiral'– with the product being passed round and round the circle of performers, altering every time it is passed on. Either cycle or spiral may be performed with as many products as there are performers, so that everyone is constantly kept occupied.

7. Machine Interface Exercise

Each performer demonstrates an interdependence between their body and a machine or item of technology. Next a second performer demonstrates a connection between themselves and the body/machine of the first performer. More than one machine or item of technology may be utilised.

8. Feat Exercise

Each performer learns how to execute a difficult feat with a chosen object.

Next they perform their attempt to execute a feat beyond the reach of their capabilities.

Robert Wilson utilised slow motion to stunning effect in *Einstein on the Beach* (1976) – an opera with music by Philip Glass. Photograph: Bob Van Danzig.

8

TRANSITIONS AS DESIRES

Having arrived at some understanding as to the nature of the drives, we must now commence an enquiry into our desires. In psychoanalytical terms there is a difference between the two terms. A desire is a wish rather than a compulsion. Desires may be conceived as emanating rivulets, separating from the main flow of one drive in order to become tributaries of another – sex perceived as feeding, for instance, which is well described in Brett Easton Ellis's *American Psycho*, where what begins as a love-bite may actually remove the nipple. Bear in mind, however, that primates eat the vermin they collect from the pelts of their partners. Thus the natural amalgam of eating and sex should be grooming, *not* psychotic cannibalism – though, again, the act of devouring concerns other organs than the mouth and instruments other than the teeth.

Among predatory animals, the hungry drive to bite may be reduced to a sign, when the mother playfully nips the cub with teeth which could tear it to shreds. Nipping therefore becomes part of a language of enactment which refers to the violence of hunting and of rivalry without actually meting out that violence. Thus a desire may modify a drive, be a sign for it, and indeed we can wish to be the sign for someone else's drive, for it is said that a desire can be a *desire to be a drive* – as when we wish to be the mother's sex requirement.

As well as singing to attract a partner, a bird may pretend that she has a broken wing to lure a predator away from her nestlings. In mediating between our compulsions and their advertisements, our desires may demonstrate a similar deviousness. In defence, before the onset of a drive, we may set out to *show* that we want to be compelled by that drive in order to prevent ourselves from *really* being at its mercy – on the basis of our (supposed) certainty that we never get what we want. Or there's the syndrome illustrated by Brer Rabbit and the briar patch, where we protest violently against being thrown into the thicket of our ultimate desire – in order that our sadistic acquaintance may actually choose to hurl us into it.

When, as a child, the playwright, Jean Genet, was accused of being a thief, he thenceforth set out to become one – and subsequently spent many years in prison. In other words, I am what the other wishes. I am the desire of the mother. I am the desire of what the mother eventually merges with – that Large Other out there.

It is the child one feeds with most love who refuses food and plays with his refusal as with a desire. For the child fed with most love *recognises*, through the mother's anxiety to feed him, that he must be difficult to feed. And having nothing else to go on, being inchoate shit, without a specular image of himself, he has no alternative but to become what it appears the mother recognises him as – a mere nothing who feeds merely on nothing.

Lacan emphasizes the power of language to transmute desires; to cause transitions from specific mothers to generalized others or notions of society. Language enables us to generate a syntax of desire, to wish for impossible things – wishes generated by the syntax alone. The child who refuses food wishes for a notion of a want which cannot be appeased merely by eating. He wants nothing – but nothing is a signifier in language. So a person whose every whim is provided for may still long to secure some imaginary object, in order to appease a sense of unfulfilled desire. By analysing a dream of one of his romantically-inclined patients, Freud discovered that what she longed for most was to possess "an unfulfilled desire".

Lacan conceives man as an animal at the mercy of language. "Desire is the effect imposed by the existence of the discourse – to make the need pass through the defiles of the signifier." Here the pre-linguistic child is a toddler cowboy corralled in the family's bosom. To reach the feeding grounds of discourse he must drive his drove of drives through the narrow canyons of language, losing many a horn to the ambuscades of meaning, while his herd is constantly being depleted by steers steering into the subsidiary canyons of linguistically-prompted aspirations.

Desires in Performance terms:

The concept, I am the desire of the Other, has repercussions for the performance artist. It implies that I am what the language (society at large) demands or projects me to be. In other words, I am the desire of the Other outside the curtain. I am what the audience desires. Yes, I am what it desires whether I consider it or not. And, since this is inescapably my condition, to consider the audience is actually superfluous and may even short-circuit its desire, or reduce that to some merely conscious manifestation of desire, rather than a powerful projection from the unconscious.

Because of the innate voyeuristic inclination of the audience, I am more what the audience desires me to be when my gaze embraces my objects than when my gaze demands that the audience serve as my object.

I have mentioned *repetition compulsions.* These are as important for art-making as they are for the satisfaction of our needs. They raise the requirement to make a performance, for instance, to the status of a drive. A drive, remember, is a need which *must* be satisfied, whatever the conditions in which we may find ourselves. If we must urinate, we will urinate in our cell, if we must eat, we will eat our boots, and if we must sleep, we will sleep standing up.

If you don't need to create a performance, or if you feel you need to create one only to satisfy academic demands or the requirements of some funding body, then your desire may rebel against the "pseudo-need" that you feel is being imposed on you.

A drive is something you must do, while a desire is something you want. We might speculate and consider desire to be the rivulet which goes around the blocking of a drive, a rivulet which may even flow into other channels. Meanwhile pleasure is release from the urgency of the drive. It is quite different to desire. To take pleasure in performing may be conducive to acting, but to *create* performances, a desire has to be generated beyond the pleasure of doing it: and then some urgency has to transform that desire into a drive. What would you love to do? Can performance art help you to do what you would love to do?

Perhaps desires are transitive – urges out of synch with the drive of the present or out of synch with the dictate of the moment's repetition compulsion: i.e., you want to be loving when you need to sleep, or you want to be sleeping when you need to love, or you want to be sleeping when you need to eat, or you want to be eating when you need to sleep, or you want to be eating when you need to love, or you want to be loving when you need to eat. For need substitute ought, and we see desire not only at variance with the drives but also jibing at the subjugating projections of the Other. And then, you can add grooming into these permutations, so that you get a statement such as, "I want to sleep when I ought to get up and brush my teeth."

Mention should also be made of the experience of a lack in (or of) the experience itself, even as you experience it: you would like to feel that you were in love when you only feel that you ought to be loving, or you would like to feel like making love when you only feel that you are being made love to. These are the lacunae which emerge from the nature of language, born out of the quandaries opened up by their possibility in the syntax, well expressed in R.D. Laing's *Knots*.

So desire suggests some transition from one drive to another – it represents a change of gear. The grass is always greener on the other side of the track, until you cross over the track. In performance terms, these transitions are "crossings over" from one primary to another. Desires may be in reaction to drives: however sleepy I am, I may desire not to sleep. In a similar way, an additive sequence can be seen as a reaction to repetition which moves the subject towards inconsistency.

Primary colours mixed together make a secondary colour. However, since performance happens in time as well as in space, our action-mixtures are often *transitions*. Of course one can still perform two primaries at the same time, such as repetitive footwork and inconsistent head movements, or maintain completely still upper parts while the legs move inconsistently. These are more in the nature of *overlays*, and they will be dealt with later in this chapter.

But having established the *primary* actions – stillness, repetition and inconsistency – we can now identify the *secondary* actions or transitions: the effect of increasing or decreasing our speed, as well as the additive actions and the subtractive actions.

As the drives approximate to the primary of repetition, our desires relate to these *transitional actions*. In performance terms, desire is the desire for a change: it leads to some transitional activity. Thus the secondary actions represent threshold-crossings: from a drive to its reverse, as in from dreaming to waking or vice versa, or from hunger to satiety and back again, or indeed from the known into the unknown. Alternatively the thresholds crossed may stand between one drive and its neighbour: between hunger and sleep, or between sleep and grooming, or between grooming and sex, or between sex and defecation. Rather than compulsions, the desires are either constructions on the drive, elaborating the sought object; or they are erosions of the drive, causing it to falter under the pressure of sleep or hunger.

There are two sorts of secondary or transitional action. The first concerns speed – slowing down or speeding up a repetitive action or an inconsistent string – that is, mixing stillness with repetition or inconsistency or removing stillness from repetition or inconsistency. The second transition concerns adding an inconsistency to a repetition, thus creating a new repetition and then adding another inconsistency to that – or a reversal of this process (subtracting from it).

We shall now look at these secondary actions in more detail.

*   *   *   *

The Secondary Actions (Transitions):

1. *The Effect of Speed:*

    Slowing down an action:
    suggests increasing *stillness*, is evocative of sleep (dreaming being the transitional state between action and sleep), can suggest fatigue or sleep-walking, can be read as satisfaction or lack of desire and can be the result of fatigue or a demonstration of unwillingness. It can also be a progression towards the 'uncanny' effect of stillness.

    Speeding up an action:
    takes it further from *stillness*, denotes increased activity, is evocative of increasing desire, consciousness, energy or impatience and can be read as stimulation, inspiration or excitement. It can also suggest matters lurching out of control or actually send matters out of control so that eventually they fly apart or result in exhaustion.

*   *   *   *

Slowing Down

As Pilinsky has Sheryl Sutton put it, "A step five-times slow is also more beautiful, but much more ungainly and more perishable than the normal." By slowing down an action, we lose the essential momentum which enables that action to occur. Try slowing down the action of sitting down in a chair: at a certain point you must lose your balance. Most actions have their own ideal performance speed. You cannot crack a whip slowly. Thus there may often be an increased clumsiness about deceleration. Throwing will prove impossible.

As actions slow down, they become more silent.

Horizontal actions may be successfully slowed. Try walking, for instance, taking a count longer to perform each step forward: the first step takes one count, the second step takes two counts, the third step takes three counts etc. As you slow down the action, you will find yourself capable of analysing it more effectively: how the foot slides forward, how the heel takes the weight first, and how, as you roll forward onto the ball of the forward foot, the back heel of the foot behind lifts up, allowing you to slide that foot forward in turn.

By slowing the walk down, you are moving it away from the humdrum practicality of its repetition, you are removing its purpose, you are ceasing to get anywhere. By removing its functionality, the movement becomes more contemplative ... you are, by slowing down, approaching the Zen of stillness. A trance-like condition results – a condition well understood by Robert Wilson.

Speeding Up

By speeding a movement up, you are removing it from the contemplative; coming out of the trance. The humdrum practicality gradually becomes frenetic. And it may be that the action becomes satirical, a comment on our society. The pressure of inconsistency, of chaos – chaos induced by too much happening at once, too many things to do, too little time to do them in – is coming into play now.

Slowing down can suggest a lack of desire to continue; speeding up can suggest an intensification of desire. Actions become less easily analysed. They turn into blurs. Skipping with a rope can only be done at speed, and a bucket swung around at speed will not lose its contents. However over-speeded action is a species of blind-spot: because it's a blur, it baulks contemplation.

Note the difference between a speeded up repetition and a speeded up inconsistency. Repetition may prove more effective at speed: its rhythm becomes more pronounced as its sound increases – and therefore there may be an enhancement of its musicality – until it gets speeded up beyond the ability of the performer, at which point it will start to fall apart. Inconsistency at speed can be devastating if it concerns a single act – the lightning flash, or the final collapse of a gradually-accumulated stack of objects. An inconsistent string of actions is practically impossible to perform at speed, since no rhythm can be established. The only way to perform an inconsistent string at speed is to rehearse it first – in which case it is really a disguised repetition.

Speed brings about a devaluation of space – we are moving too fast to appreciate the landscape through which we pass. There's a violence about speed epitomised by the increased shock of impact on contact. A harmless action can be rendered harmful by acceleration. Perhaps the combustion engine has made society more violent at the same time as it has increased accessibility. For a commentary on speed see Paul Virilio's *Speed and Politics*.

2. Additives and Subtractives

Additive   progressive   advancing

> Pressure from *repetition* towards
> *inconsistency*. Urge out of comfort
> towards the unknown. Transition from
> feeding towards intercourse (one need
> satisfied, another takes its place).
>
> Formula: A, A+B, A+B+C, A+B+C+D.

Repetition expanding to embrace a new inconsistency each round.

Subtractive   regressive   retreating

> Pressure from *inconsistency* towards repetition.
> Urge to return from the unknown to the familiar.
> Transition from intercourse to feeding
> (overextended need falling back on comfort).
>
> Formula: D+C+B+A, C+B+A, B+A, A.

Inconsistency shrinking to dwell upon a single repetition.

An additive system grows by repeating an action, adding a new – inconsistent – action, repeating the first action and the new one, adding a third – inconsistent – action, repeating the first, the second and the third, and so on. A subtractive system diminishes a string of actions by removing one action, then repeating the remainder of the string, removing another action as well as the first one removed, then repeating the remainder of the string, and so on, until no actions remain.

*   *   *   *

More about Addition and Subtraction:

Additives and Subtractives can also be *doubled*, to increase the repetitions required before adding a new unit:

A:
A, A+B
A, A+B, A+B+C:

or subtractively:

A+B+C, B+C, C:
B+C, C:
C:

Naturally one can speed up or slow down an additive or a subtractive sequence, as one can a doubly additive or doubly subtractive sequence, thus altering a transitional action by allowing it to be affected by another transition. Of course there are countless variations to this process, each altering the ratio of repetition to inconsistency. In *And*, performed at The South London Gallery in 1997, Gary Stevens and his team of performers increased and decreased the component parts of gestures and action details - as Martin Arnold does on film with the aid of an optical printer in *Passage à l'Acte* - thus enabling a small scene captured on celluloid (from *To Kill a Mocking Bird*) to repeat and to add to itself at the same time as it repeats and subtracts from itself. The notion of time reversing or subtracting is essentially filmic - we can actually see it occurring when a piece of film is played backwards - and such cinematographic tricks have inspired many performance artists.

Additives can be useful in the devising process, since they are in effect a repetitive method of working through an inconsistent string of actions. If such actions have been generated by some suggestive process, such as those described in the chapter on inconsistency, each unit of action can be modified as the performer sees fit each time it is repeated, prior to a fresh action being added. The additive actions may also be the component parts of a single coherent action - greeting someone for instance. Additives also suggest to me the Nietzschean notion of 'the Eternal Return', though it can be argued that an additive sequence is a 'reconfiguration' as opposed to Nietzsche's notion of the exactitude of time's repetition. However, each new unit of addition is itself repeated when yet another unit is added. Thus the inconsistency is forever being incorporated into the repetition. In the performance by Gary Stevens, the entire sequence of gestures, fragments of events and combined greetings which constituted the additive and subtractive cycle carried out by his team amounts to a performance of some twenty minutes which is in itself repeated many times during a six hour performance. One is what one repeats, and the world is what it repeats, and every repetition of oneself and the world causes something new, some adjustment to occur. But then, that something new, that adjustment, gets repeated in its turn during the next cycle of repetition – only to cause a fresh adjustment. Thus everything is repeating itself but also renewing itself at the same time – in the sense that something new is added only to get repeated. Doubled additives add a musicality to this process, since they increase the ratio of repetition over inconsistency in the developing sequence.

On the other hand the subtractive process is essentially an editing one. It is possible to subtract units of action in the same order as one added them – thus the first to appear is also the first to disappear – and this will produce a balanced structure. I have found it useful, though, to perform the following exercise:

Create a set of actions additively. Once the additive comprises eight actions, cease adding new actions and instead repeat that set of actions eight times. Then start to subtract the actions, one round at a time, but not in the order in which the set was created. First remove what you consider to be the weakest, the least effective action. In the next round, remove the action you now find the weakest. Thus, by the time you find yourself performing a single action, it will be the action which you consider to be the most essential one of the set. Now repeat that single action eight times.

While subtraction constitutes a transitional process leading from inconsistency to repetition, it should be noted that it also leads ultimately to stillness.

Momentum:

Having established a repetition, a performer can put momentum into it by speeding it up. Making it an additive will cause that repetition to spiral – expanding it by letting it incorporate other actions. The repetition compulsion of rehearsing a piece may also put momentum into the eventual performance – think of each repeat of the piece as one traverse in a series of traverses up a mountain: although the action is the same, you never come back to the same place, you are always a little nearer the summit.

Stuart Sherman's portraits of places or people were spectacles which incorporated some twenty vignettes: each was (repetitively) a portrait, but each was a portrait of a different place in his 'places' spectacle, or a different person in his 'people' one. Such a structure involves difference within repetition rather than inconsistency, as discussed earlier. Still, the momentum gathered was the result of both repetition and change. In a table move, I might move my furniture through ninety degrees again and again, and in each round, add or discard an item of clothing, allowing the turns to spiral into an otherness from the condition at the start.

Julian Maynard Smith may ask one performer in the Station House Opera to describe the actions of another. The person whose actions are described then attempts to mimic the description in action. Here the *transition* is from action to its signifiers and from them back into action: a basic "feedback" model. It generates momentum since the verbal description tends to exaggerate the actions which in turn tend to exaggerate the ensuing verbal instruction derived from the description. Thus distortion generates growth.

Overlayering

There is a difference between one thing diminishing as another augments and one thing being laid over another. Thus we must also consider the amalgamation of primary actions, that is, working with two primary actions at the same time. Exercise 2. in the *Stillness Workshop (page 11)* – "Stillness Repetitions" – is formed by layering an action of repetition over a stillness exercise, and Exercise 3. in the *Repetition Workshop (page 41)* – "Repeated Repetitions" – is formed by layering a further action of repetition over a repetition exercise.

Overlayering might be compared to the psychoanalytical notion of *over-determination*. "A dream-image, or any other item of behaviour, is said to be *over-determined* if it has more than one meaning or expresses drives and conflicts derived from more than one level or aspect of the personality," (see page 123 of Charles Rycroft's *Critical Dictionary of Psychoanalysis*).

Often more than a single meaning condenses on our objects or influences our actions. In performance terms, for instance, narrative can be developed by constructing a sequence of sentences additively but maintaining a repetitive similarity of subject throughout the sequence. Here the impulse away from repetition and towards inconsistency is qualified by an overlayering of repetition so far as the subject-matter is concerned.

Corps-de-ballet effects can be attained by a group of performers all performing the same stillness or repetition (thus overlayering it with an equal amount of repetition), or all performing the same (rehearsed) inconsistency (which is repetition *disguised* as inconsistency – since it has been rehearsed – and then overlayered by an equal amount of repetition). Choruses can be developed by everyone repeating the same song or sentence repetitively or additively – and of course such choruses can also be subtracted in unison. Rycroft goes on to say about over-determination that:

"it provides a 'final common pathway' to a number of convergent tendencies. Since psychoanalysis assumes the presence of a residuum of wishes dating from the past and that the various stages of development are superimposed on one another in layers, all behaviour is regarded as over-determined in the sense that it is possible to interpret it as the result of simultaneous activity at several levels."

(*Critical Dictionary of Psychoanalysis*, page 123)

This turns out to be true of our performance primaries. Take Exercise 1 of the *Stillness Workshop* – "Primary Stillness" - (on page 11), where *one performer enters the space and freezes in any position. The stillness of the silence is allowed to deepen. Then a second performer enters the space and freezes in any position.* Here the fact that the performers may each freeze *in any position* brings an overlayering of inconsistency to this group exercise in stillness.

Simultaneous actions can be humorous. Julian Maynard Smith combines looking at a watch with pouring a glass of wine. Briony Watson attempts to jump while drinking. I contrive to hide while shifting furniture.

Restrictions and Rewards:

Working to create a performance must necessarily deny you the gratification of other desires in conflict with the practice (that is the repetition compulsion) you have set up. Having established the timetable for your creativity, it is vital that you maintain it, whether or not the session proves productive. It is just as important that you are not doing anything else as it is that you are making your performance.

However, it may be useful to set a limit to each day's creative repetition of your practice, and then perhaps to reward your compulsion in some way. I used to reward myself by taking the dog for a walk after I had sat writing for two hours everyday. The reward incentive required that I denied myself the dog-walk until after I had completed the writing session, which is not to say that I had completed the writing. Some writers "break off" in the middle of a paragraph each day, in order to have something to "pick up" and complete the next day, which brings them into the swing of their work.

*   *   *   *

Most important of all, a performance requires a motive. In conventional practice, this is often confused with a subject or with some moral "motivation". In my experience, the strongest motive for a performance is a motive in its own terms. It is rarely a subject I am motivated to illustrate – what it may illustrate is only discovered after its completion, and this is often more apparent to the audience than to the creator.

More important is a motive for moving, a motive for using. The motive for using objects or others is to supply the performer with a motive for moving. Without a motive for moving, the performer has no reason to move. What was my motive for using large items of furniture in my table moves? I employed these items in order to turn them through ninety degrees. What was my motive for turning them through ninety degrees? I've claimed earlier that I turned them through ninety degrees in order to give myself *something to do.* Something to do is the subject of performance as something to paint is the subject of painting. Therefore the performer must ask, How do the objects or others (or how does the language) I have chosen give me something to do? Or, How does what I have given myself to do alter the objects or others I have chosen? The motive, the something-you-have-given-yourself-to-do, may evolve into an abiding concern.

This concern progresses via the resolution of niggles – or, in grander terms, through the resolution of critical issues. For instance, the principal motive for my performance *Homage to Roussel* was: How do I move objects through ninety degrees without using masking-tape to orientate myself in the performance space? Only the most ardent theorist of performance art would be able to identify this desire from the result.

———————

The Workshop on Transitions

1. Slowed Walks, Speeded Walks

Each performer walks the diagonal length of the performance space, counting 'one' for each pace taken. He or she then walks back down the diagonal, counting 'one, two' for each pace taken. With each ensuing diagonal the number of counts per pace is increased, until each pace takes six counts to accomplish. After this is achieved, the counts are diminished with each diagonal, until at length each performer has returned to taking one count per pace.

> *Then the performer increases speed, taking one count to walk two paces down the length of the next diagonal, then taking one count to walk three paces - and finally walking as fast as possible.*

> *During this exercise, anyone may shout 'Stop!' at any time. At this shout, all the performers should come immediately to a halt – even if this requires that they balance with their weight distributed between both feet. After not less than fifteen counts, anyone may shout 'Continue' – and the walking can continue.*

2. Slowed Objects/Actions - Speeded Objects/Actions

Each performer repeats a simple action utilising an object (or an item of clothing). This action is gradually slowed down until it is happening so slowly no one can see the performer moving. After a short period of absolute stillness, the performer recommences his or her repetitive action with the object (or the item of clothing), gradually speeding it up now, until moving so fast that the action can no longer be performed.

3. Slowed/Speeded Inconsistent Strings

Each performer chooses a fairly long suggestion string – a sentence, say – and uses each letter of that string as a suggestion for an action. This process should gradually be slowed down, either by counting out a gap of an extending number of counts between each new action or by slowing down the actions themselves. After this the performer should choose another suggestion string and attempt to speed up his or her actions as it is performed. Rehearsal may be required to create the 'appearance' of a very fast string of inconsistencies.

4. Spasmodic Speeds

Each performer chooses to perform either a repetition or a string of inconsistencies. Each then alters the speed of their performance spasmodically, sometimes allowing it to slow down, or suddenly speeding it up – keeping the change in speed unpredictable.

5. Out of Stillness/Into Stillness Exercise

Each performer prepares a repetition of about five actions. At the start of the exercise each enters the performance space and takes up a position of stillness. This stillness should be held for at least thirty counts. Each performer then experiments with breaking out of stillness, either very gradually or very suddenly, performing their repetition slowly or fast or altering its speed, and returning to the position of stillness either very slowly or very suddenly. After each performer has broken out of stillness twice and returned to stillness twice, all the performers should find themselves standing as still as they were at the start of the exercise. This final stillness should again be held for at least thirty counts. After this, each performer leaves the space.

6. Additive/Subtractive Exercise

a) Perform a sequence of actions additively, then subtract those actions starting with the action first performed and ending with the last action added.

b) In chorus, sing a song additively word by word, then subtract those words, starting with the word first sung and ending with the last one sung. Now divide into two groups. One group should sing the first line of the song additively while the second group should sing it subtractively at the same time. Both groups should finish singing together.

c) Perform a sequence of about eight actions additively. Then repeat the entire sequence eight times. Finally begin to subtract actions, not in any order other than that of ridding oneself of the action one thinks is the weakest, then, on the next round, subtracting the action one now thinks is the weakest – until one is down to one's strongest action. This should now be repeated eight times.

d) Perform a sequence of actions doubly-additively, then doubly-subtract those actions starting with the action first performed and ending with the last action added. Now try the same exercise using words instead of actions.

7. Narrative Exercise

Speaking as if to themselves, each performer should create a verbal additive, each word or sentence of which should concern the same subject.

8. Overlayering Exercise

Performers should experiment with overlayering, inventing their own action and its overlaid restriction. Examples include: performing an inconsistent string while only using the face, performing a fairly complex repetition only using the feet, performing a parallel additive for the hands, performing a repetition of some eight actions, none of which utilise the same part of the body, reciting a repetitive phrase while performing an inconsistent string of actions or performing an inconsistent string of actions with one's upper body while repetitively skipping.

Anthony Howell moving furniture through 90 in *Table Move 1*, at the Lyon International Symposium of Performance Art, 1983. Photograph: Bob Van Dantzig.

9
TRANSFERENCE, SUBSTITUTION AND REVERSAL

In analysis, 'transference' is the term used to describe the redirection of attitudes and emotions towards a substitute. A transference occurs when the subject (the analysand) redirects feelings away from someone who matters to them (a parent possibly) and towards their analyst during therapy. Remember, we, the performer-witnesses behind the curtain, are, in this case, the analysts: our subject is performance art.

Attraction towards an object can be rechannelled onto another object. The Freudian body of thought has given birth to a host of now commonly used terms to describe this rechannelling.

There are *energy replacements*, such as when the Wolf-man mourns at the grave of a celebrated poet who his sister admired instead of mourning his sister – whose grave is a few miles away from that of the poet. There are *object substitutions*, as in the fort-da. And sometimes an object is *over-determined*, that is, when several forces and desires condense around it. There is also the possibility of a *displacement* of the emotions. Here is Freud, discussing such an affect:

> "... it not uncommonly happens that obsessional neurotics, who are troubled with self-reproaches but have connected their affects with the wrong causes, will also tell the physician the true causes, without any suspicion that their self-reproaches have simply become detached from them. In relating such an incident they will sometimes add with astonishment or even with an air of pride: 'But I think nothing of that.' This happened in the first case of obsessional neurosis which gave me an insight many years ago into the nature of the malady. The patient, who was a government official, was troubled by innumerable scruples... I was struck by the fact that the florin notes with which he paid his consultation were invariably clean and smooth. (This was before we had silver coinage in Austria.) I once remarked to him that one could always tell a government official by the brand-new florins that he drew from the State treasury, and he then informed me that his florins were by no means new, but that he had them ironed out at home. It was a matter of conscience with him, he explained, not to hand any one dirty paper florins; for they harboured all sorts of dangerous bacteria and might do some harm to the recipient. At that time I already had a vague suspicion of the connection between neuroses and sexual life, so on another occasion I ventured to ask the patient how he stood in regard to that matter. 'Oh, that's quite alright,' he answered airily, 'I'm not at all badly off in that respect. I play the part of a dear old uncle in a number of respectable families, and now and then I make use of my position to invite some girl to go out

with me for a day's excursion in the country. Then I arrange that we shall miss the train home and be obliged to spend the night out of town. I always arrange two rooms – I do things most handsomely; but when the girl has gone to bed I go in to her and masturbate her with my fingers.' – 'But aren't you afraid of doing her some harm, fiddling about in her genitals with your dirty hand?' – At this he flared up: 'Harm? Why, what harm should it do her? It hasn't done a single one of them any harm yet, and they've all of them enjoyed it. Some of them are married now, and it hasn't done them any harm at all.' – He took my remonstrance in very bad part, and never appeared again. But I could only account for the contrast between his fastidiousness with the paper florins and his unscrupulousness in abusing the girls entrusted to him by supposing that the self-reproachful affect had become *displaced*. The aim of this displacement was obvious enough: if his self-reproaches had been allowed to remain where they belonged he would have had to abandon a form of sexual gratification to which he was probably impelled by some infantile determinants. The displacement therefore ensured his deriving a considerable advantage from his illness."

(*A Case of obsessional Neurosis,* Complete works, Volume X, page 99)

From a performance viewpoint, the action of ironing banknotes is intriguing. That such an action connects to such a story suggests that resonances abound when objects and actions combine in a way which seems a trifle out of kilter. However physical our actions, they will always stir some emotional response in our audience.

The key to any substitution will be the resemblance between the original and the substitute object – which may appear tenuous if preliminary substitutions have already been prohibited. Here the psyche is working in a metaphorical mode. The mouth pulls on objects exhibiting characteristics close to those of the nipple. Sublimations and compensations abound. The dynamic tension in rage repression may lead to arthritis. Apprehension could lead to asthma, since both entail shallow breathing. Apocryphal notions perhaps – but I recall a student couple: she was apprehensive, constantly on the defensive. He seemed phlegmatic – but suffered from asthma. Had he caught his asthma from her anxiety?

Repressed hostility towards a parent, say, can lead to projections where the subject maintains that the opposite is the case: that the parent is hostile. Equally, an over fussy love of one's offspring may disguise latent hostility. Here we're awash with clichés. 'I hate you' may be expressed as 'You hate me'. 'He is punishing me' may stand in for 'I am punishing myself'.

Psychoanalysts speak of *reaction formation*, where love masks hate. But reactive love protests too much. It may be detected by some showiness or exaggeration. To hide the resentment the subject must be seen to show love. Then, in a phobia, where we shun an object we may not be afraid of the object, only afraid of the wish for the object. Such reaction formations may hide a fascination with sex under a pose of chastity. Altruism may camouflage selfishness. Piety may disguise sinfulness (whatever that may be). It's invariably exaggeration which gives the game away. Hamlet's feigned madness is too fey. Excessively sane comportment suggests a screw is loose somewhere.

Other exaggerated reaction formations might include pronounced lesbianism to divert attention from femininity or intense body building to disguise 'soft' homosexuality.

The final cliché on this list of common parlance Freudian terms is *regression* – stunted growth in fear of hazards ahead. Instead we repeat the past. Thus regression is a fixation equivalent to fear of the inconsistent (unknown).

We should leave this over-tilled field and turn instead to performance. A transference may be physical instead of psychical, though of course any action must have its attendant psychical implication. So how does the performer use this term?

Performance transferences:

1. Objects can be used in more than one way. Consider first the simple *transference of action* described in the *Object Exchange Exercise,* (page 67). Consider after that how a tie can be tied round the neck, used as a belt or used to strangle someone. A hairbrush can be used in combination with a lady's shoe to provide a dustbin and brush. This is called *transference of use.* I employ most of the transferential actions above in my performance *Homage to Roussel.* To take advantage of a transference of use is the sign of the handyman; inventive transference being the gift of a *bricoleur* such as Marcel Duchamp, the first artist to present us with the 'found' object.

2. *Transference of Scale* comes next. A match can be struck on a matchbox, and then a suitcase can be struck by a riding-crop. Here the ordinary action gives rise to an extraordinary action, but the logic linking the two actions is clear.

3. *Transference of Lead:* Moving so slowly no one can see them moving, two performers may appear to mirror each other. One, though, is in the other's line of sight. The one seen 'leads'. To transfer the lead to the other performer, the leader slowly turns his head, this action being mirrored by the other performer. When that performer can no longer see the former leader, it may be presumed that the former follower is now in the other's line of sight, and thus the lead is transferred.

A similar exercise allows two performers to seem as if speaking at the same time. In fact one speaks slowly and the other echoes what is said. An appropriate trigger for transference might be that when the leader mentions the name of the follower the lead is transferred.

Analytically, these last two types of transference might be expressed thus: when I lose sight of you I lead, and you are allowed to lead till you give me my name.

There are things done best in couples. You can create a *corps-de-ballet* of followers while visually leading, but only the two performers at either end of the line get to control the actions of that line. Those inside the line are merely pawns in the game played by those two players who exchange the lead.

Among primates grooming and de-infestation by lice is best done in couples. If one passive subject is de-infested by more than one other, quarrels arise as to whose turn it is to be de-infested next. This suggests that love is *over-determined*. Grooming is as much at the root of love as sex is. Take the phrase, "You scratch my back, I'll scratch yours." This amounts to an offer to exchange the lead. Grooming constitutes a prompting quite as forceful as desire. We might infer from it that it is through grooming that love transcends the banal promptings of nature. However it is common to most animals. Sophisticated de-infestation may demand a higher level of digital organization than is available to mammals other than the primates – but horses use their teeth on each other's backs.

Buckminster Fuller maintained that all moral codes have their basis in our sanitary habits. They concern hygiene. Sex and hygienic considerations create love. So love is a fusion of the sex drive and the more sophisticated digital/aural grooming instinct which transfers the lead from being passively de-infested to actively de-infesting. This in turn creates exchanges of domination and passivity. Lead transference is better done in couples, and couples don't need outside help to do it. In *Civilization and its Discontents*, Freud observed that at the height of a love relationship, "the pair of lovers are sufficient unto themselves, do not even need the child they have in common to make them happy."

Speaking of *aphanisis*, that fading of the subject in the face of meaning, Lacan insists on a *dyad*, that is a pair, of signifiers: "As soon as there are three the sliding becomes circular. When passed from the second to the third, it comes back to the first – but not from the second." (*The Field of the Other*). Such circularity centres the nuclear family around itself while there is only one child. Once there is a second child, many of the oppositional tensions may reappear. A similar circular sliding occurs in *Philoctetes*, the play by Sophocles – which has only three main characters, two of whom are forever pairing-up, though in different relationships. Thus nobody can ever quite get the upper-hand and the play can only be resolved by a *deus ex machina*.

Transference of lead creates a binary switch to activity from passivity or to visibility from invisibility. The transference is the manifestation of how the other desires you to be. You *are* what the other wants you to be. In mirroring, the lead ego is multiplied by two, the follower is invisible (faded): then the lead switches, and visibility is conferred on the follower. You convince others of what you doubt yourself.

Poetically speaking, I am pouring my voice into her ear and it is pouring through her and out (to the Large Other), while she is pouring her appearance into my sight and it is passing through me and out (to the Large Other), and thus we are perceived as "a pair". This is true where the sight leader is the voice follower (and vice versa) – which is difficult to do, but a fair evocation of mutual love (see also page 32).

4. The shift from activity to passivity – which grooming exchanges engender in a relaxed manner (as opposed to the violent opposition of predator and prey) – enables a play activity to stand in for an activity triggered into violence by a more urgent reality.

In the same way, when animal adults play with their offspring, the bite is only a nip, a playful sign of the bite, and a safe enactment of it. This is *Transference from Action to Sign*, which has a bearing on the origin of language. In a similar way, the V in the sky came to lie in the sand where it had been drawn by a stick, signifying that the cranes were flying. As the voice pours into the echoer, the cranes poured into the sign, were transferred into it – and writing began. This transference may be reversed, of course, as when, during a live tv show, assistants hold up signs to the audience – instructing them when to clap.

Transference from action to sign should perhaps include transference from action to image of that action. Kevin Atherton created a performance in which he was dressed in a boxer's singlet and shorts. He stood close to an 8mm film of himself dressed in identical gear. His image went through the motions of boxing and he boxed it back – eventually 'punching' his image out of the frame.

8mm film is an *analogue* transference from active figure to image of that figure, based on the light coming in through the lens of the camera, as the V in the sky becoming a V in the sand exemplifies an analogous relationship of image to language. But the transference from action to sign is often rendered *digitally*. In digital transference, the signifier is no longer a tracing of the signified, rather it is a translation, a translation into a language composed of measurable units. This is the case with a video image, which must be translated into an electrical signal created in a binary language made up of sequences of 0 and 1. But it would be wrong to think that digital transference is an entirely technological phenomenon pertaining only to our times. Unlike Egyptian hieroglyphics, which are made up of representational ideograms, the cuneiform writing of ancient Ur in Mesopotamia is created out of wedge-shaped characters dependent on the capabilities of the writing tool. Thus, even in 3000 BC, it was necessary to translate a system evident in reality into a system devised for the clay tablet rather than simply to attempt to imitate it or trace it out on a flat surface.

This can be as true for the signs engendered in our minds. The internal system will have been developed according to its own prerequisites – as necessary to it as the stylus was to cuneiform. Thus it is feasible that the phallus might be translated into a mathematical formula, instead of being inscribed as some obvious symbol. Anthony Wilden's excellent *System and Structure* goes very deeply into the differences between analogue and digital usage.

5. There is also *Transference from action to language*, which is so particular a modification of the transference from action to sign that it deserves its own heading. Such transference may simply be the relation of an event in the past – "Yesterday, I fell over and hit my head." It can also be reversed, a *Transference from language to action* – "Tomorrow, I will come and collect you." But there can be other expressions of this transference, as when, in its latter form, the girl stops talking about love and actually kisses the boy (or vice versa), or as when the soldier drills for war, and then talks about what he will do on the battlefield! Thus the performer might carry out all the preliminaries to a forbidden action – and then talk about how he or she would take these actions further, were it permitted. Who is it, though, who forbids the action? The Large Other out there? Or the performer himself – or herself?

6. There are also *Transferences of place*, as in my own "table moves", where I moved items of furniture through ninety degrees in the performance space. This derived from cubism. It enabled the audience to "see" the room I had created from more than one angle. The room was defined by furniture alone. The performance also conferred volume to the furniture by showing each piece from more than one side. Transferences of place create sculptural qualities and destroy two-dimensional illusion. The game of illusion is better played when objects remain in the same place or are viewed from a single point. In this sense, Georgio Morandi, who painted many still lives without tampering obviously with the picture plane, exemplifies "the other side of the coin" to cubism. In his work, objects may obscure each others' shape and we cannot be sure of their volume.

A transference of place occurs if the entire performance space is shifted, together with its audience. Louise Maunder, who was a student at Cardiff a few years ago, laid out a trail of objects taken from her handbag. Around each corner she had hidden another handbag. The audience followed her trail-making. As she turned each corner (and moved out of their sight) she hid the emptied handbag about her person and picked up the previously hidden one, which was of course filled with more objects: this enabled her to create the illusion that her handbag contained an inexhaustible supply of items as she continued her trail along the corridor and down the stairs and finally out of the building.

Fiona Templeton employed transference of place to great effect in her performance *You: The City*. One at a time, members of the audience were confronted by a performer in a specific location (an office). At this first location, a mock interview took place, with the interviewer speaking the entire time. On leaving the office, the member of the audience was met by another performer who walked that audience member along the street, talking continuously, then introduced them to another performer in another location in the city. Later, that member of the audience was ushered into a taxi, and the driver, who was another performer, would talk as he drove to yet another location where another performer was waiting. At one stage, the itinerary looped back on itself, and one observed a performer talking to another member of the audience in a deserted bomb-site, the scene of one's own meeting with that performer some twenty minutes previously.

7. *Transferences of dimension* are possible, as in the "Anti-Gravity" exercise, where the performers use the walls or the ceiling as the floor. This may be reminiscent of flying dreams.

8. *Transferences of element* involve performances in swimming-pools or suspended in the air or in the centres of fires.

9. A *humanization of an object* may take place – with a performer substituted for an object – for instance, in *Homage to Morandi* by The Theatre of Mistakes, a tall performer in a brown warehouse coat

Transference of place: Emile Jansen talks to his single-person audience while driving a taxi in Fiona Templeton's *You: The City*, Mickery, Amsterdam, 1990. Photograph: Bob Van Dantzig.

becomes a wardrobe while others 'stand in' for chairs and suitcases. Perhaps this is more properly the objectification of the performer? Equally, though, an object may be invested with human qualities. Stuart Sherman puts shoes on the ends of a chair's legs (in *London: Portraits Of Places*), or a tie might be fastened around the neck of a jug. The performer might then address the jug – "There, you look much smarter now! "

10. *Transferences of weight* play a major part in dance and a significant one in many performances. A transference of weight occurs while one is walking. Contact improvisation utilizes this concept a great deal. A transference of weight also occurs when a liquid is poured from one container to another. When the Theatre of Mistakes performed *A Waterfall* at the Hayward Gallery in 1977, water was transferred from a bucket at the bottom of a tower built out of tables and chairs, via cups in the hands of the performers, until it filled a bucket at the top of the structure. Then it was poured directly back into the bucket on the ground. Most fluid objects may be poured from one container to another. A performer can be transferred from one person's back onto a table top, and from there slid onto the floor. Transference of weight is akin to transference of place, and most puttings in and pullings out may be considered in the light of this transference – think of Eyeore's birthday presents.

11. Finally there are *Transferences of Exertion*: shifts from repetitive modes of behaviour to inconsistent modes of behaviour, for example, or from stillness to some other form of action (remembering that in performance' terms stillness is an action in itself). Cathexis will be utilised to trigger these shifts from one activity to another.

*   *   *   *

Concerning the first transference on this list (*transference of use*), a valuable aesthetic rule has emerged in performance which particularly advocates this transference since it amounts to using an object in *more than one way*, or *for more than one purpose*. Using an object in more than one way encourages limitation (it teaches you to do more with less), and results in homeostasis – more of the load spread throughout the system. Are there analytical repercussions here? Getting back to my asthmatic student and his apprehensive girlfriend, were they just spreading the load?

Could there be transferences of weight, then, in phobias? In all probability, my student was asthmatic before he met his girlfriend. Nevertheless, her apprehensive fears encouraged him to play a calming role, soothing his own condition; while his asthma gave her something concrete to worry about, allaying some of her more irrational fears – so a condition of homeostasis resulted in the shared organism which constituted their relationship.

Humanisation: Anthony Howell, Julian Maynard Smith and Peter Stickland take the places of chairs and suitcases in *Homage to Morandi* by the Theatre of Mistakes, performed at the Mickery Theatre, Amsterdam, 1979. Photograph: Bob Van Dantzig.

Reversals:

As we have already seen when considering the positive/negative, putting on/taking off aspect of repetition (*pages 34-35*), reversal plays its role in performance as well as in psychoanalysis. Or take the question of camouflage: does the performer dressed in black who stands against a black curtain actually wish to stand out from the crowd? Her role can be *reversed* from camouflage to display by moving from the black curtain to the white wall. Here we might speak of *transference to reversal*, since the performer reverses her role simply by a transference of place.

Then we should ask ourselves what would be the reverse of our clothing – do we secretly desire to wear its opposite – garish, hippy gear instead of a grey suit? Is clothing worn to disguise our desire? Does it represent a transference onto that which opposes our wish? We might devise emotional reversals: kissing someone's shoes, say, but later stamping on their hat.

It is said that when language is blocked behaviour enacts, and that what cannot be remembered is repeated in behaviour. Prohibited remarks may be transferred entirely into action – and a sort of transgressional charades may evolve – secretly articulating taboo sentences. But while this is going on, the subject may verbally articulate polite commonplace platitudes – reversing the message of these actions. The charade thus becomes an inconsistent language, or at least a body language at variance with what is said.

Aneurisis (wetting) may be accompanied by reversal dreams (of fire/ of burning), but the secret of the reversal lies not with the subject but with the other. One becomes a masochist in order to seduce – so that the other will enjoy giving one a beating. In bed-wetting, one may be seeking the consequence – which is the punishment pleasurable to the other. The same sort of reversal occurs in sadism: one is a sadist because the beating one will inflict 'will turn the other on'. In performance the sadistic game might be displaced by a substitution – and thus transferred elsewhere: one performer may hit the upholstered chair repeatedly with a riding-crop, while, in another part of the performance space, a plump performer presents his posterior to the audience, shouting, "Do it harder! Do it harder!"

Faeces are a child's first gift. Note the substitution inherent in the *Grumus Merdae* – the excretion left behind by a burglar. The swag successfully stored in a bag brings about release of rectal tension. At the same time, the turds so deposited are 'payment' for what has been stolen.

Aversion may metaphorically transpose the bad sight for the bad smell (sense transference) – thus someone who sees a hideously deformed person might expel air as if experiencing a stink, while the sight of a lovely person might cause that person to inhale deeply. This might be considered a transference of sense.

There are also the important reversals connected with travesty (*see also page 18*). It has been noted that the term can refer to more than the mimicry of the opposite sex. Wearing the clothes of one's lower half on one's upper half, or underwear over one's suit can epitomise the supremacy of the bodily instincts over social obligations. As a transference to reversal, we might also consider the notion of the "world turned upside down". Woodcuts illustrating this subject have been popular since the middle ages. Primarily their function was educational, to show how the world is not, in order that children might learn how it is: the man drawing the cart whipped on by the horse, the wife gone hunting while the husband sits at home spinning, the pigs slaughtering the farmer. These illustrations have always been associated with the ribald spirit of carnival and with revolution. Domestic revolution might be expressed by upended wardrobes and by tables balanced on upended chairs and covered by upside down carpets. Mikhail Bakhtin's *Rabelais and his world* elaborates on these themes.

Regression:

Somebody who retires to bed with a scarf to suck their thumb may be said to be regressing. Regression is retrograde time-travel. Day-dreaming is time-travel into the future.

Freud cites three time-periods as important to daydreaming: the *now* (usually a set-back) which prompted the dream: the *then*, a particular occasion in the past when the subject got the upper hand over a similar issue or incident: the *will be* which allows the past triumph to leapfrog the present

The World Turned Upside-down. Le Monde à l'Envers, page 123.

disaster. This notion resonates with that of the three-fold compulsion to repeat which we find in plot construction: the event, its echo, and the repercussion of that echo.

Note that the timespan for a performance is a microcosm model for life. Infancy, maturity and death find their equivalents in the beginning, middle and end of a performance. So "Let's go back to the beginning" can read as a regression to childhood or suggest that time can be reversed, that we can start again and get things right this time. These equivalencies become less interesting, however, when generalised into a metaphor for history: prehistoric time as infancy, renaissance as prime of life, twentieth century as dotage. In my view cave-paintings, renaissance paintings and abstract expressionist paintings are all equally sophisticated. At all times we have done as well as we may with the tools available to us. Still, *regression to the start* trammels us in urges whose expressions have become clichés - getting back to nature, getting back to our roots, getting back to our national identity. In this light the eternal return is also the eternal regression, a regression ending in that dark, primordial nothingness pregnant with new beginnings which Freud perceives as the aim of the death-instinct. A series may *regress* to infinity: the painter painting a picture of a painter painting a picture of a painter etc. Equally a performer may copy a performer copying a performer copying a performer. This was the concept behind *Going* by the Theatre of Mistakes.

At the start of a performance, the end amounts to the future. On entering that future, a performer may "regress" to a theme first made manifest during the infancy (start) of the performance. Thus, in performance terms, regression may equate to *reduplicating the start*.

Transference from Internal Formulation:

As performers, you are looking for an "action language": one you can spontaneously "speak". By this I mean that you need to be able to think in your action language – just as you can only be said to have mastered French once you have ceased translating your sentence from English before you speak it. You become good at writing creatively once you have stopped pausing and formulating each sentence in your head before writing it down. The hand should do the writing – not the head. So you need to *think by performing*, instead of trying to complete your thinking *prior* to the performance. Your mental activity needs to be transferred into the action actually relevant to the job. You need to think in French or through the hand or by performing. Performing is not a translation from another language. As in writing, where the hand thinks the sentences, your actions must think the performance.

Here we should return to our guiding notion; that we, the performer-witnesses, are the analysts, and that performance art is our subject. A transference must be affected from subject to analyst. This is a crucial stage in psychoanalysis. In our terms, this requires that the performance must successfully transfer onto the performers. Thus the performers become the performance – consider Gilbert and George. They tell me that they have never used the term performance to describe what they do. Emphatically, they are Living Sculpture, Singing Sculpture, a Living Piece or a Posing Piece. As such they are not even separate beings. Even when they go out to eat breakfast in some small cafe in East London they remain dressed as the living sculpture: they *are* the living sculpture they proclaim themselves to be, just as they are the living sculpture when at a *vernissage*. Having been Gilbert and George from the start of their partnership, they remain in their suits or subtract down from their suits to their underwear or to a state of nudity (though I have observed that they've added a fine pair of plaid overcoats to their credible attire). Their 'sculptural' identity is now so integrated with their personalities that there is no need for specific showings to be created at specific times – except perhaps for nostalgic reasons, as when they recreated their 1974 piece, *Underneath the Arches*, in New York in 1994. When evident together, they are Gilbert and George, and being Gilbert and George is a perpetual showing, incorporating their bodily functions which get worked into their artistic presentations, and this exhibition will last as long as their bodies bear up to the strain of being sculpture...

The Transference Workshop

1. Exercises in Transference

Performers should work through the performance transferences set out in the preceding chapter – pages 137–144. They should employ:

> *transference of use,*
> *transference of scale,*
> *transference of lead,*
> *transference from action to sign,*
> *transference from action to language,*
> *transference of place,*
> *transference of dimension,*
> *transference of element,*
> *transference of exertion,*
> *a humanisation of the object,*
> *transference of weight*
> *and transference to reversal.*

2. Free Session Transference

Performers improvise in a free-session for some twenty minutes in the privacy of the performance space. They then move to another location, preferably a public one – an entrance foyer or a canteen, for instance - and repeat that free-session as accurately as they can.

3. Substitution Exercise

Performers divide into pairs. Then the first performer behaves extremely violently towards the second performer, but expends that violence on an object rather than on the other performer – meanwhile the other performer reacts as if the violence were actually being experienced. Then the second performer behaves extremely amorously towards the first performer, but expends that passion on an object rather than on the other performer – and meanwhile the other performer reacts as if that erotic passion were actually being experienced. The exercise is then repeated, with the second performer taking the initial role of the first performer and vice versa.

4. Role Projection Drama

In a free session, each performer identifies another as a member of his or her family – mother, father, daughter, son, brother or sister – and reacts to that performer accordingly. More than one performer may be so identified – one might be a mother while another might be a father, brother or sister. Gradually, during the session, all the performers should attempt to regress – ending up as infants without the ability to speak.

A language of action signs and emblems: Scotty Snyder and George Ashley in Stuart Sherman's *Taxi Dance*, premiered at the St. Mark's Poetry Project, New York, 1985. Photograph: Babette Mangolte.

10

LANGUAGE

"Even if it communicates nothing, the discourse represents the existence of communication; even if it denies the evidence, it affirms that speech constitutes truth; even if it is intended to deceive, the discourse speculates on faith in testimony. Moreover, it is the psychoanalyst who knows better than anyone else that the question is to understand which 'part' of this discourse carries the significative term, and this is, ideally, just how he proceeds: he takes the description of an everyday event for a fable addressed to whoever hath ears to hear, a long tirade for a direct interjection, or on the other hand a simple *lapsus* for a highly complex statement, or even the sigh of a momentary silence for the whole lyrical development it replaces."

(Lacan, "Function and Field of Speech and Language"
– *Écrits, a selection*, page 43)

In analysis, we may be encouraged to regress into baby talk, yet the noises we use, the pet names, the nonsense words of endearment or revulsion, will still constitute an expression open to interpretation; or we may launch into some shaggy dog story to screen our feelings, and the analyst may listen to the telling of our tale, reading into it revelations of the past we do not recognise ourselves. The past revealed by language is its own reality, a reality which is neither true nor false, and when we speak of our past we reveal more about our present state than we do about what happened to us "then" – just as the documented history in holy books tells us more about the times of those who originally compiled the documents than it does about those past events the documents purport to describe.

Freud measures the cure by the degree of continuity in memory, as the blanks are filled in and the fictitious substitutions detected for what they are during the analysis. The unconscious of the subject constitutes that subject's history. What is forgotten is revealed in acts.

The psychoanalytic method propounded by Freud strives to unearth the secret history masked by the tale told via an analytic symbolism strictly opposed to analogical thinking. Jungian analysis puts more weight on analogy: the story as a whole is considered for its similarity to some myth, folktale or religious epiphany rooted in the subject's cultural soil. Freudian analysis is more digital: it "deconstructs" the story, identifies its components within a symbolic glossary derived from the interpretation of dreams. The dream has the structure of a sentence or a rebus, and the ego may be distinguished by a tightly knit *nexus* of words which, when read like a word-square, may suggest a particular sentence for each subject.

Here, I am again reminded of the *spectacles* of Stuart Sherman, especially of his "Portraits of People". Each vignette is brief, and the actions contained in it amount to a puzzle, to be read on a vertical axis as well as on any horizontal one riding along the sequential line of the actions. This performance puzzle, so obliquely described in small object manipulations, and punctuated by the occasional enigmatic sound, may provide a key to the character of the friend.

The inquiry we are engaged in posits that we, the performance artists, are the analysts of our medium. Our audience will be the analysts of our performance. In a Freudian session, every slip is a revelation, every unsuccessful act (of language or behaviour) is a successful articulation of our unconscious. The symptom resolves itself into a language comprehensible in analytic terms because the symptom itself is structured like a language; the symptom being the signifier of a signified repressed from the consciousness of the subject. Every member of our audience translates our performance language into their own perceptual language, and of course it's a precious occasion when the interpretation of some critic in our audience provides us with an insight into our performance which has not yet dawned on our awareness.

The word itself is a presence made of absence, for the thing is not there, the word stands in for the thing. But it is not the fading of things which permits language, rather it is the world of words which creates the world of its absences, the world of the things themselves. As Lacan puts it, "Man speaks, then, but it is because the symbol has made him man." Sometimes, of course, the thing stands in for the word, as in the case with most religious paraphernalia. And in many instances, the performance artist may be striving to bring about the *presence* of a word or a phrase; citing it for itself, as an object made out of language, rather than simply drawing attention to what it signifies. Drawing attention to the narrative significance of the text is the task of the conventional actor.

On emergence from the pregenital, prelinguistic stage, the metapsychology of Freudian analysis avers that the "name of the father" gives identity, law and language to the son, metapsychology being the branch of psychoanalysis that deals with philosophical questions which go beyond the study of specific cases. The authors of the *Anti-Oedipus* would query this domination by the father, arguing that production produces its own articulation of what is produced, that production and description are simultaneous activities. The advert comes into being at the same time as the commodity. We invent a expression to describe our excretion simply because we've produced it, not because a parent has told us what it is called.

Hamlet is identified with the skull he holds. But does he contemplate the skull of Yorick the clown or his own mortality? Since his father is as dead as Yorick, and the skull signifies death, does he inherit his sense of mortality as much from his father as from this unearthed memento – as the Freudians would have it? More importantly, in performance terms, does handling the skull provide Hamlet the actor with a *mnemonic implement:* this soliloquy associated with the jaw, that other with the occiput – the skull thus providing him with his dead father's legacy of language? When he feigns madness, Hamlet indulges in a speech which seems to have given up trying to make itself recognised – but this allows the unsayable to be said, as Yorick's clowning once provided him with the licence to mention the unsayable in jest.

Neurosis may have recourse to a language bereft of dialectic, even if all the words happen to "make sense". Conversely, one's girlfriend may make herself perfectly understood by making cat noises.

A Hindu tradition Lacan refers to as *dhvani* stresses the property of speech by which it communicates what it does not actually say. Lacan illustrates this by citing a fable:

> "A girl, it begins, is waiting for her lover on the bank of a stream when she sees a Brahmin coming along towards her. She runs to him and exclaims in the warmest possible tones: 'What a lucky day this is for you! The dog that used to frighten you by its barking will not be along this river bank again, for it has just been devoured by the lion that is often seen around here...'"

(Function and Field of Speech and Language, *Écrits*, page 82)

According to Lacan, there is a fundamental difference between language and sign. For the sign is a codification of a concrete message – think of a traffic sign. Speech, on the other hand, is open to interpretation, differs with expression and commits its author to signification by the very act of investing the addressee with meaning.

If I say, You are my wife, I am saying something about myself. Speech always subjectively includes its own reply.

But as language approaches sign, it becomes more functional and thus becomes improper for speech; since speech is a matter of the *epos*, of the many interpretations of the tale, of the differences in the telling. Speech is redolent with resonances and evocations, it generates witticism and *double entendre*. It is not a bald communiqué, as is the sign, yet as it becomes too particular to the individual – too full of private jokes, personal jargon, too much its own idiolect – it loses its function as language – which is the problem of contemporary "Language" poetry; for when poetry arrives at opacity in its exploration of the frontiers of meaning it loses appeal for any but its own practitioners.

Each individual uses an idiolect in speech and in writing; a personal imprint on language as unique as the fingerprint. When such an idiolect becomes too particular, however, autism results – often manifesting itself as an inability to learn or as an absence of recognisable speech. Sometimes the autistic person will display remarkable gifts in other areas, demonstrating an uncanny ability with numbers, or recognising the exact pitch of any note, or proving capable of drawing in meticulous detail a landscape seen for a few seconds. Among such "idiot savants", mention should be made of

Christopher Knowles, who was as a young boy the inspiration for Robert Wilson. Christopher was an expert at repetition. He would reduplicate certain phrases exactly for hours on end. He provided the motive force for many of Wilson's long-duration performances.

Speech worms in and out of the unconscious; meanwhile all discourse has its *effect* through the unconscious, and often our speech may trigger some incidental effect. We may employ secret names to identify ourselves, our treasures and our gods, but who knows when someone may unwittingly use the name we have designated with a secret meaning?

Meanwhile television and conventional theatre persist in the insipid mimicry of "normal" life, and a false ordinariness prevails in which all speech is reduced to functioning dialogue – 100% communication, supposedly eliciting the expected, socially acceptable response – wife confesses to some peccadillo, husband blows his top. Pilkinsky invokes Sheryl Sutton to speak of the flat lowlands of this mimicry theatre where drama is reduced to a slavish imitation of the ordinary.

There is no real language in mimicry theatre – only a codification of reality. The sign for reality is the hyper-real – as identified by Baudrillard – in which the photographically-generated image, or the filmed or videotaped image of things, constitutes the recognised world. The abiding characteristic of this reproduced realism is its hollowness. This is a hollowness without resonance. The more "socially real" the drama, the less we derive discourse from it. It is this obsession with the mimicry of everyday life which prevents theatre from retaining its role as a viable cultural form. Sometimes, it is true, theatre perceives this danger, and turns instead to symbolism and song. All too often though it retains a) its intentionality – which makes it obligatory to convey some message via symbolic illustration, b) its illustrative use of language and the belief that its characters should still respond to each other, and c) the normality of time – even if its actions are punctuated by 'meaningful' dance and song.

Thus, despite eschewing the reality of representational narration, symbolic theatre remains a far cry from performance art.

Aristotle believed that the arts aspired to the condition of theatre – since theatre was where they all came together. But this places the arts in the condition of illustrating each other. Conversely, the American abstract painter, Ad Reinhardt, maintained that the arts strive for *emancipation from each other*. Performance art leans more towards the view of Reinhardt - in its essential modernity - than to that of Aristotle.

Speech in Performance Art:

Speech destroys action.

In conventional, text-based theatre, the action, however well done, remains a mere accompaniment. Speech destroys action by normalising it. It is quite natural for a man or a woman to speak, and when they do so, all too often their actions become natural and ordinary – albeit the convention of theatre may require some enlargement of the gestures.

In film, this enlargement undermines the illusion of absolute realism which cinema promotes, and now our sensibilities are so conditioned by the screen that we cannot help but denounce the artificiality of theatre's magnifications.

Speech destroys action either by enforcing illustration or by necessitating stillness. Stillness commands our attention when employed by the speaker, and it also ensures reception when it exemplifies the passivity expected of the listener. Then, in the most devastating way, speech muffles the language of actions.

Experimental theatre may attempt to mimic the action-language of performance art, while retaining the playwright's text. This may surmount the problem posed by illustration – where the action is subservient to the text – but it may bring about a conflict between speech and action resulting in a tension inimical to the homeostasis of the experience – it's as if we were watching two performances at the same time – and while this may be an intriguing situation there is a risk that we will end up failing to concentrate on either.

Performance came into its own as an *art in itself* in the latter half of the twentieth century: before that, the futurists and the dadaists were still making plays or ballets. As an art-form, it liberated action from being muffled:

by speech	-	which is drama
by music	-	which is dance
by illustration	-	which is mime
by effect	-	which is conjuring
by purpose	-	which is sport

All the above are either mixed media or they serve two purposes. It has been necessary for performance art to become an unmixed medium, serving only the specific dictates of action, in order for it to become evocative and resonant – that is, in order for it to become a language.

So performance art only comes into being as language when language itself is renounced. The more you use actual speech, the more your performance risks becoming a mere accompaniment to that speech. The more people speak, especially when their speech responds to the speaking and action of others, the more the performance becomes normalized, and the more the actions become ordinary.

Performance rescued from speech holds the promise of a language compounded of stillnesses and repetitions; a language of transferences and objectivizations; a language of expectations, inconsistencies and catastrophes, of regressions and sublimations. Its dumbness should release or stir the inner commentaries of its audience. It is that inner commentary which should make comparisons and assemble differences. For it is ultimately the audience who should analyse the show, and therefore the commentary should not be provided by the performers.

However, speech remains an action, and may be used when considered solely as action:

1. Words might be chosen as triggers: triggers which would cause changes from one mode of action to another or set off light changes, or, as in mirroring, alter the lead.

2. Sentences may be considered as objects, and, as such, subjected to action - as in the 'First Conversation Piece'. In this exercise, a sentence without nouns can be changed via its pronouns or in its declension, or its structure may be turned into a query or a negative statement or command, or it may be fractured so that bits of it only are used: "What did you decide for him?" "I didn't decide for him." "You did decide for him." "I decided for her." "So what did you decide for her?" "I decided you should decide for her." "I won't decide for her!" "Why not decide for her?" "You decide for her!" "I won't. Why should I decide for her?"

Tu Quoque arguments are a simplified version of this: a child responds fiercely by exact repetition. "You take it." "You take it" "You take it!" "You take it!"

3. Pilinsky's Sheryl Sutton suggests "speaking to oneself" as a strategy for speech in performance. Here language is allowed to rise vertically, like smoke, rather than to move horizontally from mouth to ear. Speech *à la Cantonade,* where a child speaks happily to no one, is a similar phenomenon.

4. Outbursts of abuse, as in *Tourette's Syndrome,* may be considered a physical activity. Terms of abuse may also be used as affectionate endearments. But only blacks may call each other 'niggers'. This prohibition reinforces discrimination: it does nothing to diminish it. Enlightened 'correctness' has never come to terms with the fundamental ambivalence of language.

5. Speech adulterated by sound or scrambled or distorted in some other way may be considered – for instance, there is *grammalot*: a term used to describe the making of nonsensical sounds interspersed with the occasional word that makes sense. Another possibility is song. Another is *distortion rhyming,* where one replaces every word one wishes to say with a word which rhymes with it.

Song is particularly interesting if used out of context: a newspaper can be sung aloud instead of read aloud. Michael Nyman's opera, *The Man who Mistook, his Wife for a Hat,* based on a case-history by Oliver Sacks, transfers everyday conversation into song in a very effective way. A sudden burst of song can constitute an inconsistency as disconcerting as Tourette's Syndrome. The horizontality of the songs in the entirety of their verses may be distorted by gaps, or by extension – the performer taking as long over any one note as would normally be spent on a phrase, and then taking as long as would normally be spent on the entire verse.

6. Speech may be subjected to rhythm or time: a regular gap or a regular emphasis will entail a rhythm, while the additive insertion of gaps of silence (the gaps growing longer and longer), will gradually disintegrate the narrative thread. Ultimately the performance will be punctuated by isolated words occurring at extended intervals.

7. Narrative may be employed to the accompaniment of consciously anti-narrative actions, for example, dancing and jumping up and down shouting out, 'They got me. Ah, I'm shot! Look, I'm hit. They got me...' But note the problem of homeostatic conflict mentioned above. Then a narrative paragraph might simply be repeated, and then repeated again, and again. This would serve to objectify the paragraph, lessening its transparency, that is, the transparency that language suffers when only its content is attended to.

*   *   *   *

Language punctuating action: Claire Hayes makes a single hysterical outburst in *Objects* by Anthony Howell, performed at Cardiff Art in Time, Chapter Arts Centre, Cardiff, 1995. Photograph: Jenni Cooper.

It must be emphasized that if you wish to avoid the cliché of horizontal dialogue, you must extricate the language you employ from a servitude to statement and response. Language should not be used to acknowledge another or to respond to another or to tell the audience anything *except as an exception to the rule* (which might afford your performance the inconsistent phenomenon of a surprise). However, if the exception to the rule is of any great duration, it will become the rule, and then your performance will normalise into horizontal theatre.

Neither should language be employed as a narrative accompaniment or commentary, except perhaps as satire, as in "Now she is scratching her head, now she is blowing her nose" – as she does it; although this also relates to *Station House Opera's* 'feedback' explorations.

Performance may also be fused with language in a way that reverses the accompaniment factor, so that the word accompanies the action, rather than vice versa. This calls for the creation of *word/action* units, where the word (or phrase) is intrinsic to a specific gesture or action. Then the actions can be shuffled – forcing an alteration in the order of the words or phrases. This may fundamentally interfere with the language's capacity to maintain the thread of narrative. Better still, a new narrative may emerge; a narrative which is ironic and subservient to the action.

Note also my remarks on the basic inconsistency of any string of words in both normal and abnormal usage (*Inconsistency, Catastrophe and Surprise, page 81*), as well as my remarks on the relation between speaking and excretion (*Drives and the Primaries, page 111*).

The Voice

It is not just a question of language, it is also a question of the voice. The voice should be considered for itself. The gaze, the hearing and the voice form an important triumvirate of receiver / expression devices which are all three part of the natural functioning of our body – and therefore essential to performance. Remember that receiver devices can also be apprehended:

We can be seen looking. We cannot be heard looking, but we can be heard looking for something.

We can be seen listening. We cannot be heard listening, but it can be deduced that we are listening through our silence.

We can be seen vocalising. We can be heard vocalising. But we cannot hear with our voice, we cannot see with our voice.

Presumably the whale "sees" with its voice. Natural echo effects might be considered as feedback about the environment achieved through the voice. If we were blindfolded, we would be able to guess at the dimensions of the space we were in by testing it with our voice.

Language as performance: Aaron Williamson performing his poetry in *Mnemonic Repositions*, I.C.A., London, 1994. Photograph: Tertia Longmire.

The voice is characterised by a wide range of polarities: loud / soft, high / low, explosive / sibilant, guttural / falsetto etc. We can deliver sound slowly or at speed. The voice can be emotive or dead-pan. Liberated from language, singing and sound-making provide the voice with a language "of its own". Liberated from communication, voices can perform in parallel – as in a chorus – or they can perform independently – as when two songs are sung at the same time.

Performance poets, like Cris Cheek and Aaron Williamson, have established an arena where noise-making comes into play with verbal articulation; a sort of penumbra of the word, or a no-man's-land between speech and sound. Williamson is deaf, and he contributed an interesting insight into language at the Performance Poetry Seminar at Dartington in 1996. Here there was much pontification regarding the 'primacy' of speech over written language – as if speech were the uncooked form of expression, the origin. Williamson followed the debate which was transcribed from speech to screen for him by two typists, and he averred that because of his condition speech had meant little to him until *after* he had grasped language through the written word. For him, therefore, it is the text which is visceral, primal. After his initial experience of a lack, text is how language has claimed him. For all that, his performances have a 'tactile' aural quality, one feels the strain of the larynx, the tension between plosives and vowels, and language overflows the voice and seeps into the body causing it to twist and contort.

One way to envisage the voice is to think of it as the *internal body of the performer*. In warm-up exercises, it is essential to activate this internal body as well as the external one. For this purpose, song is perhaps more useful than speech. But other voice exercises such as tongue-twisters should not be discounted. Voices can also be raised in chorus, which is a species of verbal mirroring. Huutajat – or The Screaming Men – is a performance art choir from Finland. Thirty men from the same small town, all wearing black suits, white shirts and black rubber ties line up in strict configuration and scream a repertoire of workers' songs, national anthems and quotes from Finnish laws!

The Language Workshop

1.   First Conversation Piece

Performers practice this exercise as set out on page 39 in the Chapter on Mimicry and Repetition.

2.   Language Adaptions and Word/Unit Adaptions

Performers should look through all the exercises so far covered in the workshops described in this book and see if they can be adapted to being demonstrated solely by the voice - either in terms of language or sound. Having performed these using language or sound alone, each performs these exercises again, utilising word/action units where possible.

3.   Language Experiments

In a free session, performers experiment with speech à la Cantonade, with outbursts of obscenities - as in Tourette's Syndrome - with grammalot, snatches of song, extended song, distortion rhyming etc. They should also try repeating a sentence and, with each repetition, adding gaps of increasing duration between each word.

4.   Narrative Exercise

See page 133.

5.   Songs Exercises

All the performers agree on a single phrase from a song. This they sing repetitively, each leaving out words whenever they choose, while keeping to the timing of the phrase as it repeats. A second phrase may be added and treated in the same manner. It may help if the group divides in half. The performers should also practice song-extension - slowing each word of a song as it is sung - as well as additive or subtractive songs - singing the first word, repeating it and adding the second and so on - or the same process in reverse.

6.   Memorised Text Exercise

Each performer memorises a brief text. It should be learnt so well that the performer is able to reverse the order of its sentences, scramble its words, add gaps between each word, say the entire text extremely fast or fuse the first half of the first sentence with the last half of the last sentence, then cutting and reforming all the other sentences of the text in the same manner - without of course referring to the written text itself.

7.   Verbal Excretion Exercise

See page 117.

8.   Additive word/action units

Spontaneously perform a sequence of five word/action units additively. Repeat the entire sequence five times. Then shuffle the units many times, according to the system of your choice. Finally diminish the number of units subtractively. Next, carefully devise a sequence of five word/action units, and repeat the exercise with these prepared units.

Peter Rasmussen and Ingrid Cullen complete building *The Tower* by Anthony Howell, at the Art Gallery of New South Wales, Sydney, Australia, 1984. Photograph: Kerry Dundas.

11
TIME AND SPACE

Time:

Time, in analysis, is usually parcelled into sessions. A regular starting time is maintained, and the sessions are of equal length. The regularity of the sessions should establish a repetition compulsion in the subject, and the issue of tardiness, punctuality or arriving early for the session can be of import to the analysis. The time of the session is dictated by the clock.

Lacan, however, identifies the rule of the clock with the malaise of our century. Just as there is no 'No', there is no concept of time in the unconscious. Yet analysis is punctuated by its endings and digitalized by them also, i.e. they divide the entire analysis into discrete units of equal length, whereas an analogue analysis might simply continue the session until some matter had been brought to a head. Obviously the pattern of modern life makes the latter method practically impossible, so far as an ongoing deep analysis is concerned, though it may apply to a group therapy session held at some weekend retreat.

Any indefinite period may be punctuated by arbitrary intervals. These intervals operate on the period, but they are not part of it. A performance session may go on until someone says, "Stop." If that someone has stepped outside the performance simply to look at a watch, then that command truncates the performance – it may not have reached its end. Indeed a performance may go on, and on. Annie Sprinkle pays this tribute to Linda Montano:

> "Linda is one of the greatest artists of our time, erasing the barriers between 'art' and 'life' by performing her fears, fantasies and taboos using sound, deprivation and humor since 1969. Her most infamous projects include "One Year Art/Life Performance" in which she lived for an entire year tied to another artist, Teching Hsieh, by an eight foot rope – and never touched him..."
>
> (Love and Kisses from Annie Sprinkle, Vol. 1)

Lacan says, "Perhaps we might get a better idea of time by comparing the time required for the creation of a symbolic object with the moment of inattention when we let it fall." Here we have a repetitive or an additive process being destroyed by a single inconsistent accident.

It is said that the unconscious needs time to reveal itself. Something akin to the unconscious of the group may reveal itself in time, during a lengthy free-session. This is not a "collective unconscious", that mythical phenomenon promoted by Jung, for none of its feelings are necessarily common to all the performers. It is simply the unconscious of each performer becoming manifest and mingling with those of the others.

A painting also needs time to reveal itself, and the large-scale pieces by Robert Wilson created in the early seventies such as *Deaf Man Glance* and *The Life and Times of Sigmund Freud* presented performance panoramas which were very still or slow moving, punctuated by sudden actions or entrances which worked rather like splashes of colour added to an already rich canvas.

When we are in the audience, a performance takes us through a series of transitions: there is the impact of the beginning, which is followed by an analytic period where we describe what we witness to ourselves. This is followed by expectation, for we are conditioned to suppose that some inconsistency or surprise will alter our original impression. The occurrence of this first surprising development or revelation in a drama is known as "the rousing moment". If this expectancy is not fulfilled then boredom may set in. A master of performance art such as Robert Wilson may be able to extend this expectancy for many hours and finally resolve it into meditation, though even he has recourse to those "sudden splashes of colour" which keep our expectancy aroused. As our expectancy gets rewarded by events, we become intrigued, and finally, in drama's classical terms, "Catharsis"' occurs, defined as a purification of the emotions by vicarious experience. In other words, the actions of the others we watch arouse emotions in us which are ultimately purged by the outcome of the piece.

If the performance happens to be an ongoing activity – a process without end, similar to a discipline of the Zen monks, or a continuous 'life-style' improvisation – then some punctuation by clock-timed intervals may be the only way to parcel the experience. But such endings, with their attendant beginnings, may not be required. Joseph Beuys spent a week in a caged room with a jackal. Some of Alastaire McLennan's performances have lasted over a fortnight. Prior to performing *Seven Years of Living Art*, Linda Montano described it as "a multilayered personal experiment in attention which will last for seven years. I will wear only one colour clothes, each year a different colour, listen to one note seven hours a day, stay in a coloured space three hours a day, and speak in a different accent each year."

Gilbert and George are Gilbert and George for life. But even Gilbert and George are subject to intervals. Gilbert is busy being Gilbert, but eventually he must fall asleep, and then when he wakes up, he wakes up as Gilbert, but how can he be sure that he was Gilbert before he went to sleep? This is a difficulty which faces George also. Descartes understood that our conviction that we are coherently and consistently ourselves is called into question by sleep, when we lapse out of consciousness. Possibly we wake up each morning entirely reinvented. Here sleep is a stillness which acts as an inconsistency interrupting the continuum of existence.

In ritual, the rite takes as long as the actions of its ceremony require – while extensive preparation time may also be part of that ritual. For the solo performer who has set himself a specific task, the time it takes to complete the task may suffice.

Clock time may get referred to (or is deferred to) in group performances where no actions have been rehearsed. In such free sessions, everyone may be going about their separate tasks, so the problem is how to know when the performance is finished, and, if one seeks to minimise imbalance for the sake of the integrity (or homeostasis) of the whole, how to finish at pretty much the same time.

Abandon the clock, and how to finish at the same time becomes the task which unites the performers.

The standard form in jazz improvisation is to play the tune through in unison; then each player performs a solo in turn, improvising on the tune – with the others providing punctuating riffs or choruses. When each player has performed their solo the tune is reprised (played through again) and so the piece finishes.

Mutual performance art has yet to identify its forms, though the notion of the free session has some currency, of course, based as it is on the notion of improvisation. I think improvisation has a key role to play in the development of performance because it allows the unconscious of the group to emerge and to be read by the Large Other which is the audience. This unconscious made evident might be considered the content of the performance.

One of the tasks of a set form might be to establish a method of time-keeping, in order that everyone would finish at the same time:

1. There might be time-keeping by turns: if five performers each establish a task of equal length, then the others are free to improvise, provided each performs their established task in turn, in order to keep time. When all 5 have performed their task the piece ends.

2. There might be a mutual task: in which case the performance will probably require some rehearsal.

Both the above systems require acknowledgement and thus introduce awareness into the performance. In the first, one performer has to notify the others when his or her task is finished, or they have to recognise its end; and also a rota of time-keepers will have to be established. In the second, rehearsal brings everything into awareness. But the greater the necessity to be aware of the structure, the more difficult it is for the performer to improvise freely and lose consciousness of the others, which is a prerequisite for each performer if the diverse unconscious of the group is to emerge (I call it *diverse* to avoid any confusion with a 'collective unconscious').

Of course, the performers can simply elect one of their number to be their metronome or time-keeper by performing some task which terminates the performance by its completion. This metronomic performer is always the odd person out however – and placed in a subsidiary role which must interfere with the homeostasis of the piece.

A performance may be timed by any extrinsic factor, and some may prove more sympathetic than the clock. The progress of the sun towards sunset might be used, or the performance might be terminated by the dinner-bell. A more integrated method, requiring a minimum of awareness, derives from the common practice of staggering the entries and the exits when an exercise is being performed:

1. One performer begins, and, one at a time, each of the others begins after a while: once the performers have been working in the space for a while, the one who started the performance leaves, and, one at a time, each of the others leaves after a while - so the first *on* is the first *off* the space, and the last *on* is the last *off* it.

This might be described as an *Accumulative* and *Decreasing* method of construction:

Mins:	5	10	15	20	25	30	35	40	45
	A	A	A	A	A				
		B	B	B	B	B			
			C	C	C	C	C		
				D	D	D	D	D	
					E	E	E	E	E

With the above method, at least you know that the performance is finishing by the progressive absence of the others - but that's all you need to know, and the only awareness you require, which is a pretty minimal amount of awareness. In performance workshops, when this structure is used, I stress the need to allow the performance to "deepen" before each new entry. That is, at first we have a solo. Let that solo "deepen" before the first performer is joined by a second performer, turning that solo into a duet. Now let the duet "deepen" before the third performer turns it into a trio. A similar allowance should stagger the exits towards the conclusion - don't rush to exit just because someone else has left the space.

By "deepen" I mean "register". If you are waiting to enter, first register what the solo is. A stillness? A repetition perhaps? And the duet - are we now watching a repetition with an inconsistency in juxtaposition to it - or two differing repetitions? Registering the nature of the performance into which you are about to enter will help you sense what to do.

2. The lozenge structure the above method produces can be inverted – everyone beginning at once, then becoming still or leaving the space,

one at a time, until everyone is still or no one is present, then, one at a time, re-entering the action, recognising that the performance will cease a while after everyone has re-entered. However, this creates an anti-homeostatic situation where the performers work on the space for unequal lengths of time. Equalizing their performance times produces the following structure:

This might be described as an *Inverted* method of construction:

Time:	5	10	15	20	25	30	35	40	45
	A					A	A	A	A
	B	B					B	B	B
	C	C	C					C	C
	D	D	D	D					D
	E	E	E	E	E				

The inverted lozenge it produces has certain imbalances, and may demand more awareness from its performers. By turning this structure around, however, the period when all the performers are working on the space together can be transposed from the start to the close, creating a larger climax at the end than at the beginning.

The *Accumulative and Decreasing* method gives a solo beginning, builds to a five-performer climax, ebbs away to a final solo: the *Inverted* method gives a climax at the beginning, a lull in the middle of the performance and a climax at its end, which can either be larger or smaller than the one at the start.

The phrase "ending together" has obvious sexual connotations, as does the phrase "coming together". In the lozenge, performers come together in the middle of the performance, in the inverted lozenge they come together at the beginning and almost end together, or they almost begin together and come together at the end. One could talk about a peaking crisis, which then ebbs away, as opposed to an undulant crisis which ebbs away only to climax later, more powerfully or less powerfully than at the start. It is tempting to extrapolate masculine and feminine tendencies from these patterns, concluding perhaps that, rather than necessarily coming at the same time, the dovetailing of male and female in coitus might incur a climax in the male in the midst of intercourse, whereas the female might have several climaxes, these being climaxes in waves.

Another method of structuring time with the minimum of acknowledgement might be derived from *serial music*:

Each performer works through an initially inconsistent string of actions an agreed number of times, extending or altering any unit of action in that string. Naturally an inconsistent string becomes a repetition once repeated, albeit an extended repetition and, in this case, a repetition with differences in the times of its units.

One might agree about the number of units in each string as well as the number of repetitions of it – but acknowledgement is unnecessary after that.

This might be called Serial structure.

Accumulative, Inverted and Serial structures require no rehearsal. Rehearsed performances however naturally allow the construction of more elaborate forms – fugues (time-lagged repetitions), shared tasks', spectacles, pre-arranged vignettes etc.

Musicians experienced in the field of free improvisation, such as the guitarist Derek Bailey and the musicians who gather together to play in company with him, seem to rely on no pre-ordained structure whatsoever. Free improvisation is discussed at length, together with an examination of improvisation techniques in traditional forms such as Baroque music, Indian music, Flamenco and Jazz, in Derek Bailey's book – *Improvisation: its Nature and Practice in Music*. There appears to be a natural end, an end which simply occurs, to which improvising musicians are highly sensitized, so that even without structure, the conclusion is practically simultaneous. To achieve this, they must rely on a perception of each other close to that described by Theodor Reik, when he describes "listening with the third ear" – which is quoted in Chapter 6: *Cathexes and Chaos, pages 89-95*.

And what of catharsis – that "purification of the emotions by vicarious experience"? In lieu of that, performance posits an identification with the unconscious generated by the group. This identification may have as purgative effect similar to that of catharsis, but it may be experienced by the audience individually rather than as a unity. In August 1978, in an article entitled *Subjective Denouement*, I wrote this about Robert Wilson, when reviewing his piece entitled *I was sitting on my patio when this guy appeared I thought I was hallucinating*, which he performed with Lucinda Childs at the Royal Court Theatre:

> "My 'realisations' are subjective. I remember a moment during *Stalin* (*The Life and Times of Joseph Stalin*, another of Wilson's performances) when I leapt to my feet to shout 'Bravo', and noticed that at the same time someone was weeping in the audience, while yet another roared with laughter. Wilson employs the single point of view ironically to achieve diverse effects. Each member of his audience will experience realisations of their own, with all the intensity of personal detection. His work allows such freedom to breathe. Previous artists, in all fields, have been concerned with arriving at their own subconscious – now, whatever 'the subconscious' may mean, there is much territory of thought rarely returned to, not necessarily barred to one at conscious moments, simply seldom visited. Often, the artists of our own time are concerned not only with getting to their own subconscious but also with getting to the particular subconscious of each receiver of their experience..."

(Artscribe No. 13.)

Today I would use the term 'unconscious', but the notion of an individual, subjective reaction still applies, I think, and operates in a similar way to the group experience of "catharsis".

*   *   *   *

I have observed earlier that repetition suspends time by annulling progress, while inconsistency creates time by supplying it with a history of significant events. Time seems capable of shrinkage and of magnification. People say that directly before a catastrophe, and during it, time appears to move slowly. We remember each instant we experienced in a car-crash – provided we can remember anything at all. So the inconsistent incident may very well magnify time. Surprise wakes us up. Gives us a rush of adrenaline and thus gives us a sense of time-enlargement. Conversely, repetition may lull us to sleep, but I am not sure that it inevitably causes a shrinkage. We might think of repetition as either hot or cold. A hot repetition in a jazz club may be pleasurable – and pleasurable moments are soon over. The cold repetition of daily drudgeries, or an interminably repetitive but dull performance, may cause time to pass extremely slowly.

This alteration in the size of the instant as it passes can be used to effect. A sense of monotony can serve as a fine prelude to a surprise, since the span of time when one is beginning to become bored is a time of slippage, of drift – one is dislocated slightly from the event, and this enables one's own dreams to merge with what is before the eyes. And being lulled into a restive state, slightly impatient, with an attendant loss of concentration, enhances the surprise that follows: one is "jerked out" of a reverie, and the adrenalin rush this causes is greater than it would have been had the surprise occurred when one was already fully alert.

Additive and Subtractive Time

In *Beyond the Pleasure Principle*, Freud considers the compulsion to repeat and differentiates it from the pleasure principle which seeks to expel unnecessary tension and restore homeostasis. He can perceive no homeostatic gain in the repetitive dreams of those traumatised by war. Before an experience can be identified as pleasurable or non-pleasurable, it must first be assimilated and parcelled up by cathexis – cathexis being apprehended as a form of mental digestion which appropriates raw experience, preparing it for utility or expulsion. When the subject is grossly over-stimulated by an experience – for example, when the unprepared subject has suffered an unexpected fright – that experience, violently *inconsistent* with the subject's expectation, amounts to a sudden psychical wound without any physical manifestation to accompany it (for a physical manifestation such as an amputation might focus the trauma and eventually heal it). The dreaming which performs the digestive task of responding to this experience (cathexis) is compelled to repeat it on numerous occasions in an attempt to keep parcelling up the massive dose of excess simulation which initially flooded the system.

Here an attempt is being made to restore the organism to its condition prior to the shock. It shows the natural elasticity of the organism, which endeavours to return it to the state it was in before the psychical wounding: and it can be interpreted as an urge to return to an earlier state of being - eventually to some sort of primeval inertia. Freud contrasts this death instinct with the sex drive which he calls a life instinct, which ostensibly struggles against the death instinct, but he detects an attempt to restore a previous state of things even in sexuality on the hypothesis that living substance at the time of its coming into life was torn apart into small particles, which have ever since endeavoured to reunite through the sexual conjunction. Thus even the pleasure principle has the death instinct beyond it, and, for Freud, 'the aim of all life is death'.

Freud equates this drive to return to a previous state as a drive towards our ultimate state, since everything dies for internal reasons. But it is here that his argument goes awry. Our language may not differentiate between ante-life and after-life, but nevertheless a difference is evident. It is true that a repetitive reverberation may shake a mechanism apart, just as a bridge may be destroyed by torsion in a high wind, and in this sense we may all eventually be destroyed by the wear and tear of our own repetitions. Even so, a compulsion to return to a previous state of things is quite different to an urge to disintegrate, and we know, from the theory of "the selfish gene", put forward by John Maynard Smith as well as Richard Dawkins, that while a decrepit mare may instinctually sacrifice herself to the pursuing wolves, this is to ensure the survival of the herd. The gene values the species over the individual. Thus the pleasure principle may be overridden by a genetic instinct rather than by a death instinct, even among lemmings - the mass sacrificing themselves in order that the few remaining alive may find sufficient sustenance to survive. Anyhow recent research suggests that the lemmings' "suicide" is a myth.

Freud is right, though, to insist on the existence of a drive to restore things to a previous state, characterised by the compulsion to repeat. Perhaps this should be called a *back instinct* rather than a *death instinct*. Borrowing terms from mechanised vehicles we might then be able to speak of *forward drives* and *reverse drives* rather than of life and death instincts.

We can perceive the drive to return in both additive and subtractive performance structures, since the one keeps 'returning' to its initial action while the other keeps 'returning' to its ultimate action. Presumably, there's a forwardness about the additive, since it contributes more and more actions. But does the obligation of the subtractive to contribute less and less make it in any way a reversal? Despite appearances, both push on through time.

There is as much repetition in an additive sequence as there is in a subtractive one, but the former moves from repetition towards inconsistency, while the latter moves from inconsistency towards repetition. We can detect the reverse drive in the necessity for most repetitions to incorporate their reversal if they are to repeat at all, but then they must move forwards just as often. This suggests one drive: a *forward and reverse* drive, an AC/DC instinct, thrusting us forwards over our thresholds and then pulling us back again, an oscillating action Lacan associates with pleasurable feelings – as opposed to being either fully in or fully out.

As performer/witnesses we will notice that in additive sequences of action, the initial action always seems more significant than any subsequent action. Its significance may be caused simply by the fact that it repeats more often than subsequent actions, but it seems to us more than that, for here again we experience an effect of magnification as powerful as that induced by adrenaline. It is the significance of the 'first throw', the first card laid down, the first mark on the canvas. All subsequent actions grow out of it. In that dawning moment of the first action the spatial environment of the performance is made apparent to us, together with the objects (*o*) visible on that space, so that first action crystallises the event, announces it and provides its key. The actions that follow tend to do so in a diminishing order of significance. Significance is only restored by an action on some scale quite other to those of the previous actions or after a "quiescent" period of stillness. This is the moment for inconsistency to bring about its surprise.

I have already remarked that the timespan for a performance is a microcosm model for life, and that life's stages find their equivalents in the successive stages of a performance (*see page 146*). It is also the case that the significance of the initial action in an additive sequence can be equated with the significance of childhood memories, and with the drastic effect of experience before speech, an effect exerted upon us, creating a memory which we cannot articulate, an experience about which we cannot speak – recalling that phrase of Wittgenstein's advising us that we must pass over in silence that about which we cannot speak: a metaphysical effect, perhaps, but still a pressing reality.

Memory itself must work additively, first recalling early experience, and then overlaying that with later experience, and eventually having very little capacity to memorise fresh events. When memory starts to fail, though, a subtractive process occurs, starting with a diminution from the top of the sequence rather than from its inception, and therefore it is our earliest memories which persist the longest.

Addition *creates* the event - because it is an amalgam of repetition and inconsistency it partakes of inconsistency's power to create a history. Subtraction, on the other hand, relies on history. One can build an additive sequence out of nothing and then subtract it. One can subtract its units of action by starting to take away its initial units or by starting to take away its

When flour is showered from a sieve in the roof, performers in Station House Opera's *Black Works* erase floor-drawings while creating others. Antwerp Festival, 1991. Photographs: Cor Hageman.

concluding units or by subtracting units at random. What one cannot do is subtract from nothing. Thus subtraction can never occur at the start, for even were one to begin a performance by removing the objects on the space, this would not read as subtraction, rather it would read as a repetitive act of removal. Actions have to have accumulated before subtraction can occur. And then, finally, significance will accrue to the last unit of subtractive action, to the unit of action left at the end of the subtractive process. This is the significance of the conclusion, of last words and final outcomes - another magnification of time, and one which should be the most important of all, both to the performer and to the spectator of the show.

*   *   *   *

Space:

It is very often the case that performance art questions the single-sided view of proscenium arch theatre. In my introduction to *Elements of Performance Art*, I wrote:

> "Situations exist in the round. Any performance conceived for the proscenium arch presents a situation as a single surface .... (But) our view of the predicament depends upon our vantage point. If the performance space occupied a square mile hearing would be affected as drastically as vision... A new sort of performance must be considered for theatre in the round: a performance where the point of view of the spectator is an integral part of the drama, an integral part of the dance. (As if cubism were turned inside out.) Thus "main characters obscured by a crowd" might be a moment in the drama seen from one point of view at the same time as "main characters with a crowd in the background" might be that moment in the drama seen from the opposite point of view. One might visit the performance again, simply in order to change seats. There need not be any seats..."

Our diagram on *page 44* could easily be adjusted. The performance could be moved into the centre of the studio, and the curtains altered so that they formed a square around the performers and their objects (*o*). Now the Large Other of the Audience (**O**) would surround the performance. These days, the occupancy of the centre is common enough in performance art and in theatre. Note also the remarks on *Transference of Scale* on *page 137*, on *Transference of Place* on *page 140*, and on *Transferences of Dimension and Element* on *page 141*. Spatial possibilities are also discussed in relation to gravity on *page 116*.

Just as performance art requires some dislocation from the normality of the 'horizontal' theatre of narrative and acknowledgement, it requires a dislocation from the accepted notion of the set, and a dislocation from the central vanishing point concomitant with the view through a proscenium arch. Thus tables are as much for standing on as they are for sitting at - or they may be turned into towers or used as shields. The performer may place himself in the centre of his audience, or above his audience or below it - Vito Acconci masturbated beneath his audience, and David Alexander begins his performance buried beneath his audience's feet. Stelarc hovers high above his witnesses. In Station House Opera's *Black Works*, the principle point of focus is the floor which is used as a sort of enormous blackboard for large drawings which get erased by the performers as other large drawings get created.

In the performance space, one should feel that one's movements constitute a drawing on that space. If one walks diagonally across a space, the audience will read this as a diagonal line drawn across it. If one circles it, or frames it by turning at right-angles at each corner, these actions will read as linear descriptions. It is important therefore not to amble about the space - unless you wish to *project* a lack of clarity by ambling about - since this will read as a lack of clarity and may indeed interfere with a perception of the geometries laid down by the travelling actions of other performers. Inexperienced performers tend to move around too much. Stillness deepens on a fixed spot. And a fixed spot may be utilised as an anchoring reference to an entire set of travelling actions which move further away from it, around it or nearer to it.

Remember that a square performance space is actually a cube of space. New geometries become apparent if one decides never to touch the floor, or never to remove one's back from the floor. One might attempt to remain invisible on the space - hiding behind curtains or items of furniture. Ideally, one should be able to suspend oneself from the ceiling, to scale the walls or to disappear through the floor. However, a performance can feel 'caged-in' by too many spatial rules and the excessive use of barriers, meshes and masking-tape (*see Cathexis versus Simplicity - page 92*). Of course though, if you *want* to feel 'caged-in', rules may be the way to go about it.

This issue of space in performance is capable of expansion! Performances can take place in drawers, chests and wardrobes. Performers have taken over houses and invited their audience inside as their guests. In his book, *The Poetics of Space*, Gaston Bachelard discusses the psychological implications of the house from cellar to garret. He considers nests, shells and corners, and the effects of miniaturization - all of which may be of use to performers.

Miniaturization of the space is used to particular effect in the solo performances of Stuart Sherman - which often occur on the surface of the small table he removes from his suitcase and erects at the start of his 'spectacles'. His work reminds me of the now almost forgotten flea-circuses which used to be the marvel of every fair. When Sherman coughs above his objects it is God coughing above His world.

Interactive performance may require specific locales. Consider Orlan's use of the operating theatre or Claire Shillito's use of the hotel room.

Quite obviously, space needs to be appropriate to concept. But whereas conventional theatre may represent space – creating a stage-set which looks like a hotel-room, say – in Shillito's case, it is crucial to the effect of her work that the performance should take place in a real hotel room. For if performance deals with the reality of actions rather than their mere representation, then naturally it must deal with the reality of the spaces in which those actions occur.

Topographical considerations of psychical phenomena concern themselves with the whereabouts of those phenomena, and whether they may be located in the id, the ego or the super-ego. Freud also considers the mind in terms of a spatial metaphor when he likens analysis to excavation and considers the unconscious in the light of buildings now unearthed at Pompeii after many centuries of burial under the detritus of Vesuvius.

In 1982, I performed *Active Circles*, a piece devised by the Theatre of Mistakes on Lake Goongarrie, a dry lake some eight miles in diameter, in the desert of Western Australia:

> "...It's a performance The Theatre of Mistakes abandoned in 1977 because the company couldn't find a flat space in England large enough for it. It's like a game really, the performers forming two radii of a circle which can accelerate towards the centre or towards the perimeter - and when both radii form a single straight line, a new, larger circle can be started, with either end of the line-out as its pivot... In the long, hot summer of 1977 we did perform it on Hartley Wintney village green, which has a sizeable cricket-pitch... It had to be abandoned after 9 hours though, because the performers were beginning to circumnavigate the village during their circling - thus losing sight of each other..."
>
> (*Performance Magazine*, UK, No. 33)

> "...We go out to the lake for a last session of circling, with a seven-person line-out and no witnesses - I haven't seen humans other than our party since we got here, and I've only heard civilization in the far distance - the rare lorry on the road beyond the mines.... During this last session we get one wonderful vortex audible line" (the sound sent from performer to performer when the two radii form a new line on a circle rotating faster at its centre) "...What are we doing, out here in the wilderness, performing for ourselves alone, unable even to document the most exciting moments because all are engaged in the attempt? Is it art? I am reminded of Willa Cather's remarks in 'Death Comes for the Archbishop': *When they left the rock or tree or sand-dune that had sheltered them for the night, the Navajo was careful to obliterate every trace of their temporary occupation. He buried the embers of the fire and the remnants of food, unpiled any stones he had piled together, filled up the holes he had scooped in the sand.. Just as it was the white man's way to assert himself in any landscape, to change it, make it over a little (at least to leave some mark or memorial of his sojourn) it was the Indian's way to pass through a country without disturbing it, like fish through the water or birds through the air...*"
>
> (*Performance Magazine*, UK, No. 34)

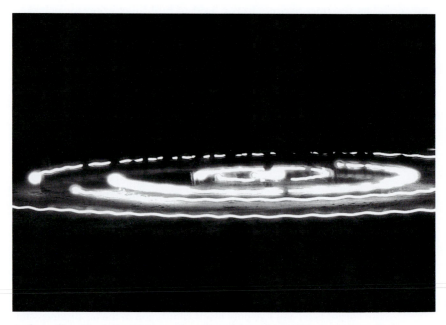

Anthony Howell's *Active Circles*, performed at night with portable gas-lamps on Lake
Goongarie, a dry lake in Western Australia, 1982. Photograph: Alan Vizents.

The Time and Space Workshop

1. Accumulative and Inverted Free Sessions

Performers start a free session by entering one at a time, and end it by coming off the space one at a time.

Next, the performers start a free session by all entering at the same time and each leaving the space, one at a time, during the performance. Then re-entering the performance space one at a time and finally finishing the performance at the same time.

2. Long Duration Site-Related Free Session

After preparation - to collect objects, clothing required, lighting which may be necessary - the performers choose a site and perform in it for the length of the day.

3. Speed and Contraction Exercise

A free session is performed slowly in a large space. Gradually the performance speeds up as the performance space grows smaller. When the space grows so small that all the performers find themselves in contact with each other, the piece ends.

Now the opposite is attempted. The performance begins in a constricted space with all the performers in contact with each other. They perform at speed, their actions gradually becoming slower as the space expands. The piece ends when the performers come into contact with the walls of the space or no longer remain within sight of each other.

4. Cubism Exercise

Performers create a performance which continually turns through ninety-degrees.

5. Audience Locations

Performers devise methods of working above their audience.

Performers devise methods of working below their audience.

Performers devise methods of working at a considerable distance from their audience.

Performers devise methods of working with the audience very close to them indeed.

6. Object Spaces/Stages

Create a performance inside, underneath or on top of an object. The performers may either share one object or perform in conjunction but in isolation, each inside, underneath or on top of their own object, or they may all utilise each other's objects.

7.   Miniature Performance

Create a performance for a very small area such as a table-top or a part of one's anatomy.

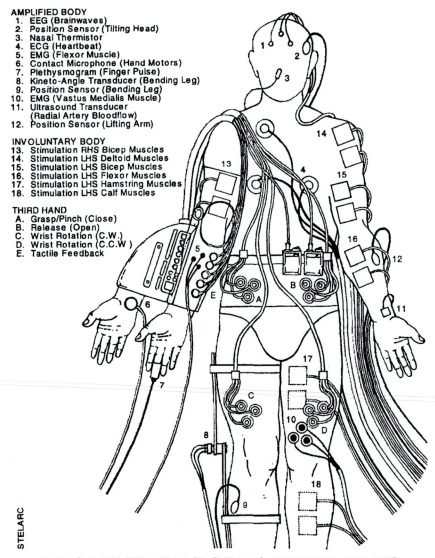

AMPLIFIED BODY
1. EEG (Brainwaves)
2. Position Sensor (Tilting Head)
3. Nasal Thermistor
4. ECG (Heartbeat)
5. EMG (Flexor Muscle)
6. Contact Microphone (Hand Motors)
7. Plethysmogram (Finger Pulse)
8. Kineto-Angle Transducer (Bending Leg)
9. Position Sensor (Bending Leg)
10. EMG (Vastus Medialis Muscle)
11. Ultrasound Transducer
    (Radial Artery Bloodflow)
12. Position Sensor (Lifting Arm)

INVOLUNTARY BODY
13. Stimulation RHS Bicep Muscles
14. Stimulation LHS Deltoid Muscles
15. Stimulation LHS Bicep Muscles
16. Stimulation LHS Flexor Muscles
17. Stimulation LHS Hamstring Muscles
18. Stimulation LHS Calf Muscles

THIRD HAND
A. Grasp/Pinch (Close)
B. Release (Open)
C. Wrist Rotation (C.W.)
D. Wrist Rotation (C.C.W.)
E. Tactile Feedback

STELARC

INVOLUNTARY BODY / THIRD HAND

Stelarc's technological extensions are wired to respond to his body's muscular contractions.

12

CATHEXES OF DESIRE
(*The Language of Performance*)

We are now in a position to utilise a comprehensive grammar of performance, understanding the psychical significance of our actions as well as their physical characteristics. We have our primary actions – stillness, repetition and inconsistency – and our secondary actions – acceleration and deceleration, addition and subtraction, together with the qualifying properties of overlayering. We understand the transferences, substitutions and reversals which may effect what we do, and we realise that these characteristics of what can be done can be manifested not only in action but also in sound, or in language, or in units fusing sound and action or language and action. We are also aware now that we can magnify the significance of our actions or diminish that significance by organising how those actions occur in time. What remains is to bind these abilities together into a coherent syntax – an effective vehicle for executing our performative desires in their entirety.

To do so, let us return to the notion of *Cathexis*, discussed earlier in relation to the primary actions. The appropriative property of cathexis allows experience to be digested. Cathexes bind stimuli in a psychical sense, parcelling-up these stimuli so that they may be identified by the pleasure principle and disposed of, and as such, they are psychical enzymes, breaking up experience and deconstructing it so that its conflicting components may be stored in appropriate files or ejected via the dream's appropriate channels.

Hypercathexis signifies alertness, a sort of mental salivation. We experience such alertness as a rush of adrenaline, as when we prepare for flight or fight. Interminable suspension in such a state debilitates the system. In performance terms, such alertness can be translated as a readiness to change, an awareness of triggers and a preparedness to react to them.

We have considered triggers for change in relation to the primaries. Now we need to bind primary and secondary actions, drives and desires, into a unified system of operable response, thus giving our performance language a working syntax.

To do so we will need to adjust our model, and it may be that for this advanced operation the initial analogy of colour theory as applied to action will no longer be of help to us. Instead of it, let us focus on a new triad of terms: *Speed, Difference and Development*.

Each of these terms exhibits polarities. On the axis of speed, we can move faster or slower – becoming utterly still at one extreme or moving "at the speed of light" at the other. On the axis of difference we can incline towards

repetition or towards inconsistency. On the axis of development we can construct our actions additively or diminish them subtractively.

Let us call these three axes the *Active Cathexes* of action, and our ability to qualify our movements by our positioning between their poles the *Qualifying Cathexes* of action – just as the verb is the "activator" of speech while the adverb qualifies it.

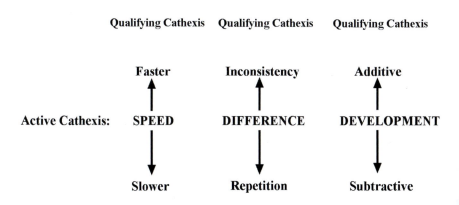

As an exercise, we might employ preordained triggers to switch between speed, difference or development but choose our adverbial cathexis by intuition.

It is difficult to hold more than three triggers in the head at the same time, which is why it may be appropriate to choose one's location on the scales of speed, difference and development intuitively.

Here is an example of how the above cathexes might be used:

Seeing an inconsistency is the trigger for a switch to the speed axis (though fast normal, slow, altering or still is chosen intuitively): seeing stillness is the trigger for a switch to the development axis (though whether one starts to add actions or subtract them is chosen intuitively): seeing an additive sequence is the trigger for a switch to the axis of difference (though whether one's actions become more inconsistent or more repetitive is chosen intuitively).

Two observations may be made now:

1. That a switch to another active cathexis may sometimes suspend the performer in the condition he was in on another axis. For instance, I am performing a repetition and I see an inconsistency and alter my speed but not my repetition. This is not the case, however, if next I see an additive sequence being performed, for now I might switch my repetition to an

additive build-up of actions, although my speed would now be unalterable – unless I had already chosen alteration of speed intuitively while on the axis of speed, in which case I would have to continue altering it.

2. That the triggers chosen will be constructed from the vocabulary of action possibilities already identified by the above cathexes. For while one might choose a door slamming as one's trigger for a change of action, that slam of the door will still be defined within the grammar – in all likelihood either as an inconsistency or as a repetition.

Observation 1. suggests that in many cases the locking-on of one cathexis causes the suspension of another. Observation 2. suggests that systems of recognition and response exhibit homeostasis in that their terms are sufficient unto themselves, that the application of one trigger is the signal for another, and that trigger-systems do not lie outside action: they are actually the actions in themselves.

"Seeing" was the term used to simplify these issues. But in the reality of a performance, an additive action may be heard, an inconsistent action may be felt, a repetitive action may be tasted. And therefore any sort of sensory impression may be utilised as a trigger, just as that trigger may be activated by any item of action and not simply by those cited as examples.

A fourth trigger might be required to complete the above system of responses. This would be a trigger which designated an adverbial shift while *remaining on the same axis* – i.e. a shift from fast to slow, or from repetitive to inconsistent, or from additive to subtractive action.

Further Appropriations

The syntactical possibilities so far described may be sufficient for our system, but of course there are other systems, other ways of grasping the performance. One might appropriate it by first identifying its *gestalt* – getting an overall view of it. For instance, is the performance sculptural or expulsive?

If it is sculptural, then throughout the piece its homeostasis will remain intact: there will be no additions from outside the performance space, no destructions or ejections on the space. Objects may be moved around, but essentially what is there at the beginning of the performance will be there at the end of the performance. The performance itself will come full circle, so that the arrangement of objects and performers at the start will be the same as the arrangement of objects and performers at the end of the performance.

If it is expulsive, then the homeostasis of the piece may be altered or destroyed during the performance. Objects may get broken, fluids may get spilt, food may get eaten or waste-products expelled. Performers may get hurt or hurt themselves, so that they end up in a different state to the state

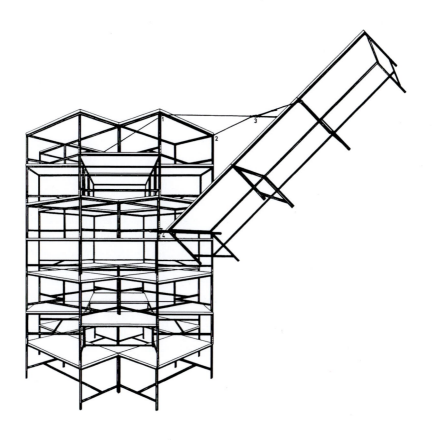

BY ANTHONY HOWELL

CONNECTION SYSTEM AND TACKLE DESIGN BY PETER RASMUSSEN
DRAWN BY DILYS BIDEWELL

THE TOWER

UPPER CHUTE PERSPECTIVE

Sculptural performance: a diagram for *The Tower* by Anthony Howell.

they were in at the start of the performance. Changes of state will occur, and the conclusion of the piece will be fundamentally different to its beginning.

Most performances by the Theatre of Mistakes were sculptural, as are the performances of Gilbert and George. My own table-moves are sculptural. Most performances by André Stitt are expulsive, as are the performances of Franko B and Orlan.

One might devise triggers to switch between various *specific types* of action, since, apart from its immobile, repetitive or inconsistent nature, action may be:

1. *Fixed or Transportive*: that is, it can stay in the same spot or it can move the performer from one place to another – as do the walk, the run, the jump, the crawl etc.

2. *Supported or Supportive*: that is, the performer can be supported by something or someone, or he or she may support some object or performer. One may be supported by a chair or a bed or by another performer, or one's hand can support one's chin, or one's knees can support one's arms while one sits on a chair.

Naturally actions can be both *transportive* and *supportive*: one can carry or drag another performer, or be supported by wires while travelling through the air. Equally, actions can be *Fixed* and *Supporting* – or combine in any other way.

3. *Gestural* actions constitute another type: actions which have no function, often performed by unemployed limbs – the tapping foot, the clenching and unclenching hand. Sometimes such actions seem to evade description since they are not clearly resolved, but more often they signify some emotional state – anger, impatience or boredom. Then there are also *linguistic* gestures – which clearly mean something: the wave, the handshake, the nod or shake of the head, the warning finger etc. Sometimes these gestures may be involuntary – the yawn, for instance, or the shiver.

4. *Task Oriented* actions comprise the largest group. These are actions which achieve some result. They may be:

a. Exchanges – incorporating the simple transference of objects from one place or utensil to another – water poured from a flask into a cup, glasses taken off the nose and put into a case, one pair of shoes exchanged for another. And this class of actions must include transportations, exchanges or transferences of place.

b. Creations or Destructions – consider the making of a paper hat or the burning of a letter, or the construction and subsequent dismantling of a tower or a wall. Note also my remarks above concerning expulsive performances.

c. Miscellaneous task-oriented actions – often repetitive: scratchings, sweepings, brushings, washing etc, actions concerned with eating and grooming – chewing, for instance. Consider turning the pages of a book or looking for lice in someone's hair. The repetitive actions which transport one (walking, running, crawling etc) also figure here.

Thus an alternative system of triggers might cause the performer to switch from supportive action to gestural action, from a small repetitive task to a major exchange. Equally, the triggers for such changes of action might be brought about by responding to a destruction, say, or by responding to some specific linguistic gesture – such as the yawn *covered by the hand* – the action of the hand making the yawn's involuntary nature linguistic.

In performance terms, the great difficulty with cathexis is that one's systems of response can easily become too complicated. There are too many possibilities to choose from. Indeed, a multiplicity of choice can as easily lead to inaction as can a situation which seems to offer no choice at all. In order to preserve all one's options one may devise a system which demands too much thought – in which case one's performance becomes hesitant.

It's self-obvious that singularity is opposed to cathexis, as simplicity is opposed to elaboration. And in seeking the essential concept that might dynamize an action, refinement often produces a statement of that action in its simplest terms. Just because we can identify every single part of speech

The Maybe – Tilda Swinton asleep in a glass case – an example of the simple use of a single primary action (stillness) to create a performance. *The Maybe* was conceived and performed by Tilda Swinton in an installation created by Cornelia Parker at the Serpentine Gallery, 1996. Photograph: Hugo Glendinning.

grammatically, we are not obliged to utilise every part of speech in every one of our sentences – though such a rule might well produce an interesting text.

We have seen that a comprehensive system might require at least four triggers. But a good performance might require no more than one: a single trigger switching the action from one state to another. As already noted (*on page 92*), it might require none – one could simply remain fixed in stillness and be very effective indeed – Tilda Swinton sleeping provides an example. One could limit oneself to performing an additive sequence for the duration of the piece, ignoring all external stimuli. A performance which utilised the full diapason of possibilities would in all likelihood be a hotch-potch – incapable of development in any significant direction. Better then to perhaps set oneself no more than two responses and to give oneself no more than two options for the nature of one's actions. Even this may prove too complex. The key thing is to be immersed in one's actions, and to be guided by the homeostatic necessity of the work, rather than to be forever struggling with some unwieldy system.

Lacan maintains that the unconscious is structured like a language. Ultimately the language of performance should be treated as an unconscious. Indeed performance art might be defined as the *unconscious of theatre*, since its repetitions distance it from theatre's more constructed goal – which is to represent. In the arena constituted by this new art, response by intuition is just as important as the adoption of a deliberate mechanism. At this point it might be advisable to re-read the remarks of Theodor Reik on "the third ear" – which concluded my chapter on *Cathexes and Chaos (pages 89-95).*

The Germ of a Performance

Reik's sense of subliminal listening brings me to an important difference between performances. Put simply, the difference is this: a solo is radically different to any piece involving more than one performer.

In each other's company, on the space, performers may adopt triggers for their reactions, while still avoiding conventional, horizontalist acknowledgement of the other or others. Each may use the 'third ear' to listen to the performance and grasp its development. Naturally the solo is a more isolated affair, unless the performer takes his or her triggers from the audience.

This has a bearing on the germ of the performance. Equipped with a grammar and a vocabulary, any performer can create variations on any given action or event. The 'given' act may constitute the kernel, the instigating gist of the piece. In a free session involving several people, even in a duet, this germ of the action makes itself evident in the first minutes of the performance, perhaps in the first few seconds. One performer contributes a word, another contributes a phrase: someone else performs an intriguing movement. The unravelling of these events and their subsequent re-weaving, the way they are adopted and modified by others, provides enough material to work with – the performance already has a life. Certainly there will be surprises: catastrophes, even, may emerge – and loud cacophonies and serene silences will occur. All of these grow out of the germ created at the outset, and some law of 'eternal return' will keep the beginning reiterating itself in everything that subsequently comes about.

This may not be the case with a solo. In a solo, which can never be as reactive as a group performance – unless it is highly interactive – it may be necessary to prepare the germ. Great solo improvisers, like Min Tanaka of Japan, might disagree. But I think that a kernel of personal content, and even some rehearsal, may be more necessary to the soloist than it is to the performance artist working in a group.

This is an observation based on the felicities which emerge in free sessions involving very aware performers. Of course groups can and do rehearse, and can prepare their content prior to their performance. Most duets and groups have been highly rehearsed in recent years. The Theatre of Mistakes carried rehearsal to fairly obsessive lengths. But today I am intrigued by the notion of the audience as analyst, and it seems to me that groups provide their audience with a unique opportunity to witness the performative unconscious as it unfolds in front of their eyes. A rehearsed piece will be different every night, it is true. But the group free session should be capable of carrying this difference to the highest level of unpremeditated stimulation.

Punctuation

How do we punctuate a performance language?

When performing certain sequences of action, situations arise which require breaks. The simplest way of creating a break is through stillness. Almost all actions will be read more clearly if a pause is placed in between them. These may be pauses of one or two counts. After that, the pause becomes 'a stillness' – and constitutes an action in itself.

If that is not a problem, then the length of these breaks may fluctuate. For instance, they may be intuited, and perhaps depend on the emphasis one needs to place both on the action just performed and on the action about to be performed. Formally though, such gaps can be built upwards or downwards according to a system, as in *The Gaps Exercise* from *Elements of Performance Art*:

> Extend the duration of a sequence of units (of action or sound / language) by increasing the number of counts between each unit.

> Diminish the duration of a sequence of units (of action or sound / language) by decreasing the number of counts, between each unit.

Or:

Extend any sequence of regular gaps by increasing the number of action/speech/language units between each gap.

Diminish any sequence of regular gaps by decreasing the number of action/speech/language units between each gap.

Another method of punctuation is to adopt some interrupting action which one uses in between sequences of other actions. So just as one might stand up (pause), remove a jacket (pause), hang the jacket on a chair-back (pause), one could stand up and cough, remove the jacket and cough, hang the jacket on the chair and cough again.

Interruption actions are particularly useful when the sequence or method of building adopted requires a reversal. Say you are repeatedly performing a complex sequence which involves standing up, walking round your chair, taking off your jacket and hanging your jacket on the chair-back. Then you reverse these actions – taking your jacket from the chair-back, putting it on, walking round to the front of the chair and sitting down again. When repeated, an action is immediately followed by its reversal both at the conclusion and at the returned-to start of this sequence – either you hang your jacket on the chair-back and then immediately pick it up again, or you sit down and then immediately stand up again.

But the performance of an action immediately followed by its reversal reads as an artificial vacillation. The contrivance of your system is made all too apparent by the purposelessness of this hinge. However, if an interruption action is placed between the action and its reversal, some semblance of purpose camouflages the U-turn: so now, you stand up, walk round the chair, hang your jacket on the chair back, *blow your nose*, remove your jacket from the chair-back, walk back round the chair, sit down, *blow your nose*, stand up, walk around the chair...

Blowing your nose actually involves an action followed immediately by its reversal (as will a cough when you bring your hand to your mouth), but it is an action whose immediate reversal happens naturally in everyday behaviour, and so it serves as a viable interruption device. At least it allows you to remove your hands from your jacket before placing them back on it again. But remember to keep your handkerchief in a trouser pocket! Note also that at the kernel of the action there is in fact a non-reversible inconsistency – the actual clearance of the nostrils. The cough itself is a similar non-reversible inconsistency.

Taking off one's glasses, giving them a polish then returning them to the nose is an action followed by its reversal but punctuated by the repetitive, circling act of rubbing. It is a fairly complex action involving both the glasses and a handkerchief. As such it may be too complex to serve as an interruption action. Wiping one's nose with a finger, on the other hand, is almost too easy – and it may not enable you to remove both hands from the object utilised in the previous action which will be re-used during that action's reversal (i.e. the jacket hung on the chair-back). In psychical terms, interruption actions may well be employed to disguise compulsive repetitions – but then they become compulsive repetitions in themselves.

I realise that the interruption actions used as examples here have a certain masculine slant. Feminine interruption actions might involve the application of lipstick ("reapplying"), the adjustment of a strap, the patting of a curl – though of course women blow their noses and clean their glasses.

Obviously this opens up the issue of stereotypes. And the truth is that both sexes readily adopt the other's signs. In performance, however, stereotypical dress can be useful. For both males and females, stereotypical dress, together with its component objects, constitutes a specific uniform and a fine arsenal of usable objects. Still, men can dress as women and utilise the female arsenal, and women have no qualms about trousers. What is undeniable is that these stereotypical components come in handy when devising interruption actions to punctuate one's performance, since these components usually accompany the person of the performer. It follows from this that performing naked will call for a different vocabulary of interruptions, and indeed a different vocabulary of the actions one intends to use sequentially. I have mentioned earlier that I have found it useful to stipulate that the performer wear only that which he or she can find an active use for during the performance. Such a stipulation governed the choice of objects and of clothing in my performance *Homage to Roussel*.

Returning to the issue of punctuation. Our very nature may dictate the nature of the break, since our lives are themselves punctuated by the requirements of the drives. In performance these become our technical considerations. Thus a freeze may be timed by the punctuating need to urinate. A strenuous repetition will demand recovery time. In a performance called *Objects*, where I lift and carry an inert female from one location to another, my punctuation is to sit and mop my brow.

The Workshop on the Language of Performance (Advanced Cathexis)

1. Speed, Difference and Development Exercise

Performers choose preordained triggers to switch between speed, difference and development, but choose their qualifying cathexis by intuition.

2. Sculptural and Expulsive Performances

Performers are given a week to prepare solos, duets or trios - these may be either sculptural or expulsive.

3. Specific Alterations

Performers create additive solos which vary the specific types of action with each new addition -fixed and transportive, supporting and supportive, gestural and task-orientated actions should be utilised, and the task-orientated actions should include exchanges, creations, destructions and repetitive scratchings, sweepings, brushings etc. A variety of objects should be used in the carrying out of this exercise, and then the exercise should be repeated utilising only one object.

4. Solo Free Session

In front of an audience of the other performers in the workshop, each performer should perform a solo free session.

5. Freedom versus Rehearsal

Performers should divide into two groups. One group devises and rehearses a performance to be watched by the other group. The second group prepares for a free session and subsequently performs it in front of the first group. The differences between the two performances should then be debated. Another option is for both groups to perform in the same space at the same time.

6. Interruption actions

Each performer experiments with a sequence of actions which subsequently reverses before being repeated. He or she devises interruption actions to punctuate the 'hinges' of this sequence.

The use of heated quicklime creates stunning effects during Station House Opera's *Limelight*, Copenhagen, 1996. Photograph: Erik Sokkelund.

13
LOOKING AT LIGHT

The time has come for the Large Other we excluded, in order to create the performance, to be admitted into it via the gaze, now that we consider it ready to be seen. There will be a primitivism about what the Other sees. The performers 'grant an audience' as do Kings or Queens. The audience is ushered in, tamed by the atmosphere of the performance space. One of the signs of weak theatre is that it is too willing to accommodate its audience – to acknowledge it – and thus for its performers to become 'just like their audience'. A compère may invite a member of the audience onto the stage – pretending that any member of the audience is 'just like him', and as good as any performer. Usually the contrast between audience-member and performer causes the opposite effect – the volunteer seeming inept – a laughing-stock for the rest of the audience.

An accommodating 'demystification' such as this robs the performance of its intrigue, as one might expect it to do. In those demystified shows as are frequently concocted by television to solicit the phantom participation of its viewers, the stage is invariably bright, and the studio audience – a surrogate for the immaterial, networked audience – is usually well-lit also, so as to be visible to the gaze of the camera. The studio audience amounts to no more than a pseudo-audience – it's as if an actor should perform only to his *claque* (or a King only to his courtiers, even if they are dressed as shepherds).

When it retains its intrigue, its mystery, the arena of the performance enables the gaze of the Other, or society at large, to regress into primitivism. It is a primitivism which recognizes touching the ground as cheating, just as in certain forms of tag. Even the performance artist must take the word *play* seriously. The audience watches the performer at play – as royalty may be watched playing croquet: for play is, after all, the prerogative of royalty. Slaves are not at liberty to play, any more than adults are for most of the working week. Melanie Klein, the pioneer of child analysis, set great store by the playing of children, the observation of which provided the basis for her interpretation. Her biographer, Phyllis Grosskurth, describes how she came to attach such importance to play:

> "On one occasion Rita, then seven years old, blackened a piece of paper, tore it up, threw the scraps into a glass of water and, as if drinking from it, muttered under her breath 'dead woman.' Klein saw at that moment how revealing drawing, paper and water could be in the symbolic expression of anxiety. Rita, who disliked school intensely, had shown no interest in

drawing; but when Klein, on impulse, fetched her some of her own child's toys – cars, little figures, a train, some bricks – the girl immediately began to play, and from the various catastrophes to which she subjected the cars Klein interpreted that she had been engaged in some sort of sexual activity with another child at school. Rita became alarmed by this interpretation, but after the first onset of anxiety subsided into a state of relief.

This experience, supplemented by others, convinced Klein that it was essential to have small toys, nonmechanical, varying only in colour and size, and that the human figure should represent no particular profession. The very simplicity of the toys enabled the child to express a wide range of phantasy or evocation of actual experiences. The equipment she gradually began to assemble for each session consisted of wooden men and women in two sizes, cars, wheelbarrows, swings, trains, aeroplanes, animals, trees, bricks, houses, fences, paper, scissors, a knife, pencils, chalks or paints, balls and marbles, modelling clay, and string. In addition, the child could bring some of his own toys, although she preferred that he concentrate on those that were locked away in his own individual drawer."

(*Melanie Klein: a Biography*, page 101)

The list described is very like a list of props for one of Stuart Sherman's spectacles performed on the small table he takes out of his suitcase. It is through his play in a privileged space, the space beneath the gaze, that the performer and his objects become symbolically charged, just as the table-top where the child's toys are arranged and re-arranged becomes a symbolically charged arena for the child's analyst. In both spaces, the objects and the actions at play are there to be focused upon, invested in readability, subjected to the most intense degree of scrutiny.

Like some basic drive, such playing is conservative, i.e. unwilling to renounce the appetites of infancy; regressive and repetitive. But to the observer, the play of a performer can exert considerable fascination – a fascination similar to that of the analyst observing a child. Joan Rivière, another child analyst, made this observation in The International Journal of Psychoanalysis (page 376):

"Psychoanalysis is Freud's discovery of what goes on in the imagination of a child – and it still provokes opposition from us all; this 'childishness', these unconscious phantasies are abhorred and dreaded – and unwittingly longed for – by us even yet; and this is why even analysts still hesitate to probe these depths. But analysis has no concern with anything else, it is not concerned with the real world, nor with sickness nor health, nor virtue nor vice. It is concerned simply and solely with the imaginings of the childish mind, the phantasied pleasures and the dreaded retributions."

To my mind, these "phantasied pleasures and dreaded retributions" constitute the drama of our time, just as Freud's case-histories rank with the greatest fiction of the twentieth century. Performance art enables its audience to witness the enactment of our dreams and traumas, and to interpret our living imaginings as they occur. I have said earlier that performance art is the 'unconscious' of theatre. Dreams and traumas are the content of this unconscious, and the performer's art is to externalize these and enlarge them, so that they become available, ultimately, to the gaze of the Other.

As I have stated, this play is conservative, and, in our dream actions, our regressive and repetitive appetites "come into play". We are often less sympathetic, more cruel, in our dreams, than we are in everyday life. The wishes of the libido are expressed without the shackles of consciousness hobbling its impulses. The "Mystery-play" at the heart of a dream-like performance enables its active contenders to assume that uncanny state, particularly when their repetitive field utilises stillness and slowness. Participating via its own gaze, the audience identifies with the primitivism made manifest on that privileged space, sympathises with revenge or passion – or with actions which seem emblematic of such states – beyond its willingness to do so under the disciplined strictures of mature behaviour.

In my childhood I went for several years to a Kleinian analyst. For two sessions a week, I would play under the gaze of my interpreter. Later, but while still at school, I created a puppet theatre. The puppets were glove-puppets: my own hands brought about the plays. After a long training, I danced for a while with the Royal Ballet. The Royal Opera House was an exceptionally privileged space, for a performer, but being in the corps-de-ballet felt more like being enlisted in the army than it felt like play. I became a writer, playing with words, you might say, and then became a performance artist. Perhaps a Kleinian past influenced my choice of careers, and contributes even now to my notions concerning the essence of performance. At the same time, the discipline of the ballet was important. Disciplined play is my ideal, for these contradictory terms are not necessarily in conflict.

When I am in the audience, at a performance of some integrity, I am drawn out of myself by what I watch. The picture I see is in my eye, but I am not in the picture. My body is pacified by my watching. However, bits of me remain visible to me, though evident only on the margin of my consciousness: the edge of my nose, my knee, perhaps my hand. Partly seeing myself in this way, while looking out of myself, recalls the pre-mirror-stage, when an infant's vision of itself is still fragmented: the eyes gazing upwards from the cot, helpless, enclosed in a nest of extremities – toes, fingers, knees, perhaps the breast.

The act of remaining passive while watching thus induces a state akin to the pre-genital, pre-linguistic state in the observer, eliciting a preparedness to regress. Then the comparative darkness in which the audience often sits edges the observing gaze further into regression; and the observer becomes mere eyes and ears, lays aside that specular image which requires so much effort for its maintenance, and each iris widens to accommodate play, willing now to accept the dream before it as that beneath its own lid. The eye looks from darkness, as if asleep.

The darkness of the auditorium prepares for the performer an eye seeking the fulfilment of its wish, gratified by pools of colour and big voices. Compare any state of looking at light from a place of darkness with the depression of staring at darkness from a place of light; the darkness of a tunnel or of the shadow behind a dustbin observed in daylight. And yet this perceived dark is not everlastingly dull, for it consists of the muff of pleasure too, the gate to the forbidden. Even as we gaze at that illuminated by the magic lantern of the theatre, we seek out its shadowy places for inconsistencies and secrets. Light may attract us still, but the less seen the better, so far as our imagination is concerned. Consider the daughter of a publican sitting on the top stair in the private quarters of a public house, her chin in her hand, gazing at the light coming from the cracks around a closed door below. She listens to the noises caused by various unseen actions, and she imagines an adult world of festivity which will never be matched, later, by her own mature experience.

That the use of light enhances the mystery is obvious. As a young artist allied to conceptual realities, I used to revile lighting grids as the very instruments of theatricality: the spots and floods supported by the grid enabled an external source to render the performance fictive. The 'rig' reinforced pictorial clichés of drama.

In the early days of the happenings, those who pioneered performance art would often do actions in daylight, or in bright gallery spaces. Again, the urge was to demystify the presentation. Here, though, there was no wish to substitute for the mystery a fictitious, participatory farce, as in compèred television shows. The artists who created the happenings were after truth to action; action stripped of anthropomorphic, metaphorical or melodramatic significance. If there ever was participation, it was genuine involvement, as in Carolee Schneemann's *Meat Joy* performances when the audience would be invited to perform nude – or practically so – and in close body contact, with the artist and with each other.

Action perceived as action: Stuart Brisley simply digging a hole for the duration of a "Documenta" show: Ulay and Marina Abramovic driving a truck which leaked oil round and round in a circle until a perfect circle of oil was left on the paved square below the Museum of Modern Art in Paris, during a Paris Biennale. The heyday of such daylight actions coincided with the period when the art world was preoccupied with minimal concept art.

In those days one researched into lights one could carry oneself – so that the light could become an integral part of the performance, incorporated into its homeostasis; a genuine component of the living sculpture the performance was intended to be. Candles were used (too often), torches, and camping-gas cartridge lamps. I remember Annabel Nicholson suspending a bonfire from a sort of cauldron, at the Acme Gallery. There was also an interest in lights one could operate oneself. searchlights, and pull-switch overheads. The light was therefore intrinsic to the performance, not projected onto the performance from outside it. Thus was expressed a general antipathy to the theatre. The performance artist used objects; and spoke of equipment, not props. The light source was another object – turning it up, rotating it, transporting it and extinguishing it – these actions were all part of the performance.

Visually inclined students often have an image of what their performance will look like, but can think of no action to go with it. Remember that the action can simply be the construction of that image. You are dangling by your ankle from a beam, half-buried in shredded paper, against a backdrop of sellotaped newspapers. All your actions require preparations. These preparations can constitute the performance. If there is any development of the piece, it is likely to occur while such preparations are taking place. Usually the lighting of a piece is part of that preparatory process.

Light, fire, heat: these can all be treated as sculptural elements – as ice can be, or steam, or water. And the way the image of your performance is put together through a process of construction rather than a process of depiction, reinforces the fact that performance, unlike theatre, has more to do with sculpture than with painting. The proscenium arch favoured by conventional theatre is very similar to the frame of a picture, and the narrative nature of the dramatic text enables a scene to be depicted within that frame. In contrast to this, performance art breaks down the image into those components required to build it, eliciting, through this process, a sequence of actions which, naturally, occurs in time. Performance, therefore, can be considered a form of time-based sculpture.

No one should underestimate the influence of sculpture on the development of performance art. Sculpture encouraged a materiality to emerge concerning the elements employed. Its thinking taught the performer to consider the action of his actions, i.e. the effect of his actions upon his privileged object: how the ice or the wax melted, how the honey dripped, how the furniture broke or floated. Sculpture attuned the performer to material changes of state. Light is one such material.

But electricity remains a problematic material. The performer may experience an aversion to cables and leads trammelling the performance space. These restrict the action, and their connections may prohibit the use of water or fire. On the other hand, electricity enables the performers to use a new range of physical objects on the space – objects such as standard lamps, or hoovers, or key items of technology – video monitors, slide projectors etc. But whether actually located on the space or projected onto it from an external source, electricity remains an element pumped into the performance from outside. Its source is other than the performance. The National Grid distributes it.

However, if we are not to be left with darkness or daylight as the only options other than torches or gas lamps, we must come to some entente with electricity. As a potentially lethal material, it was crucial to certain performances by Chris Burden when he gave the spectator the option for an action which would electrocute the performer. A strategy for utilising electricity as a source of illumination might be to associate the electric light with the gaze of the Other, the Large Other (**O**) out there, in the auditorium, who can now see us, since we have drawn aside the curtain which lent our preparations privacy, having decided at last upon the ethos of our performance, whether that be an entirely rehearsed structure, a one-off event or some improvised manifestation. For what is revealed by the lights equates with the viewpoint of society at large and the language inherent to it which encloses us and interprets our performance.

By observing it, the light which is the gaze of the Other also shapes our play, since our performance of that is always the wish of the Other. The light is that looking, which defines us, but which is ultimately shaped by our obstruction of it. It's as if the bath-water had more solidity than the figure submerged in it – indeed, as if the figure itself were the liquid, since the performance is protean, changing its shape through time. As performers we make a space, but are shaped by what we displace.

Corresponding to the gaze, projected light may beam on the performers, and thus the performers obstruct it both with their own bodies and with their objects: they are the screen upon which it falls, and so they're revealed by their shields, and, by allowing it to reveal at least that much of them, they acknowledge it. But this acknowledgement hides what lies behind it.

The process of a star passing in front of another star and hiding it is called occultation. Every night the moon occults several stars, which disappear from our view. In the same way, a performer can be occulted by a wardrobe passing between him or her and the source of light. Both lighting and looking see only the surface presented to their projection, and so they are both intimately connected with what gets hidden from that point of view, that is, what gets occulted. The occult is associated with magic, and occultation influences our horoscopes. In these the eye is our birth bestowing upon each of us a particular point of view, apparent only at that moment.

Any single source of light creates a more distinct shadow than that generated by several simultaneous sources. We might talk about conflicts of light, lights fighting against each other's shadows, mutually weakening each others' distinction. The spotlight pins the performer down, as if he were a specimen in a butterfly cabinet: the footlight foreshortens him, and stares up his nostrils, aggrandizing him even so: the backlight makes a silhouette of him, or gives him a halo. The gaslamp is a pool, however, rather than a gaze – similar to the embers of a fire, which may be gazed into, but does no gazing out.

Lacan talks of the seer's shoot – we are squirted by another's gaze. The visible performers depend on that which places them under the gaze of the seer. They are squirted with light as he squirts them with his gaze.

What the darkness does for the audience is to lessen self-consciousness. No one can look at them looking. In everyday dealings, I see from one point while I'm looked at from several sides. The fixture of the theatre seat locks the direction of the gaze when all else but the stage is steeped in darkness. Breaking such a convention causes problems for "theatre in the round", as it does for "performance in the square". The audience can see the performers from all sides, but at the same time, they can be seen themselves, not only by the performers but also by other members of the audience. This makes the audience self-conscious, and its capacity to regress gets arrested.

"Mystery", "miracle", "passion" – all these words have preceded the word "play" when definitions have been sought for the religious theatre of the middle-ages. Consider, then, that the eye is the nest of the gaze; and, when nested in darkness, while falling, or shooting, onto the stage, it may register a mystery amounting to a miracle. That mystery is felt as a practically physical sensation. It is one which gives the audience goose-bumps. How is it that the eye may observe characters so caught up in their drama that they do not acknowledge the gaze of the Other, "actors" for whom the Other is invisible? This is the mystery which lies at the heart of Colderidge's notion of *the suspension of disbelief*, a trick which turns the entire audience into one "Cyclopean" voyeur - since the initial fiction, about which it is passionate, is that it "cannot" be seen by the players. These mysterious individuals may not even acknowledge the gaze of some other "on stage" unless that other happens to be their treasure, their privileged object. We are used to the everyday eye – it looks, and of course it is looked at. But here are beings whose eyes are looked at without showing any recognition of the fact.

Yet how important they are, these eyes. In everyday life, we read them first, before we glance at the genitals. And as we read, we are read. Not only does the gaze look, it shows. However, in a performance, under a lighting grid, the eyes of the audience cannot be seen, though the light blares at the performer. The light shows. And now a metaphor occurs: the flood becomes the view, and the spot becomes the gaze.

Lacan considers the voyeurism of Acteon spying on Diana as if it were a smell which arouses her nostrils by his presence. Perhaps the opposite of theatre in the round should be explored: the curtains parted no more than half way, or even less than that – *only the smell of seeing leaking through*. Members of the audience on the left would see more of what was going on to the right of the stage than members of the audience on the right, who would see more of what was going on to the left, while those at the ends of rows would see still further behind the curtains. This would disintegrate the all-seeing unity of the audience and place each in the position of an *isolated* voyeur, spying the action from the privacy of their own vantage point.

In terms of an art speaking an action language capable of making the unconscious evident, an audience of "Peeping Toms" might be intriguing to play to. For here, the Large Other would be peeping in at its unconscious self. Then, if some member of our audience happened to espy a performer engaged in *watching the action*, hidden by the curtain from all but that audience-member's gaze while witnessing the performance from an all-but-hidden vantage point, our audience member might recognise that he was now watching himself watching himself watching, or herself watching as the case might be.

Isn't this the first stage of a regressive series? – in itself a classical device, epitomized by the Greek chorus, and elaborated in Shakespeare when Hamlet puts on the play within the play – or when Bottom plays Pyramus – watched by other members of "the cast". Once a performer/witness is observed watching, any member of the audience may be recognised as the start of such a regressive series: looking at them looking at them looking. This is a condition that Magritte returned to again and again, emphasizing that occultation the condition necessitates – seeing only the back of one's own head.

At the start of *Homage to Morandi*, three performers enter and sit on chairs facing backstage at 45 degrees to the audience. After a pause, these performers clap in unison at the blank screen of the back wall. Then they begin the performance, returning to this "audience" position at the end of each of its acts.

Psychoanalysis would connect the regressive series to the relation of the conscious to the unconscious, and the unconscious to whatever lies below it: the audience watching the watchers of the play within the play. Privileged objects will appear to be at the heart of this, but of course they are inscribed on the first skin of the onion to be peeled away, just as much as at its heart.

Each layer is a screen or a veil, distinguished, perhaps by back lighting, from the layer behind it, and certainly requiring light to achieve its shadow relation to the next screen. The American theatre director Richard Foreman devised a play for a long, narrow room. This was called *Pandering to the Masses*, performed in 1975. The stage and audience area were only fourteen feet wide, but the stage was far longer. Roselee Goldberg describes it in her book on performance:

> " ...The stage itself was seventy-five feet deep, the first twenty feet being at floor level, the next thirty feet running at a steep rake, finally levelling off at about a six foot height from the remaining depth. Sliding walls entered from the side of the stage, bringing about a series of rapid alterations to the space. This specially constructed space determined the pictorial aspect of the work: objects and actors appeared in a series of stylized tableaux, compelling the audience to view each movement within the picture frame of the stage.
>
> These visual tableaux were accompanied by aural tableaux: sound blasting from surrounding stereo speakers. Foreman's overlaying of taped voices and sound with the action attempted to penetrate the consciousness of the audience – the voices that filled the stage with the author thinking aloud as it were. These clues to the intentions behind the work – presented within the work – were meant to trigger off similar unconscious questioning in the audience. In this way, the Theatre of Images gave considerable importance to the *psychology* of making art..."

> (*Performance: Live Art 1909 to the Present*, page 123)

I witnessed this performance, and, not crediting the reality of the stage, believed that Foreman was using mirrors in some ingenious way to give the appearance of impossible length: mirrors facing mirrors on the back of screens – reflecting greater depths than were actually there in the loft in which his piece was performed.

Clearly, I was deluded about these mirrors. However, the New York artist Dan Graham has utilised mirrors, to create the very opposite of a "theatrical" effect. Far from wishing his audience to lose their awareness of themselves, Graham has often imposed an uneasy, self-conscious state on them, in order to reduce the gap between them and the performer. His work comes from that modern tradition that would break down illusion and present things as they are. In a piece I saw at the ICA in London, in the mid-seventies, he placed a very large mirror directly in front of his audience, and proceeded to describe individuals among them, observing them in the mirror, discussing their choice of apparel, or his hypotheses as to their nature. The audience thus became integral to his performance, but in a more clinical way than is ever required by our compères.

Discussing the use of mirrors recalls the psychological stage to which this artifact gives its name – the mirror-stage – and its physical substitute in the theatre; the notion, illusion or reality of twins: the notion being when one actor assumes these binary roles on alternating appearances, the illusion being when an actor works with a mirror, the reality being the performing presences of actual twins, or two clowns working on either side of a mirror's empty frame. Plautus makes use of two of these devices in his wonderful farce, *Amphitryon (see also page 107)*: one actor alternates in the roles of Amphitryon and Zeus – who are never on stage at the same time, while a pair of twins take the roles of Hermes and Sosia – who do appear on stage together. The long tradition of mistaken identity in theatre stems from the mirroring notions twins inspire in us.

In terms of performative action, twins are two cards, one 'occulting' the other, in the infinite pack of a regressive series. They can, of course, be separated, so as to be seen in their entirety. However, in terms of their regard, their condition is similar to that in which only the backs of the heads can be seen: one twin is looking at the other, who in turn is looking at a twin. This is the condition of the performers in the *Mirror Exercise* described under Transference of Lead *(page 137)*, where the one following is only able to mirror that other who may be leading the action by looking at that performer. However, the leader must also look away, as if looking at a virtual leader in the line of sight.

Twins therefore are performer/witnesses of their own condition – watching as well as performing, and performing by watching, as does any member of an audience. If "identical", they may seek to break their condition by separation - for then perhaps each will cease to be regarded as a twin. Yet how will they ever evade a mind's eye view of their sibling or cease from a replication of the actions of their virtual triplet? Meanwhile, in the theatre, seduced by backlit silhouettes, trapped in the regressive series of painted wings and mirror images, each member of the audience may be twinned with an attendant, a watching bear, a member of the chorus, and so tiptoe onto the stage.

But now, in the darkness behind the lights, the audience is settling into its role, and performing being what it is, that It, or Other, which emerges when several are unified by all being able to see everything at the same time. To see everything still more, cubism turned its subjects around, presenting sides and backs to the view from the front. Unity of viewing constitutes a version of divinity: the audience becomes the all-seeing One.

If that unity was broken down when the notion of cubism suggested *theatre in the square* to the Theatre of Mistakes, and if self-consciousness thus permeated the audience – who could now see each other, being seated on all sides – nevertheless the arrangement brought closer contact between audience and performer without weakening the action. Meanwhile the mirror performances of Dan Graham brought about contact between the performer and the image of the audience, and encouraged the audience's scrutiny of its own image. Earlier, the People Show had placed their audience in cages located within the space. Later, the Mickery Theatre used mechanised seating to move raked banks of the audience into different configurations for viewing, shattering the unity of the audience still further; for different banks would watch different vignettes at the same time.

Ultimately, the performance cubism of the Theatre of Mistakes derived an ironic singularity of vantage point from the notion, of the *shausseite* – or "showing side" – which is often a condition of sculpture, even though the statue be sculpted in the round. Several of my own solo performances in the eighties, which evolved from my work with the Theatre of Mistakes, concerned furniture vignettes which were moved through right-angles repeatedly, rotating before an audience who only sat on one side.

And though it remains an entertaining concept, it is doubtful whether "Peeping Tom" theatre would put to rest self-awareness, given its individual vantage points behind the less-than-fully-drawn curtain. People would feel that they were not able to see properly. A solution might be to arrange the audience into four groups; each in front of a quarter-drawn curtain, each located near one corner of a four-sided space. Here the viewing constraint would be felt as equally limited from all vantage points.

Another possibility is to show the performance to one member of the audience at a time. This was pioneered by Fiona Templeton, herself an ex-member of the Theatre of Mistakes. As discussed earlier, in *You: The City*, her audience was fed individually through a long chain of performers – (see Transference of Place, *page 140*). Templeton's concept of a "theatre of privacy" evolved out of an all-night workshop, when each member of our group (there were seven of us then) chose a location in the farmhouse where we lived, or in its outhouses or fields, and, at that location, created a performance for each other member of the company in turn: thus each created one performance and experienced six on a one-to-one basis.

To return to more conventional conditions: whatever the arrangement, seating decisions are always intimately connected with those governing the lighting. And just as lights can be suspended above or set up below the performers – as with spots or footlights – so the seating can be raked above or set below the performance space. Looking down on something is different to looking up at something: the former suggests seniority and divinity, the latter suggests infancy and hero-worship. Looking down also evokes intimacy, the opening of presents, or that moment just before one blows out the candles on one's birthday cake – infancy attaining seniority as it blows. There is a greater all-seeingness about looking down on the action. When in "the gods" in an opera house (an apt name for the highest circle of the auditorium) one gets an eagle's eye view, and the main ground to the performance is the floor, rather than the backdrop. On the other hand, looking up at the action from the stalls increases the audience's sense of the presence of the performer, but always restricts the view somewhat: one cannot see the tops of tables, one cannot see the back of the stage. From this view-point, a member of the audience can feel small, inadequate and human, while the performer appears divine, larger than life, inhabitant of unseeable areas such as tabletops.

"The treasure of the signifiers" is a phrase used by Lacan to evoke the nexus of the unconscious. Thus the treasure of our concern, when looking down, might illuminate our faces, as in the paintings of Georges de la Tour or Joseph Wright of Derby. In such "school of light" paintings, the light source our gaze is directed at is a hidden component of the picture – screened by a palm or placed in a bowl. When this condition obtains, we evade the tyranny of the Other's gaze and the glare of the light flooding in from the audience or pin-pointing us with a spot from the watcher's point of view. Instead, lights are hidden in boxes, wardrobes and suitcases. Torches, candles and gas-lamps are used, and recently, in *Limelight* (1976), Station House Opera have heated quicklime. The resulting flare from that is dazzling but short-lived, and naturally the candle gutters and the gas-lamp putters out. A self-sufficient internal light-source is always "mortal". We are watching the embers glow – since it is always a dying light, you will note, if dependent on a tangible fuel or battery, though the space will remain clear of leads.

Is this also the case with our personal treasure of signifiers, our own privileged objects – that the light they emit, which fascinates, is always a dying light? Certainly, since this treasure is *repeatedly* illuminated by our fascination, our gaze into it is compelled by the 'death instinct' of the Freudians, that supposed reverse in us – that urge to return to a previous state. In one sense the treasure which draws our gaze to it *is* fading, since indubitably it concerns our early days and we are everyday further from these. On the other hand, since memory is created additively, ultimately we retain best what was remembered first. The object of our regression is forever further from us, but I believe that this impels us back in time more forcefully. It does not urge us towards that disintegration which lies in store for us – as Freud would have us believe.

Well, we inherit these treasures, just as we owe our lineaments to our parents; and we become aware of our parents' mortality as soon as we perceive our own, which we do as soon as we assume the mantle of language. Our unity of (pre-linguistic) expression fades as we assume this mantle, and, at the same time, our consciousness dawns upon us, and with it comes our sense of time and of time's passing. With language comes 'enlightenment' – but enlightenment is also loss of innocence and *knowledge destroys us* in that it makes us aware of our own mortality. Meanwhile the language is immortal, in the sense that it is inexhaustible, and about as ubiquitous as electricity.

When the full diapason of its effects is available, electricity constitutes a *language* for the stage, not a collection of signs. It is primarily descriptive. It informs us about that which deflects it and is both resonant and evocative. Meanwhile *practical light*, that is, light operating from within the performance space, often not electric, reveals itself as a privileged object, a personal treasure, being its own source – *object light*: whereas *electricity* is the light of the Large Other – *language light* – articulate about the shapes which it bathes in conjunction with the gaze of the audience, and pushing out from its source towards its future.

Ultimately, the practical, stage-located light of embers, candles and gas-lamps is 'nostalgic', of the past, encouraging the gaze to regress towards infancy – and a feeling is there that 'it won't last', that is, that inexorably even our sense of our childhood must fade as we become more mature. So poignantly do we sense this that ultimately it is our childhood which re-emerges in our senility, and so we come full circle, and once again we may concur with Freud that the urge to regress is indeed a 'death instinct', and one producing an inversion of the Christian ethic: that which comes first shall be last.

But all light is either source or deflection – and language light is utterly deflected, never a source so far as the audience is concerned. Many things deflect it, fluids as much as solids may do so: certain objects soak it up instead.

There is one condition where the light of electricity ceases to be the describing light of language. This is the condition which obtains when the electric light beam is directed from the stage at the audience. In performance terms, the source of such a light constitutes a 'blind spot'. Confrontational rock groups such as *Laibach* employ sequences of such powerful lights, connected by cables to the external circuit. Indeed the stage is a snaky area comprising wires and cables. This is an aberration. Language light employed as an object. The blind spot scrutinizes us, as we sit there. Now it is the audience which is subjected to the unremitting gaze of interrogation. We are dazzled by the stage, scrutinized by the spectacle. The beams strake the audience like searchlight beams. Lights, instruments and voices are all connected to the world outside the stage by massive doses of electricity.

At the heart of the aberration is the sense that here we have the Large Other (O) scrutinized by the Large Other Itself. A sort of mirroring of society by society. *Laibach* is a group which comes from Slovenia, and *Laibach* is the German name for the Slovenian capital, Ljubljana. Performances by *Laibach* are paradoxical. They present the audience with the strident message-hammering ambience of a totalitarian rally and accompany it with the war-mongering gestures we associate with dictators. Only the "over-the-topness" of their presentation implies that it is a critique – as exaggeration may disguise a contradictory feeling. In the present context of the Balkans, their work has proved to be a prophecy. Slavoj Zizek has written perceptively about *Laibach* in his book, *Metastases of Enjoyment*.

The blind spot is that which we cannot scrutinise. The intensity of its brightness blinds us if we are forced to look into it. Merely a prolonged glance at it leaves a stain on our retina which obscures part of whatever we look at next. But the unseeable is also the unmentionable. And there are also messages which deafen us and unbearable revelations. It was enlightenment which caused Oedipus to put out his eyes.

At other concerts the lighting may play over us, but the key ingredient is contrast – the audience kept in the dark, the stage intensely bright. At such concerts, the sound blinds us and the light deafens us. The vibration of the beat coerces us into regression, and the strength of the light ahead of us acts as a lure. Hysteria is experienced *en masse*. The humans on stage become extra visible, over-exposed. We are drawn to them – and, by identification, to our own narcissism – as moths are drawn to the flame.

Laibach performing in London, 1996. Dazzling light is projected from the stage onto the audience. Photograph: Milica Vukovic.

But when the blind spot bears down *on us*, we become the performers. We perform as *the herd*, as those under the beams of the searchlight in some inescapable compound. When this occurs at a *Laibach* concert there's a chilling irony about it, a detachment. We perform mass hysteria instead of being consumed by it. It provokes a fear we appreciate since after all we paid to experience it. Fright can cause trauma, but at the same time we will queue up to be frightened. Choice makes all the difference – it diffuses the threat to the system and translates it into pleasure. There is something in this of a dog's voluptuous grovelling when confronted by a larger animal. Menacingly present, but without becoming visible, the performer behind the spot is grilling his audience.

———————

The Workshop on Light

1. Darkness/Daylight Exercise

The performers hold a free session in the dark. Next they hold a free session out-doors and in daylight.

   Then an attempt may be made to perform the darkness free session out-doors and in daylight, and to perform the daylight free-session in the dark.

2. Single Light Source

Performers decide on a single light source – either external to the performance space or intrinsic to it. Each performer places an object – it could be an item of furniture – on the space.

   There is no other action, other than the placing of such objects, the adjustment of their position or their removal. The presence of each object is allowed to deepen before its position is altered or any other object is added or removed.

3. Sculptural Light Exercise

A performance is created which only uses lights intrinsic to the performance space (no external source of light). No cable-connected electricity should be used. Performers may carry the source of light on their own persons.

4. Lighting Free Session

One performer remains off-stage, adjusting the lights, while the others perform a free session – or each performer adjusts the lights once during a free session.

5. Confrontational Light

A performance is devised in which the lights are directed at the audience: that audience may be an audience of one.

6. Hidden Audience

Performers devise a piece which is watched by an audience that cannot be seen. This may require that the performance is watched through a keyhole or through a telescope or via a video monitor.

Suddenly, out of the darkness, a rocking-chair bursts into flames ... in Martin Burton's *Deconstruction Symphony*, Avignon Festival, France, 1993.

14
PRESENCE OR PUPPETEERING

There is the presence of the cobra; an aggrandizement of its being – designed to fascinate and finally to destroy the object of its gaze. Then there is the Navajo's ability to be there without being seen, to move with leaving a trace, or to crouch, immobile in the undergrowth. To eat without being eaten oneself necessitates an aesthetic of invisibility. Many animals marry their background and seem to blend into the distance by dint of their countershading or by their resemblance to natural objects of no food-interest to their enemies.

There is the presence of a performer like Rudolf Nureyev: the classical dancer who has learned how to 'make a presence' – and how to expand the chest, not outwards, but sideways, as the arm moves first upwards and then outwards, opening the body and the gaze to the audience. His entire frame now seems elevated by the breath inhaled. The nostrils flare; and the eyes' strength of regard recalls that of African tribesmen presenting themselves as objects of sex-appeal to the women: haughty demeanour, flashing teeth, piercing eyes.

There is also, though, the anti-presence of the Bunraku puppeteers of Japan, who remain quite visible when they manipulate their small figures of samurai and courtesans, which they carry through intense dramas of revenge or suicide. The Bunraku puppeteer wears a black costume: sometimes a hood covers his face. His is an ability to be there without being seen.

"In what we see, much inscribes itself in the picture which is not of the picture," says Lacan. Much of the picture may also be edited out. As the action of the Bunraku play intensifies, the puppeteers fade away, and we see only the courtesan falling on her lover's sword.

All regard is self-regard, the puppeteer might say. Narcissus is crucified by his own simulacra – he is the clown stuck to another in the frame emptied of reflective glass.

But a creature must adapt to its environment. Say your performance group is using an additive system of entrances to build a piece, and there are already three performers working on the space. It is now your turn to enter the action. Do you disrupt what they are doing by your own violent presence, or do you adapt to it, meekly becoming invisible within it? Is to disrupt simply another adaption, as the tiger adapts to the presence of his prey by going into a preparatory crouch?

Camouflaging oneself may not be a matter of embracing absolutes: instead, a sort of democracy may obtain. For if one can only be hidden by standing with one's back to the audience against a black backdrop, one will show up markedly against any other background and in any other posture. Effective camouflage may require one to become mottled within the variegated colours, textures, actions of the performance; or you may have to resort to some sort of camouflage by display, painting onto yourself an eye larger than that which is stalking you.

Camouflage by display demands that you hide by your presence. But now consider the presence of the striptease artist. Any lure must involve the establishment of 'what you want' within the condition of 'what you can't have.' The 'can't have' part increases the desire. Thus the attraction of the lure increases as you pull the noticeable thing *away* from the cat, or as the fisherman's "fly" drifts downstream. Fear of loss increases desire. However, according to Lacan, the retreat of the lure also identifies the offer. It is as if one were saying, 'Look, I could be offering you what you can't have.' This implies that it could be more alluring to begin naked, and to start dressing, since to undress ultimately leads to a state of demystification which can result in an anti-climax.

What might therefore be achieved by increased revelation under diminishing light?

Let us return to the cobra. Intimidation, which is the hood's business, concerns that overvaluation a subject always tries to attain by his appearance. But an overvaluation of what? Unlike cobras, street musicians do better by appearing pathetic. An old man used to go busking with a violin held together by a rubber-band. He was more successful than the young man with the "stainless" steel guitar. So perhaps it's wise to arrive at some overvaluation of an advantageous aspect, so long as you can identify where your advantages lie. Perhaps it's unwise: overvaluation implies and indeed reads as lack of confidence in that advantage. Thus the grand manner of one performer may prove convincing only as a humourous expression of pomposity.

Lacan believed that the painter might wish to take over your gaze, or wish you to lay down your gaze before his vision. But surely we must distinguish between one canvas and another. Where the nervous strength incorporated into the brush-strokes suggests a strong emotional expression – as in a Pollock or a violent Picasso – the canvas may well 'stare' at you. But what of some receding Appollonian scene, rendered by a Wilson or a Claude? Here surely the eye of the spectator is invited to penetrate the vista laid out before it.

The intrigue of *trompe l'oeil* suggests the lure, and so is much favoured by Lacan, since it suits his theories: but these hardly accommodate the deliberate crudity of Basquiat, whose ribald marks deliver a mocking commentary on all signs and on figuration itself. The presences of paintings differ: so too do the presences of actors and performers.

An actor may wish to be looked at, especially as he delivers his lines; and if he is some grandee, he may wish to be admired for his costume even while he stands listening to some plaintive address. On the other hand, a performer may wish to appear as transparent as some variable animal confounding its predator by its non-appearance. He may desire to become only the 'ghost in the machine' – activating the performance without asserting an emphasised, human presence which might interfere with the homeostasis of the action.

Martin Burton's performances occur mainly in the dark: objects drop from heights, vignettes suddenly occur which may contain no human presence – briefly there is a rocking-chair before our eyes, and it is rocking though no one sits there. Later, in a piece entitled *Deconstruction Symphony*, it may reappear from out the darkness – this time in flames. Here the object constitutes the performer, while the performers are 'stage-hands', and thus never seen. Like the Bunraku puppeteer, Stuart Sherman may ask his performers to lay down their gaze, which otherwise might sweep outwards to embrace the auditorium. Instead, he instructs them to lower their eyes, without emphatically casting their gaze down to the floor, but basically so as to adopt a neutral presence. Their deferred gaze deflects the audience's gaze down onto the objects they use.

Stuart Sherman's performers are instructed not to use their gaze – in *Hamlet*, Mickery Theatre, 1979. Photograph: Bob Van Dantzig.

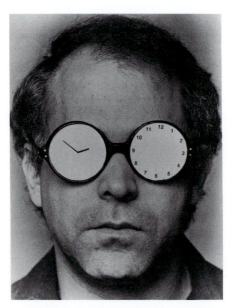

The gaze of Stuart Sherman: from his 13th Spectacle, *Time* – premiered at The Theatre for the New City, New York, 1983. Photograph: Nat Tileston.

The gaze engaged: Glenys Johnson addresses another performer with her eyes as well as her mouth in *Going* by the Theatre of Mistakes, F.I.A.C., Paris, 1977. Photograph: Kirk Winslow.

In this way the performers come to terms with their roles as the manipulators of these privileged objects that show themselves to the audience via their manipulators' actions. Sherman's work concentrates the performer's ability to focus the audience's attention on what he wishes them to watch. He may wear opaque spectacles on his eyes, so that his eyes become small circular pictures – objects to look at rather than objects which look.

Conversely, many actors and performers wish to engage the Other with their gaze, to survey the audience and to command its attention. But then it is their eyes which demand to be looked at.

In *Going*, one member of the Theatre of Mistakes was watched intensely by the others, in order that his or her actions might be copied as accurately as possible. Very soon, one performer began to copy the previous actions of the first; and later the scene which then developed between the instigator of the action and his first *doppelganger* was copied accurately by another pair of performers. In this piece, the gaze was similar to the beam of a laser – rebounding off one surface only to intensify as it rebounded off another. The five person performance created a sort of molecule of the gaze, with each performer under the scrutiny of another.

A prototype production of *Going*, utilizing the same structure but admitting of improvised movement (which only became rehearsed movement after the piece was re-named) was called *Homage to Pietro Longhi*. Take a look at the work of this wonderful Venetian genre painter who specialized in conversation-pieces similar to, but more refined and less satirical than Hogarth's. The eyes of the figures in his paintings are almost invariably directed at another figure within the box-like space he usually depicts. It is only the main character, the lady who is the centre of attention, who sometimes looks out at her audience. His paintings were often inspired by Goldoni's comedies of convention – and the lady's outgoing gaze is the outcome of all those gazes which concentrate on her, and of all those gazes which concentrate on those who gaze upon her. Many of the figures wear masks; and sometimes the masks are turned away from the faces of their wearers, as if they were decoys, harbouring the gaze of vacuity or deceit.

Attention can be held by the gaze and also by our ability to switch from one mode of performing to another, to "turn on a button" from anger to humour, as it might be, in conventional theatre, or from slow repetition to sudden inconsistency, as it might be, in performance art. If performance artists concern themselves with being rather than acting, then what is this ability to switch from one state to another, is it necessary, and can it ever be authentic in performance terms?

If it seems inauthentic and unnecessary, then the performance artist is stuck with one consistent mode of being, the one which constitutes that artist's 'identity'. However, without having recourse to acting, the performer might consider the notion of the 'alter-ego'. Every one of us contains the antithesis to their own personality. Judge Schreber felt that the light of God shone fondly on him when he dressed in female finery and posed in front of the mirror. His public life was a life of stern decision, responsibility, firmness and conviction. How pleasant to be lax and indecisive, giddy (as a female was conceived to be in the Victorian age), irresponsible, weak and uncertain – (see Freud's "Psycho-Analytic Notes upon an Autobiographical Case of Paranoia" in his *Collected Papers*).

This points to the need for a good grasp of the cathexes or the triggers which may prompt one's switch from ego to alter-ego. But ego and alter-ego hardly exist in some sacrosanct state of identity unaffected by any framework. For the performance artist, the framework is supplied by the particularity of the piece which is being performed. So a grasp of the cathexes which govern the piece is equally important. The audience will respond to our ability to respond – albeit, in performance, as opposed to theatre, this response concerns the conceptual plan both of the piece and of each individual performer rather than some normalising 'acknowledgement' of the other. It might be necessary to switch from method presence to puppet manipulation, according to some pre-considered plan for one's responses. 'Normality' might suddenly be switched on, and then as suddenly switched off, or, conversely, gradually subtracted.

In the more conventional terms of theatre, the comparison of presence with puppeteering amounts to an old chestnut which admits of no resolution. Should the actor ingest the sacrament of his character and become that character? – as Stanislavsky would ordain, who describes the metamorphosis of the actor into the role in his book on the theatre, *An Actor Prepares*. If he does so successfully, he will breathe in that character's nature and breathe out that character's presence, exhaling it onto, or into, the audience. This is achieved by a total identification with the character. If one is white, one must first change the colour of one's skin before one can play *Othello*. This is 'method acting'. In preparation for one's part, one eats only what the character would eat, and practises inhabiting the character's environment long before one goes out onto the stage. I have tried method acting while playing a peasant in *Giselle*. A sort of elation ensues, and one plays with a zest untarnished by envy of the principals. Ultimately there is no stage, only the forest of the Wilis. As propounded by Lee Strasberg in America in the fifties, method acting created a host of fine movie stars including Marlon Brando and Marilyn Monroe. Method acting is opposed to the ensemble acting of traditional theatre – where the actors perfect a comedy as if they were a string quintet. But note that the Russian performance artist Oleg Kulik has taken method acting to an outlandish extreme in his performance as *Pavlov's Dog* (Manifesta, Rotterdam 1996). Kulik identifies with (his notion of) the canine psyche, and has shown it by savaging certain curators in his audience and, more recently, copulating with a bitch. But isn't this an expression of his own emotional relationship to curators and to bitches? It was different when Simone Forti became a lizard or another animal in her performances during the seventies, for her movements were the result of a precise analysis of the movements used by the creature which were then adapted to meet the requirements of the human body – she did not merely empathise with the lizard.

On another continent, the oriental performer of the Kathakali dance is the puppeteer of himself. He wears an elaborate costume, which may have taken a very long time to get into, so that dressing for the part becomes a ritual in itself. The dancer wears a mask: his actions are utterly choreographed. He is the manipulating instrument within his externalized shell, the hand in the glove, as it were. His entire concentration is spent on producing those elaborate actions and expressions that affect the surface which is outside himself. He draws on a repertoire of time-honoured gestures, and, as with the Noh Theatre of Japan, the performance is a ceremony at which the actors officiate, re-enacting each 'sacred' stage of the drama's progress. The mask actor remains a conscious handler of the effigy which incorporates him. He is the motor, the genii within the ikon. His aesthetic is radically opposed to that of Stanislavsky and the method.

Gary Stevens is able to make a mask of his own face. His face is in itself a theatre, containing an entire repertory of expressions. As Stuart Sherman concentrates the focus by looking *at* the object, Stevens concentrates the focus by looking *out* of it. On stage there are always focal points to which we are directed by the performers – and such a point may be what the performer is looking at or the look on the face of the performer. But there are also conjurings – dependent upon some aspect not being noticed. Thus the unobserved may be as important as the observed. Miranda Payne, a performer with The Theatre of Mistakes and with the Station House Opera, used to employ a species of negative energy: a passivity in the midst of action which gradually gathered more attention to it than the contortions of her colleagues. And there's always a danger in improvisation that one person's loudness will inexorably engender a group crescendo – when it may prove a more interesting session if some performers swim against the current and become quieter when most are becoming louder.

Not only are there important matters such as conjurings which must go unobserved, there are also things which depend for their effect on being seen out of the corner of the eye or in diminishing light. Again we are in the territory of the retreating lure. It's as if we hid, in order to hypnotize our audience: for hiding always encourages the search – as when the villainous puppet hides by poking outside the booth, just as another demands of the children where he may be hiding, and as in the hysterical responses to some menacing approach on tiptoe during a pantomime. Then there is also the lure of the screen – its silhouettes, and the items which may be flipped over it. What is behind the unfolded screen in the intimate chamber - another provocative stocking?

Now think of some archetype villain, gloating over his victim, bathed in the glow of his victim's innocence or in the light from the footlights. Now his menace comes shitting out of his emphasized eyes. Worse is the glance of envy, especially when we envy most the other person's point of view, and particularly when we accuse them of never seeing things from our own point of view. This is the gaze epitomized by a lack – wanting the object privileged by our need, the local other of some other – a phallic object, a cloth, a cake or a turd. This lack closes in on the missing thing about all visual experience, the lack which must be there right in the midst of it: for the subject is presented as other than he is, and what one shows him is not what he wishes to see.

Perhaps the opposite to this Lacanian analysis of seeing in life occurs to seeing in theatre; for in theatre the subject of pretence *is* showing himself as he is, i.e. a pretender, and he – seeing nothing across the glare of light (which is the Other's gaze) – sees what he wishes to see, i.e an audience who have suspended their disbelief. Such mutual delusions, make theatre a pretty satisfactory experience so long as one agrees to some complicity in the pretence projected. Cinema, with its greater 'realism', has made this complicity more and more difficult to sustain where the stage is concerned.

In improvised performance art though, when each performer is either working vertically within himself or only through his own privileged objects, without acknowledgement of any others (for I am not talking about the closed circuit of acknowledgement and its appropriate, horizontal response), the *accidental* contact, when one person's performative itinerary coincides or clashes with another's, may well be perceived by the audience as no accident but as an *ideal union*; an outcome of a cause, an effect; for their envy reads coherence into these clashes. Such envy amounts to a desire to appropriate the meaning, though that meaning is more likely to reside in the unconscious of the watcher, and it is only through the performance that such a meaning has been allowed to rise to the surface.

This is the lure of performance art; that it allows the audience to construct a meaning, and thus the performance becomes a cobra by supplying fascination rather than pretence, ultimately taming the gaze and inducing a productive submission. Thus is the breath 'baited', held at the pregnant moment of some arrested act, the swaying hood become still, and the gesture achieving the scene by deepening its impasse. Think of the arresting punctuation of the Peking Opera, when all their flying spears suddenly seem to stop in mid-air.

While the action moves, the audience follows, busily reading its text: but when the scene stops and the primary of stillness asserts itself and the trigger-finger freezes in mid-curl, then the gesture is perceived as a half-utterance. Time stands still, and arrests its witnesses. Units of stillness operate as full stops. A prolonged period of stillness can draw attention to itself. The freeze confronts its audience. It fascinates.

Such cobra-control of the audience can be the gift of the actor of presence or of the puppeteer. The personality which has eaten the sacrament of its role can achieve it, as can the ghost in the machine. On the other hand, it may be brought about simply by the concept which governs the piece. An audience can be amused by the exaggerated, trigger-switching manipulation of one's own images, as epitomized by Rowan Atkinson, but on the other hand there is still the simple, magnifying presence as epitomized by Nureyev. It should be reiterated that such magnification does have a great deal to do with the breath. Actors, dancers and performance artists have this in common. If talented, they all know when to inhale and when to exhale. Inhalation prepares. It gathers tension into the system. To a degree, it disturbs homeostasis. It alerts the audience to the need for some ensuing catharsis. One can see this operating very clearly in circus acts. Once the difficult trick is performed the breath is expelled; homeostatic equilibrium is restored and we all 'breathe a sigh of relief'.

It is not just the breath. There is also a certain rigidity which needs to be attained in order to instill tension into the performance 'atmosphere'. As with the breath's expulsion, this rigidity can also be relinquished, enabling relief to re-establish itself. Again we seem to be dealing with life forces versus death forces, inconsistency versus repetition, irregularity versus regularity. Perhaps it is simply the play of these forces against each other that the audience has come to watch. The rigidity I refer to amounts to a tension in the shoulders, in the elbows; a certain level of dynamic tension in the system. Masters of many sports, from tennis to fencing, would argue against this in their own fields, advocating instead an alert form of relaxation. Art differs from sport, however, in that to some extent we are making apparent tensions which exist in society and in the psyche rather than simply performing as healthy organisms.

Performative rigidity amounts to a sort of erection of the body – I will not call it a virility since then I would need to refer to its necessary softening as a feminisation whereas this quality is necessary and available to performers of both sexes. Think of it as a Ying/Yang alternation, a suffusion of the blood followed at length by its drained aftermath. Japanese performers have evolved stamping exercises to develop this quality.

Thus there is presence and puppeteering, and also action and stillness, and also inhalation and exhalation, rigidity and softness. Just as repetition usually requires reversal, being in the performance space usually requires some manipulation of opposing forces. All in all, I believe we should be looking for a fusion of these, or at least we should grasp how to rapidly alternate their seemingly contrary powers. For although there is presence of soul, if you like, this can actually be deconstructed, and indeed must be, for the inhalation to successfully magnify the presence. This, after all, is why the dancer trains: it is not all empathy and feeling. There is a foot presence, a knee presence, a buttocks presence, a chest presence, and finally a face presence – all these go together when one is making one's body *conscious* to oneself and to one's audience. These forces affect the voice also, and with presence we achieve resonance. But equally, for any successful adaption to occur, there must be a degree of cold-blooded construction in order that a presence can first be established inside the shell, so that the shell can be convincingly manipulated, coming alive beneath the external gaze. As a performer, ultimately, one needs to be wearing oneself – like a glove.

———————

The Workshop in Presence

1.   Puppeteering Exercise

Performers devise a performance in which they remain invisible.

2   Performance Interpretations

A short solo is devised by one performer, and this solo is sufficiently simple to be learnt quickly by the others. The solo is then performed by each of the others in turn, and the qualities of presence brought to it by their interpretations are discussed. Then another performer devises a short solo, and again each of the others performs it. This process continues until everyone in the group has created a solo, each of which has been interpreted by the others.

3.   Loud and Soft Presences

Performers create a series of duets. In the first duet, one attempts to assert his or her presence while the other seeks to diminish his or her presence. In the second duet, both seek to assert their presence. In the third duet, both seek to diminish their presence. In the fourth duet, one starts with diminished presence but ends up strongly asserting it while the other starts with asserted presence but ends up considerably diminished. These duets may be performed simultaneously by the entire company of performers.

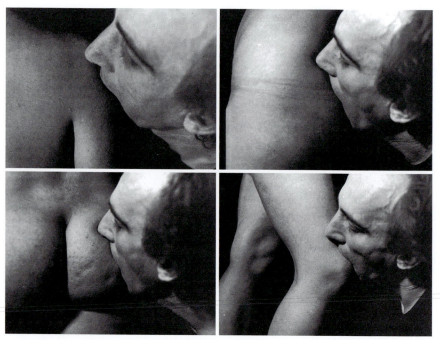

A sculpture described by the mouth: Neša Paripović's *Examples of Analytical Sculpture,*
SKC Gallery, Belgrade, Yugoslavia, 1978. Photographs courtesy of the artist.

15
CONCLUSION

"The owl makes its flight in the twilight."

(Hegel)

Wisdom's pronouncements come after the event. Artists are as intrigued by the junk-shop as by the shop-window setting forth the advantages of the latest technological product. Knowing by intuition that art serves few purposes and has, fortunately, very little effect, the obsolete item appeals perhaps more than the up-to-date and efficient one. The 'old crocks' of outmoded beliefs can be readily adapted to the irresponsible purposes of the imagination. It is for this reason that artists remain fascinated by heraldry, by alchemy, by phrenology, long after the practical and progressive world has moved on. Psychoanalysis is a case in point. I distrust it as a therapy, and would distrust it still more as a therapy wielded by an artist. It is only artists with ambitions, artists seeking recognition by the establishment, who claim that art has any moral, social or curative purpose.

Freud's adherence to the evolutionary theory of Lamarck – which asserts that the characteristics acquired by an individual can be inherited by his descendants – smacks of old testament religiosity. Perhaps because he felt obliged to suppress a proportion of the 'sins of the fathers' when he abandoned his seduction theory, their sins came to haunt his meta-psychological projects. Equally suspect is the confusion over what might be termed a 'reverse drive' and what Freud insisted was a 'death instinct'. There is a distinct difference between the notion of a period prior to birth and the final 'period' of death. Set against a background of fascism, Zionist aspirations for a return to 'the promised land' might well have seemed doomed – and perhaps eventually history will prove this to be the case. But I find Freud unnecessarily pessimistic as regards repetition and the fatality of its aim. Nietzsche's notion of the 'eternal return' seems more balanced.

Discussing Woodruff's biological experiments with a ciliate infusorian – which repetitively reproduces by fission into two individuals – Freud concluded that "the *immortality* of the Protista (protozoa) seemed to be experimentally demonstrable," though other observers found that "after a certain number of divisions these Infusoria become weaker, diminish in size, suffer the loss of some part of their Organisation and eventually die, unless certain recuperative measures are applied to them." He goes on:

"It is probable nevertheless that Infusoria die a natural death as a result of their own vital processes. For the contradiction between Woodruff's findings and the others is due to his having provided each generation with fresh nutrient fluid. If he omitted to do so, he observed the same signs of senescence as the other experimenters. He concluded that the animalculae were injured by the products which they extruded into the surrounding fluid..."

(*Beyond the Pleasure Principle*)

Surely this suggests that the waste products which result from the tension-releases of the pleasure principle are more lethal to us than the reverse drive of the repetitive instinct Freud associates with death? If the dinosaurs died from the stink of their own shit, then perhaps a similar fate awaits our own species. However, it is only through pleasure that we conjugate, and only through pleasure that we evolve. Novel delights alone will enable us to abandon the debilitating excrescences of our present ones. Any agenda based on repression will fail. It will fail because the ensuing build-up of tension will eventually overturn its restrictive policies.

The contrast between these two ideas might be expressed in performance terms by a duet in which one performer works expulsively – perhaps until impeded by his detritus - while the other works sculpturally and repetitively – until exhaustion prohibits further action (*see page 185-6*). We have seen that many psychoanalytic ideas are readily transferable into such action models, and that this makes for a rewarding discourse between the two disciplines.

Another aspect of Freud's thought which has increasingly come under question is its paranoid phallocentricity. What is surprising is the way so many contemporary feminists endorse this. Melanie Klein's explanation of pre-linguistic trauma is far more convincing, yet seems to have fewer adherents. I can see that the notion of being castrated by the opposite sex could form part of an agenda of resentment – if it were only the father who did the castrating. But phantasy is full of toothy vaginas, and it was the mothers in China who used to insist on the practice of binding the feet.

A theory with so many drawbacks should be reserved strictly for the ineffectual conceptions of artists. To seek to apply it to social and political conflict seems just as dubious as to employ it as method of healing, except in so far as it may prove a sometimes effective placebo. Smollet was a rather good doctor: he never prescribed anything but water! In his day, that was distinctly better than most medicines. Freud reminds me of Columbus. He thought he had discovered India. Certainly he had discovered something – but it wasn't India.

Deleuze and Guattari's critique of Freud in the *Anti-Oedipus* provides us with a refreshing antidote to Freud's familiar medicine; however, their factory-like concept of desiring-machines relies somewhat heavily on the notion of a 'collective unconscious' as promoted by Carl Jung, and while this may have emerged from their interest in a materialist theory of psychiatry, an underlying Marxism gives this notion of the unconscious the status of a belief or a numen. For me, it amounts to a religiosity which undermines their logic. Even so, their deconstruction of the Oedipus Complex is refreshing, for it throws new light on the play of children, a play of significance to the performance artist:

> "A child never confines himself to playing house, to playing only at being daddy-and-mummy. He also plays at being a magician, a cowboy, a cop or a robber, a train, a little car. The train is not necessarily daddy, nor is the train station necessarily mommy. The problem has to do not with the nature of the desiring-machines, but with the family nature of this sexuality .... The small child lives with his family round the clock; but within the bosom of this family, and from the very first days of his life, he immediately begins having an amazing non-familial experience that psychoanalysis has completely failed to take into account..."
>
> (*Anti-Oedipus*, page 46.)

Oedipus is simply a template which endeavoured to accommodate the strait-laced claustrophobia of the middle-classes between the wars. It ineluctably reflects the approved condition, the rigid triangle of the nuclear family. But it fails to take into account the diversity of our conditions, for we are as often as not the children of single parents, children without parents, or children of parents who have had other children with previous partners. And thus there are alternative templates, since we each grow up in some familial particularity. Deleuze and Guattari quote the *Diary of Vaslav Nijinsky*:

> "I am God I was not God I am a clown of God; I am Apis. I am an Egyptian. I am a red Indian. I am a Negro. I am a Chinaman. I am a Japanese. I am a foreigner, a stranger. I am a sea bird. I am a land bird. I am the tree of Tolstoy. I am the roots of Tolstoy ..... I am husband and wife in one. I love my wife. I love my husband."
>
> (pp. 20, 156)

Conventional psychoanalysis fails to admit the infinity of myths, the multiplicity of productions, fantasies, compulsions. After all, it is as frightening to imagine having an aperture sewn up and irreversibly sealed as it is to fear the removal of an organ. Our imagination is monstrous. Alien sexual parts can be grafted onto us. We can grow breasts, sprout penises, scoop vaginas out of our armpits. We can be clothed in turds and appalled that we take pride in our raiment. Equally we can fear being flattened by cars, falling from planes or being trussed up by combine harvesters. The machine is just as powerful as daddy.

Shame is more likely to traumatize than is the "abuse" to which it refers, and often this repercussion comes a good while after the event and after some shift of context has occurred. Shame is the flip-side of pleasure's coin, and we have learnt from our study of action that most repetitions incorporate their reversals. How does the artist vanquish shame? How is the artist to deal with these amputations, piercings, grafts, flows from the body, ingestions, burials, disinterments? How is anyone to cope with the plurality of their obsessions without Oedipus, without this cast-iron clothes-hanger which purports to deal with every one of our hang-ups?

The answer is to celebrate the unconscious rather than to cure it. When Judge Schreber dresses as a woman he is acting rationally – his dementia is to suppress the urge to do so. We can now make use of compulsive counting, and of the snips of wicked seccateurs. We can sew our fingers together, bury ourselves, eat our faeces, bite like rabid dogs. Once it is taken seriously as an action, each bizarre practice will suggest a discipline, invoke a form - we will discover that there is a right way and a wrong way of eating our faeces. This is the way to avoid the fate of the dinosaurs.

Every career has its own humdrum considerations. A male prostitute may keep his turds in the fridge – in order to have them available should a client demand a scatophagous session. Nowadays he is not the instrument of some unmentionable trade, but a sex-worker, helping people to cope with drives which have little hope of finding accommodation in "polite" society. Our drives are largely demonised, and it is not they but the shame which attaches to them which causes us to live our lives in fear and self-loathing. Performance artists often work directly with their obsessions in order to restore them to light, thus enabling these all-too-human practices to shed condemnatory shadows.

To return to psychoanalysis. Whether outmoded or not in its therapeutic application, its significance for me is that it has brought about a fundamental shift in our perception of art; for since the advent of modernism the analytic approach has taken over from the aesthetic notion of judgement. As early as the 1880s, psychologists were beginning to deduce the character of the artist or author from the work that artist or author produced. The "obscurantism" of James, Conrad and Meredith – which constituted the prelude to the difficulties of modernism – may be attributed to the desire of these writers to 'muddy the waters', thus evading the often banal reflections on their own characters brought about by this tendency (see *The Uses of Obscurity* by Allon White). Freud himself attempted to analyse the character of Leonardo da Vinci through his work, but today this is largely seen as a failure. More successful was his analysis of the novel, *Gradiva*, by Wilhelm Jensen. In his essay on this work, Freud carries out an analysis of the fiction, not of its author.

The aesthetic is preoccupied with an assessment of the effect of a work of art on the spectator whereas the analytic concerns a scrutiny of the work itself. Prior to our century, philosophers considered consciousness the goal of being, and artists aspired to a state of serene consciousness and created works of beauty with surfaces which demonstrated this. It was a consciousness of what was harmonious, pleasing to the senses – whether it proved stimulating to the spectator's consciousness, inspiring a heightened sense of something harmonious and pleasing, as was its aim, was what required some judgement. There was also the notion of the 'sublime' – that one could contemplate the awesome height or the ghastly precipice and have one's consciousness stirred by its effect. A celebration of consciousness was still the aim. Today we are not so sure that consciousness is the goal of existence. A goal in whose eyes? In the eyes of some supreme being? The transcendental 'reality' of such an abiding presence is doubtful – and its dubiety brings about a doubt about ourselves, our reality and our consciousness. Consciousness may be a mere by-product of evolution.

And so we have turned from judgement to diagnosis. The contemporary work of art is as much a symptom as an edifice of our society. Analysis allows us to deconstruct it – to identify its contradictions. We describe its surface to ourselves, as before, but we are also intrigued by the process which caused it to occur, by the symbolic language it releases, fully aware that the symbols it stimulates in our minds may not carry the same meaning for its author. Aesthetic judgement concerned an appreciation of the object: analysis concerns a reading of it. There is an appreciation still, but this includes the complete organisation of the work, its homeostasis, the resonance and the richness of the multifarious readings it permits, together with its relation to the environment in which it manifests itself, its siting – we could perhaps speak of its 'integrity' – which may be anything but harmonious, which may be abusive rather than pleasing, disturbing rather than inspiring.

Still, there is an aspect of abuse and disturbance that should be discussed, and that is their bearing on humour. Idealism plagues aesthetics, and obliges it to turn with due seriousness to the cerebral Platonism of 'high art', which emphasises an exalted sense of enlightenment and utopian form. This is as true of the recent emphasis on minimalism as it is of orthodox ikons. In all such formal manifestations there is a certain denial of the body and its functions. A Botticelli nude displays no openings – it is indeed a 'body without organs'. However, Mikhail Bakhtin understood that the functioning body – the body that consumed and gave birth and excreted, still at one with a nature which sprouted and decayed at the same time – could inspire a primordial sense of gestation born out of death (a far cry from Freud's doom-laden death instinct). This was celebrated in its seasonal repetitions by the grotesque parodies of solemnity which persisted into the seventeenth century as a vital folk tradition. He stressed that, in the middle ages *and* in the Renaissance, laughter had a rejuvenating effect – and in this he followed a lead Karl Marx provided, who understood that laughter contained something revolutionary. Bakhtin suggests that we reassess our over-Florentine view of the Renaissance, which, less Platonically:

"... expressed its attitude toward laughter in the very practice of literary creation and appreciation. Neither was there any lack of theoretical opinion that justified laughter as a universal, philosophical form. This theory of laughter was built almost exclusively on antique sources. Rabelais himself developed it in the old and new prologue of the fourth book of his novel, based mainly on Hippocrates, whose role as the theorist of laughter was at that time important .... his prestige founded on the comments contained in his medical treatise concerning the importance of a gay and cheerful mood on the part of the physician and patient fighting disease."

(*Rabelais and his World*, page 67)

I remember my uncle telling me that his squamous cancer sounded to him like "squeamish". The grotesque nature of our symptoms can indeed render them absurd – and we are at liberty to laugh at them. Now performance art is particularly 'symptomatic' in its manifestations. It celebrates its fetishes and readily pursues its own obsessions.

Of course there is no money in it, and it is often criticised for being solely of interest to its practitioners. It is less object-orientated than any other art, except that of music, and leaves representation to the cinema – having witnessed enactment's descent into cliché, on television, and on the stage. For these reasons it is seldom influenced by any critic's assessment of its effect on the spectator – as theatre remains, still taken up with how a piece is received – that is, aesthetically appreciated in the consciousness – and often confusing this with an appeal to the 'social conscience', being anxious to retain a paying audience. Indifferent to such considerations, Richard Long, the landscape artist and walker, has created pieces in mountainous places which nobody has ever seen. Performers are as likely to perform for each other as for any spectator. All this suggests that their work is eminently suited to an analytic reading rather than to the assessment of some conventional aesthetic. Analysis takes more than what may be consciously contrived into its consideration, and it has already been observed that performance can be thought of as the unconscious of theatre, since as a form it is more liable to utilise the dynamic of repetitive action than to engage in dramatic illustration.

Performances occur 'at the time', and if performance is to emancipate itself from other arts by positing an enquiry into its own essential nature – as has already happened in visual art and in literature – then its ability to provide us with an action print-out of the forces condensing around the present is an ingredient closely connected to that essence. It is something which should be taken advantage of by means of improvisation – particularly by artists performing in groups. Freud advocated the 'stream of consciousness' as the way for the analysand to bring his or her unconscious to the surface. The tapestry of actions instigated and occurring in the present on a performance space should prove a particularly fertile field for analytic readings.

Rehearsal would fictionalise the event, just as the news turns events into fiction simply by reiterating them. But there is also a danger that constant improvisation would grow predictable. Freely improvising musicians have a tendency to stop when they all run out of steam, whereas a musical composition can end on a climax. A key question for performance artists must be, how do we keep the improvisation diverse, how do we ensure that even our spontaneous actions read ambiguously, so that our audience finds it difficult to decide whether it is watching something improvised or something rehearsed?

In the same way as a performance might occupy some uneasy ground, a no-man's land between rehearsal and improvisation, Freud's case-histories occupy an ambiguous textual space between documentation and fiction. To have identified and utilised such an area constituted a major development in the field of writing. I believe Freud's greatest contribution is to literature and to the imagination. And there is something about the topography of his thought that fits strikingly well with a similar topography as we have charted it in the sphere of our actions. "Mens sana, in corporae sano. " As we move, so do we feel. Most psychical states appear to have physical counterparts, indeed we can know of the psychical only though the physical or through the *epos*, the spoken – only through that which is expressed. The unconscious is hidden: but we know of it through its externalisations. All action may be read as an emotional signifier, and is so read.

Yet I now feel less than comfortable with Lacan's dictum that 'the unconscious is structured like a language'. Too readily accepted, this statement is, at the least, open to debate. The unconscious may be structured like a language in so far as its externalisations can be decoded – just as a geographer can read a landscape. But in this general sense all phenomena are languages. If Freud's thought must be qualified by taking into accounts its Hebraic hue, then Lacan's thought should be acknowledged as suffering from a Roman Catholic bias: too much emphasis on the 'word made flesh'. Lacan takes language for his Eucharist.

Language is a series of contiguous, inconsistent events – its prosody may lend a pattern to its parts which will therefore display repetitive characteristics in the same way as charades will generate inconsistent actions which nevertheless exhibit a readable reiterated logic. So it might be said that inconsistency is structured like a language. In what sense? In the sense that most everyday actions amount to utilitarian strings of inconsistencies incorporating local repetitions, and words picture such facts as these actions narrate. Inconsistency may be a sudden blow – but in multiplicity it becomes a filigree, a veil of nodes and connections. Not so, the unconscious, which is simpler, and, in its convulsive repetitions, structured like an alimentary and digestive system dedicated to appropriation and expulsion.

If we go beyond the generality that what is readable is a language, we will acknowledge that language is a tool we put to conscious use, whereas the unconscious is a phenomenon of our nature; and while the analyst may gauge the effect of the unconscious on the language used by his subject this does not make the unconscious a language, it simply gives it a voice. If language acts as a mediator between inconsistency and repetition in that inconsistency is its surface characteristic while repetition organises the deeper nature of its components, then perhaps some expression of the additive/ subtractive mediation *between* repetition and inconsistency is the state to which it best approximates, in terms of overlayering and transition; though here we might expect to find a difference between the written word and speech.

As well as language, Lacan lays stress on vision. This aestheticises the analytical process. I think though that we put ourselves together through a combination of all our sensory inputs – thus in addition to what is said to us and what we look like, we experience the gravitational pull in our feet, and our distance from the floor in our heads: we smell right to ourselves, and others smell right to us or they do not: we have an internal sense of our own voice and only of our own voice – all other voices are outside us – and we know our external shape because we've been touched all over.

This last point is well illustrated by the work of the Serbian artist, Neša Paripović: in *Examples of Analytical Sculpture*, a performance evident as a sequence of photographs, "the author of the idea touches a naked female figure with his lips along an unimagined spiral around the figure starting from the head (ear, cheek, shoulder, back, stomach, hips, legs) with lips parted in a kiss and with closed eyes" (see Miško Šuvaković's essay on the artist in Neša Paripović: *Autoportreti*). Just as "the act of devouring concerns other organs than the mouth" (Lacan), so we comprehend form through other senses than our eyes.

In addition to these specific quibbles with specific practitioners, I take psychoanalysis in general to task for expending far less effort on inconsistency than has been expended in the name of repetition. Inconsistency is certainly as appealing, and besides *to maintain inconsistency is as problematic as it is to abandon a compulsion.*

A psychoanalyst might speak of freedom, when seeking a term to oppose to repetition. We have seen that inconsistency is not exactly freedom – simply another part in the grammar of action. But however much I may hope that this book has achieved its purpose – to set out that grammar the actionist employs together with its psychical relations – let me conclude by stressing that I've no wish for the book to become the standard for a generation of grammarians. A piece of writing does not become a work of literature merely because it happens to be correct. This is where freedom comes in. Performance artists are exhorted to question every tenet of my grammar. Rules are drawn up in art only that they may be broken. Narrative texts and dramatic characterisation, for instance, should not necessarily be avoided, nor should acknowledgement of the audience or acknowledgement of another performer become a strict taboo. The terms of conventional theatre may be adopted at the onset, in order that they may be perverted as the piece evolves. The manner of the chat-show host or the public lecturer may be used as a mask which is later abandoned as some other game takes over.

This alterality of the specular image of ourselves is also the alterality of our art. In a sense, each new piece of work must demonstrate as much inconsistency with that which has gone before as it entails some repetitive reflection of it. This requires that while a grammar of performance may help to lay out the possibilities, each new work must invent its own rules.

Annie Sprinkle. Photograph: Amy Ardrey.

Pleasure returns as the subject of the final issue to be touched upon. This concerns the chance that the phenomena which this book describes may be queried by some moralist impulse. How can the performer permit the pathological manifestations of so much suffering to act as the inspiration for creativity? The ironing of banknotes may sound wonderful to someone looking for a surreal action to perform in front of the public – but it remains the pathetic evidence of psychical confusion and very real abuse. Surely it must be wrong of artists to so blithely appropriate such sources and use them in their work?

I can only point out that the arts have always utilised the appearance of suffering. The Greek tragedies concern incest, rape, patricide and infanticide. The painters of the Renaissance sought out the worst instances of martyrdom, the bloodiest incidents of the Bible. Psychical anxiety is the pain most readily experienced in the peaceful reaches of contemporary western existence. Small wonder then that the forms it takes should prove of interest to artists inhabiting that condition of querulous placidity. As artists, it's our duty to exaggerate – to carry things to extremes. But this is better done with things which remain within our ken. It is no good sitting in a coffee-bar in Hampstead and imagining that we are in Auschwitz. Contemporary suffering in Eastern Europe or in Africa may attain a dimension we find hard to grasp: however, if we work with that which is within our grasp, we may find that the intensity of our vision resonates in situations far removed from our own more domestic concerns.

————

APPENDICES

APPENDIX 1

Gargantua and Pantagruel

by Francois Rabelais

Book 3, Chapter VIII

Why the Codpiece is held to be the Chief Piece
of Armour amongst Warriours

Will you maintain (quoth Pantagruel) that the Codpiece is the chief piece of a Military Harness? It is a new kind of Doctrine very Paradoxical: For we say at Spurs begins the arming of a Man. Sir, I maintain it (answered Panurge) and not wrongfully do I maintain it. Behold how nature having a fervent desire after its Production of Plants, Trees, Shrubs, Herbs, Sponges and plant Animals, to eternize, and continue them unto all Succession of Ages (in their several Kinds, or Sorts at least, although the individuals perish) unruinable, and in an everlasting Being, hath most curiously armed and fenced their Buds, Sprouts, Shoots, and Seeds, wherein the above- mentioned perpetuity consisteth, by strengthening, covering, guarding, and fortifying them with an admirable industry, with Husks, Cases, Scurfs and Swads, Hulls, Cods, Stones, Films, Cartels, Shells, Ears, Rinds, Barks, Skins, Ridges, and Prickles, which serve them instead of strong, fair, and natural Codpieces: As is manifestly apparent in Pease, Beans, Fasels, Pomegranates, Peaches, Cottons, Gourds, Pumpions, Melons, Corn, Lemons, Almonds, Walnuts, Filberts, and Chestnuts; as likewise in all Plants, Slips, or Sets whatsoever, wherein it is plainly and evidently seen, that the Sperm and Semina is more closely veiled, overshadowed, corroborated, and thoroughly harnessed than any other part, portion, or parcel of the whole.

Nature nevertheless did not after that manner provide for the sempiternizing of the Human Race: But on the contrary created Man naked, tender, and frail, without either offensive or defensive Arms; and all that in the Estate of Innocence, in the first Age of all, which was the Golden Season; not as a plant, but living Creature, born for Peace, not War, and brought forth into the World with an unquestionable Right and Title to the plenary fruition of all Fruits and Vegetables; as also a certain calm and gentle Rule and Dominion of all kinds of Beasts, Fishes, Reptils, and Insects. Yet afterwards it hapning in the time of the Iron Age, under the Reign of Jupiter, when to the multiplication of mischievous Actions, Wickedness and Malice began to take root and footing within the then perverted Hearts of Men, that the Earth began to bring forth Nettles, Thistles, Thorns, Bryars, and such other stubborn and rebellious Vegetables to the Nature of Man; nor scarce was there any animal, which by a fatal Disposition did not then revolt from him, and tacitly conspire, and covenant with one another to serve him no longer, (nor in case of their ability to resist) to do him any manner of Obedience, but rather (to the uttermost of their Power) to annoy him with all the hurt and harm they could. The Man then, that he might maintain his primitive Right and Prerogative, and continue his Sway and Dominion over all, both Vegetable and Sensitive Creatures; and knowing of a Truth, that he could not well be accommodated as he ought, without the servitude and subjection of several Animals, bethought himself, that of necessity he must needs put on Arms, and make provision of Harness against Wars and Violence. By the holy Saint Babingoose, (cried out Pantagruel) you are become, since the last Rain, a great Lifre lofre, Philosopher, I should say. Take notice, Sir, (quoth Panurge) when Dame Nature had prompted him to his own Arming, what part of the Body it was, where, by her Inspiration, he clapped on his first Harness: It was forsooth by the double pluck of my little Dog the Ballock, and good Senor Don Priapos Stabostando, which done, he was content, and sought no more. This is certified by the Testimony of the great Hebrew Captain Philosopher Moyses, who affirmeth, that he fenced that member with a brave and gallant Codpiece, most excellently framed, and by right curious Devices of a notably pregnant Invention, made up and composed of Fig-tree leaves, which by reason of their solid stiffness, incisory notches, curled frisling, sleeked smoothness, large ampleness, together with their colour, smell, vertue, and faculty, were exceeding proper, and fit for the covering and arming of the Sachels of Generation, the hideously big Lorrain Cullions being from thence only excepted; which swaggering down to the lowermost bottom of the Breeches, cannot abide (for being quite out of all order and method) the stately fashion of the high and lofty Codpiece; as is manifest, by the Noble Valentin Viardiere, whom I found at Nancie, on the first Day of May (the more flauntingly to gallantrize it afterwards) rubbing his Ballocks spread out upon a Table after the manner of a Spanish Cloak. Wherefore it is, that none should henceforth say, when any Country- Bumpkin hyeth to the Wars, Have a care (my Royster) of the Wine-pot, that is the Scull, but have a care (my Royster) of the Milk-pot; that is, the Testicles. By the whole Rabble of the horned fiends of Hell, the Head being cut off, that single person only thereby dieth: But if the Ballocks be marred, the whole Race of Human Kind would forthwith perish, and be lost for ever.

This was the motive which incited the goodly Writer Galen, Lib. 1. *De Spermate*, to aver with boldness, That it were better (that is to say, a less evil) to have no heart at all, than to be quite destitute of Genitories: For there is laid up, conserved, and put in store, as in a Successive Repository, and Sacred Ware-house, the Semina, and Original Source of the whole Off-spring of Mankind. Therefore would I be apt to believe, for less than a hundred Franks, that those are the very same Stones, by means whereof Deucalion and Pyrrha restored the Humane Race, in peopling with Men and Women the World, which a little before that, had been drowned in the overflowing Waves of a Poetical Deluge. This stirred up the valiant Justinian, L. I. 4. *De Cagotis tolendis*, to collocate his *Summum Bonum, in Braguibus, et Braguetis.* For this, and other Causes, the Lord Humphry de Merville, following of his King to a certain warlike Expedition, whilst he was in trying upon his own Person a new suit of Armour, for of his old rusty Harness he could make no more use, by reason that some few Years since, the Skin of his Belly was a great way removed from his Kidneys, his Lady thereupon in the profound musing of a contemplative Spirit, very maturely considering that he had but small care of the Staff of Love, and Packet of Marriage, seeing he did no otherwise arm that part of the Body, then with Links of Mail, advised him to shield, fence and gabionate it with a big tilting Helmet, which she had lying in her Closet to her otherways utterly unprofitable. On this Lady was penned these subsequent Verses; which are extant in the third Book of the Shitbrana of paultry Wenches.

> When Yoland saw her Spouse, equipt for Fight
> And, save the Codpiece, all in Armour dight,
> My dear, she cry'd, Why, pray, of all the rest,
> Is that expos'd, you know I love the best?
> Was she to blame for an ill-manag'd fear?
> Or rather pious, conscionable care:
> Wise Lady, She! In hurly-burly Fight,
> Can any tell where random blows may hit?

Leave off then (Sir) from being astonished, and wonder no more at this new manner of decking and trimming up of my self as you now see me.

APPENDIX 2

"Imaginary Conversations"

Janos Pilinsky's

Conversations with Sheryl Sutton

Janos Pilinsky was a Hungarian poet. He lived in Budapest. In this extraordinary book he tells us that his aunt was a Mother Superior, and that he spent most of his childhood among primitive nuns and juvenile prostitutes, half in prison and half in reformatory. Conscripted in 1944, he spent the last year of the war moving from prison camp to prison camp in Austria and Germany. His first book of poems appeared in '46, but he was banned from publishing for ten years after the communist takeover in '48. Nevertheless his poetry got to be known: it was translated into English by Ted Hughes. Pilinsky's work was admired for the austerity of his controlled poetic forms.

In 1973, in Paris, he saw *Deafman Glance*, an early spectacle by Robert Wilson. This had a profound effect on him and may have contributed to the evolution of his style into a more flexible free verse. In the same year, or thereabouts, I witnessed another spectacle by Wilson, and this had a similar effect on my own work. The show I saw, *The Life and Times of Joseph Stalin*, contained many of the elements previously seen by Pilinsky in the Paris spectacle. It began at 7.30 pm, in the Brooklyn Academy of Music, and ended at 7.30 the following morning. At least a hundred performers took part in it; some deaf, some blind, I believe – as well as professional actors and dancers and people Wilson had plucked out of everyday life. There were several acts, each at least three hours long. Motionlessness, or motion slowed to a fraction of its normal speed, seemed to have descended upon the stage and suspended the performers in the midst of some dream. Occasionally a swifter action would be dropped into the pervading honey of stillness – a wide-girthed, spinning negro in evening dress created one such incident – and these sudden events would leave an afterimage created out of their rarity. The sets and the costumes were both lavish and incredible: somewhere in the depths of a vast cave a seal fanned itself sporadically for ages – once an hour a huge metal pole would drop with a crash into place – sealing up the entrance to the cave and cutting it off from the golden sands outside where deaf fairies danced silently by distant wavelets. At greater intervals, a runner would pass in front of the mouth of the cave.

In a Parisian café, the Hungarian poet met a black artist / actress from Wilson's company. Her name was Sheryl Sutton. In one act of the performance, Sheryl had sat erect on a throne for some three hours before standing suddenly up – and breaking into a sweat. Pilinsky met the actress once again. They talked for several hours. And then Sheryl went away, returning to New York with the company. After this, Pilinsky imagines himself falling ill in Paris. Sheryl nurses him. She feeds him potato goulash soup. Sometimes she sleeps on the floor by his bed, curled up in her clothes. He speaks feverishly, and she talks with him about her life and about books and about performance art.

Conversations with Sheryl Sutton is ably translated by Peter Jay and Eva Major. This magical novel is the outcome of the fictional conversation which transpires during the fever which beset the poet, or which he imagined, that winter in Paris. The projected Platonic affair provides Pilinsky with a framework which can accommodate his ideas about poetry and memory, about dreams, and about the unprecedented, iconic theatre of Robert Wilson. The book itself is infused with a dreaminess which perhaps only those who have seen Wilson's spectacles will recognise as described reality. The description is here in the hands of a master poet who weaves his own essential concerns into it, transforming the dialogue into a modem classic; a text for which De Chirico's novel *Hebdomeros* is the only precedent – aside from the work of Walter Savage Landor, whose *Imaginary Conversations* bring together such figures as Diogenes and Plato, Leofric and Godiva.

Aside from being a consumate work of literature, the book provides us with the best analysis of the work of Robert Wilson that I have yet read. Pilinsky observes that masterpieces are beyond boredom, and not before it; that contemporary writing dare not run the risk of boredom. We pin our hopes on success, when failure is inherent to the greatest work: once failure is 'built-in', the work begins to write itself. "Modern art .... cannot avoid this bitter, murderous and suicidal element, which alone is redemptive."

"Quality is that which has no time," says Sheryl. She mentions Chekhov: "Walking and standing about, that's what all his plays are ... He began where you need to yawn." She speaks then of the beyond-boredom richness and patience of plants – reminding me of the movement of Min Tanaka whose action sometimes shows us the slowness of vegetal growth.

In his spectacles, Robert Wilson managed to bring about a revaluation of normal time. In this he departed radically from the dialogue-laden "mimicry theatre" which still dominates the British theatre establishment and the media. For this establishment, the message-orientated model for art so beloved of sociology-imbued historians and politically correct critics continues to hold sway. The structure of their politics remains authoritarian, conceived as a message from above, and judged by the effectiveness by which it is 'got across'.

But just as Wittgenstein, in his *Tractatus*, passes over in silence that 'about which we cannot speak', Pilinsky asserts an existential dumbness in the face of our incomprehension concerning the world we inhabit. In the aftermath of our knowledge that concentration camps have existed and indeed do exist all messages are reduced to a stammer. Imitation theatre occupies a lowland of impersonation and simulated dialogue. Something is always being 'got across', whether by illustration or by symbol. Wilson, however, immobilises the message. His stillness suspends the spectacle in a globe of his own mere being. It is as a bonfire may be, or a waterfall or a rainbow: an entity we contemplate or dream about. As Robert Frost puts it, "I want the poem to be like ice on a stove - riding on its own melting." Frank Auerbach quotes Frost, and then adds that "a great painting .... is a shape riding on its own melting into matter and space, it never stops moving backwards and forwards." This rocking motion is another form of stasis and reminds me of the music of Philip Glass, which has often accompanied Wilson's performances. Here the sociologically-inclined arts person might only note that Auerbach was born in '31, in Berlin and was sent to England before his eighth birthday, after which he never saw his parents again. Once more, I think of Wittgenstein's remark.

Pilinsky's reading of Wilson is essentially, therefore, a European reading of an American phenomenon, and perhaps he interprets the work in a way Wilson himself would find strange. In a more American way, his imagined muse talks about something important happening, which doesn't really happen – like saving up all one's pocket money to go to a swimming-pool one doesn't ultimately enter. It is this motionless drama the conversations attempt to come to terms with: a drama which informs the still-lives of Morandi, perhaps painted simply as a testimony to the value of the time spent painting them. Let us not jump in here and exclaim disdainfully against the self-referential nature of art. This phrase suggests that the self of the artist is involved, yet it is hardly the case. Art, including any masterpiece of performance, is more it-referential than concerned with any self. Even to 'refer' suggests some connotative translation into extrinsic terms. But nothing is referred to, and it is not a question of the performance being 'about' anything. You might as well ask a waterfall what its motives were.

Anthony Howell, unpublished review,
October, 1992

APPENDIX 3

The Structure of *'Going'*

by
The Theatre of Mistakes

There are five acts in the play. Each of the five acts is a repetition of the first act, each is begun by a different performer. In each act a further element is introduced by the first performer to enter in that act. Each new element is repeated in all subsequent acts.

Example: ACT 1.

Scene 1: Metronome.
Entry of the first performer.
First performer executes an action with words.

Scene 2: Metronome.
Entry of the second performer.
First performer executes an action with words.
Second performer repeats all actions and words employed by the first performer in scene 1.

Scene 3: Metronome.
Entry of the third and fourth performers.
Second performer freezes – only turning in order to observe the actions of the first performer.
Third performer repeats all actions and words employed by the first performer in Scene 1.
Fourth performer repeats all actions and words employed by the first performer in Scene 2.
Exit of the first performer while executing an action with words.

Scene 4: First performer as Metronome.
Entry of initial Metronome as the fifth performer.
Second performer repeats all actions and words employed by the first performer in Scene 3.

Third performer repeats all actions and words employed by the first performer in Scene 2.

Fourth performer freezes – only turning in order to observe the actions of the second performer repeating all the actions and words employed by the first performer in Scene 3.

Fifth performer repeats all actions and words employed by the first performer in Scene 1.

Second performer repeats the exit of the first performer in Scene 3.

Scene 5: Metronome.

Second performer begins Tone Poem Chorus.

Third performer freezes.

Fourth performer repeats the exit of the second performer in Scene 4.

Fifth performer repeats all actions and words employed by the first performer in Scene 2.

Scene 6: Exit of the third performer.

Metronome.

Second performer continues Tone Poem Chorus.

Third and fourth performers begin Tone Poem Chorus.

Fifth performer repeats the exit of the first performer in Scene 3.

―――――

ENTR'ACTE:

Metronome begins Slowed Songs while all other performers continue Tone Poem Chorus.

Metronome pulls light-switch. Slowed Songs cease. Metronome turns the set through 90 degrees.

There are five performers in the play. Since Act 1 was begun by the first performer, Act 2 will be begun by the second performer, Act 3 by the third performer, Act 4 by the fourth performer and Act 5 by the fifth performer.

Thus each performer instigates an act, elaborating on the actions already instigated.

In each act another performer begins Slowed Songs instead of the Tone Poem Chorus – thus, by the end of act 5, all the performers will be engaged in Slowed Songs.

APPENDIX 4

"Trigger Possibilities"

(An exercise extracted from **Elements of Performance Art** *by Anthony Howell and Fiona Templeton)*

Before performing any exercise, decide:

1) When to start performing that exercise and/or when to start performing that exercise again.

2) When to stop performing that exercise and/or when to stop performing that exercise again.

3) When to modify that exercise and/or when to modify that exercise again. When to stop modifying that exercise and/or when to stop modifying that exercise again.

Any of these decisions may be required in a performance, and any of these decisions may be made in accordance with chosen triggers ... (*Certain exercises are designed with triggers intrinsic to them*).

Trigger Examples:

Either perform, modify or stop performing exercise x

    for the duration of the performance
    for as long as it may take you to count to a chosen number
    for as long as it has taken or will take to perform exercise y
    for as long as you can see performer A
    for the duration of exercise z etc.

    at a touch
    at the sight of performer A in contact with performer B
    at a sound or at a silence
    at the sight of a particular movement
    at a particular word
    at a change of light, change of set etc.

until the exercise you are performing exhausts you
until you make a mistake (2, 3, 4 mistakes etc.)
until all the other performers are prone
until reaching the edge, centre or any chosen area of the performance
space
until reaching the end of any particular series of actions or counts
demanded by the exercise
until all the other performers are performing the same exercise etc.

when all the other performers start performing exercise y
when performer A enters / leaves the performance space
when any two performers speak / move simultaneously
when you can see no other performer
when chosen members of the audience stand up / sit down / cough etc.
when travelling in a straight line, curve etc.

Any trigger can apply to one, some or all the performers or to any exercise. Practically any aspect of a performance can be employed as a trigger for another aspect of that performance.

Decisions as to which trigger to employ for what aspect of which exercise may be made by chance. Triggers may be the common knowledge of the group during the performance. Secret triggers may be employed during a performance.

BIBLIOGRAPHY

Adams, Parveen: *The Emptiness of the Image*, **Routledge**, London and New York, 1996.

Alsop, Ric & deLahunter, Scott (editors): *The Connected Body? An interdisciplinary Approach to the Body and Performance*, Amsterdam Readings on the Arts and Education, **Amsterdam School of the Arts**. Amsterdam, 1996.

Armstrong, Elisabeth & Rothfuss, Joan: *In the Spirit of Fluxus*, **Walker Art Center**. Minneapolis, 1993.

Bachelard, Gaston: *The Poetics of Space*, **The Orion Press. Inc**, New York, 1964.

Bailey, Derek: *Improvisation: its nature and practice in music*, **The British Library**, London,1992.

Bakhtin, Mikhail: *Rabelais and his World*, **Indiana University Press**, Bloomington, USA, 1984.

Baker, Kenneth: *Redemption through Painting: late works of Morandi*, in *Giorgio Morandi*, catalogue of an exhibition organised by the **Des Moines Art Centre** in 1982, USA, 1982.

Battcock, Gregory & Nickas, Robert: *The Art of Performance*, **E.P. Dutton**, New York, 1984.

Baudrillard, Jean: *The Evil Dream of Images*, **Power Institute of Fine Art. University of Sydney**, Sydney, Australia, 1987.
The Illusion of the End, trans. Chris Turner, **Polity Press**, Oxford, 1994.

Beckett, Samuel: *Waiting for Godot*, **Faber**, London, 1959.

Büchner, Anton: *Danton's Death*, **Heinemann** , London, 1983.

Chard, Chloe: *Spectral Souvenirs*, paper delivered as part of *Emma Hamilton, Naples and Enjoyment* – **The Paul Mellon Centre Seminars 1996-97**, organised by Chloe Chard & Helen Langdon, London, 1997.
'*Women who transmute into Tourist Attractions: Spectator and Spectacle in the Warm South*', in *Romantic Geographies: Discourses of Travel in the Romantic Period*, edited by Amanda Gilroy, **Manchester University Press**, Manchester. 1998.

Childs, Nicky & Walwin, Jeni (editors): *A Split Second of Paradise, Live Art, Installation and Performance*, **Rivers Oram Press**, London, 1997.

Dawkins, Richard: *The Selfish Gene*, **Oxford University Press**, Oxford, 1989.

Deleuze, Gilles: *Difference & Repetition*, **Athlone**, London, 1994.

Deleuze, Gilles & Guattari, Felix: *Anti-Oedipus: capitalism and schizophrenia*, preface by Michel Foucault, **Athlone**, London, 1983.

Descartes, Rene: *Discourse on Method and Other Writings*, trans. F. E. Sutcliffe, **Penguin Classics**. London, 1968.

Dunne, J.W. *An Experiment with Time*, **Faber & Faber**, London, 1927.

Ellis, Brett Easton: *American Psycho*, **Picador**, London, 1991

Euripides: *Hercules Furens (Hercules Distracted)* in *The Plays of Euripides in English in 2 Volumes*, trans. Shelley, Dean Millman, Potter and Woodhull, with an introduction by V.R.R., Everyman Library, **J.M. Dent & Sons**. London, 1906.

Fisher, Joel: *Exhibition Catalogue*, **Nigel Greenwood Gallery**, London, 1974.

Fluxus: *In the Spirit of Fluxus*, **Walker Art Centre**, Minneapolis, USA, 1993.

Forti, Simone: *Handbook in Motion*, The Nova Scotia Series: Source Materials of the Contemporary Arts, **The Press of the Nova Scotia College of Art & Design**, Halifax, and **New York University Press**. New York, 1974.

Foucault, Michel: *This is not a Pipe: with Illustrations and Letters by René Magritte*, Translated and edited by James Harkness, **University of California Press**. Berkely / L.A. / London, 1983.

Freud Sigmund: *The Standard Edition of the Complete Works of Sigmund Freud*, translated under the general editorship of James Strachey, adapted and slightly abridged for **The Penguin Freud Library**, London,1991.
> *Collected papers: Authorised Translation under the Supervision of Joan Rivière*, **Basic Books,** New York, 1959.

Gilman, Sander L.: *Seeing the Insane*, **John Wiley and Brunner/Mazel**. New York, 1982.

Goat Island: *Hankbook – Process and Performance of 'It's Shifting, Hank'*, Adrian Blundell documentarian, **Goat Island** Chicago and **Ferens Art Gallery**, Hull, 1994.
> *Goat Island Schoolbook – textbook of the 1996 Goat Island Summer School in Glasgow*, **Goat Island**, Chicago and **Centre for Contemporary Arts**. Glasgow, 1997.

Goldberg, Roselee: *Performance: Live Art 1909 to the present*, **Thames & Hudson**, London, 1979.
> *Performance: Live Art Since the Sixties*, **Thames and Hudson**, London, 1998.

Gracián, Baltasar: *The Oracle: a manual of the art of discretion*, **J.M.Dent**, London,1953.

Grosskurth, Phyllis: *Melanie Klein: a biography*, **Hodder & Stoughton**, London, 1986.

Hall, Calvin S.: *Primer of Freudian Psychology*, **Mentor**, New York, 1956.

Hegel, G.W.F.: *Hegel's Science of Logic*, trans. A.V. Miller, **George Allen and Unwin**, London, 1969.

Howell, Anthony: *Subjective Denouement: the work of Robert Wilson*, **Artscribe no. 13**, London, 1978.
> *Five Figure Exercise* (article on Lucinda Childs, Philip Glass, Sol Lewitt, Stuart Sherman and Robert Wilson) in **Harpers & Queen International**, May 1979.
> *Performance Test* (article on Bruce Mclean and Nice Style) in **Harpers & Queen International**. London, November, 1979.

Performance Land Art, in **Performance Magazine**, No. 33 and No. 34, London, 1985.

Performance, **Tate Gallery Catalogue**, London, 1985.

Memory and the Body, (symposium paper), (Re)Membered Bodies Symposium, Drama Dept., Lancaster University, 1995.

Howell, Anthony & Templeton, Fiona: *Elements of Performance Art*, **Ting Books**, (now at 21 Augusta Street, Adamsdown, Cardiff CF2 1EN), UK, 1977.

Ibsen, Henrik: *Four Major Plays*, **Signet**, New York, 1970.

Irigaray, Luce: *Gesture and Psychoanalysis* – reprinted in *Sexes and Genealogies*, **Columbia University Press**. 1993.

Jaspers, Karl: *Man in the Modern Age*, trans. by Eden and Cedar Paul, **G. Routledge & Sons**, London, 1933.

The Perennial Scope of Philosophy, trans. Ralph Mannheim, **Routledge & Kegan Paul**, London, 1950.

Jensen, Wilhelm: *Gradiva*, trans. Downey, **Sun & Moon Classics**. Los Angeles, USA, 1993.

Jones, Ernest: *Papers on Psychoanalysis*, **Bailliere, Tindall & Cox**, London, 1977.

Kelly, Mike: *The Uncanny*, exhibition catalogue for *Sonsbeek 93*, **Gemeentemuseum**, Arnhem, Netherlands, 1993.

Kierkegaard, Soren: *Writings 1813-55*, **Princeton University Press**, USA, 1990.

Klein, Melanie: *The Selected Melanie Klein*, edited by Juliet Mitchell, **Penguin**, London, 1991.

The Writings of Melanie Klein, **Hogarth**, London, 1984.

Künstlerhaus Bethanien: *Performance: another dimension*, **Frölich & Kaufmann**, Berlin, 1983.

Lacan, Jacques: *The Four Fundamental Concepts of Psychoanalysis*, **Penguin**, London, 1979.

Écrits: a selection, **Norton**, New York, 1980.

Seminars, volumes I & II, **Cambridge**, 1988.

Laing, R.D.: *Knots*, **Penguin**, London, 1967.

Lévi-Strauss, Claude: *Tristes Tropiques*, trans. John and Doreen Weightman, **Penguin (Peregrine)**, London, 1984.

Marston, John: *The Dutch Courtesan*, edited by M. L. Wine, **Edwin Arnold**, London, 1965.

Maynard Smith, John: *On Evolution*, **Edinburgh University Press**, Edinburgh, 1972.

The Evolution of Sex, **Cambridge University Press**. Cambridge, 1978.

Evolution and the Theory of Games, **Cambridge University Press**, Cambridge & New York, 1982.

McLuhan, Marshall: *The Gutenberg Galaxy: the making of typographic man*, **Routledge & Kegan Paul**, London, 1962.

McLuhan, Marshall & Fiore, Quentin: *The Medium is the Massage: an inventory of effects*, **Penguin**, London, 1967.

Morgan, Stuart: *The Death and Rebirth of British Performance*, essay in *Cinq Ans d'Art Performance à Lyon*, catalogue, **CEP**, Lyon, France, 1984 – reprinted in *What the Butler Saw*, selected writings by Stuart Morgan, **Durian Publications**, London, 1996.

Nietzsche, Friedrich: *The Joyful Wisdom*, **Frederick Ungar**, New York, 1960.

Nijinsky, Vaslav: *The Diary of Vaslav Nijinsky*, **Simon and Schuster**, New York, 1936.

Orlan:*This is my Body .. This is my Software*, edited and produced by Duncan McCorquodale, **Black Dog Publishing Ltd**, London, 1996.

Pilinsky, Janos: *Conversations with Sheryl Sutton*, **Carcanet**, Manchester, UK, 1992.

Plautus: *The Rope and Other Plays*, trans. Watling, **Penguin Classics,** London, 1981.

Rabelais, Francois: *Gargantua & Pantagruel*, trans. Urquhart & Le Motteux, **Chatto & Windus**, London, 1979.

Racliffe, Carter & Rosenblum, Robert: *Gilbert & George: the singing sculptures*, **Anthony McCall,** New York, 1993.

Reik, Theodor:*Listening with the Third Ear*, **Farrar Strauss**, reprinting 1998/9. (extract quoted is in Gilman, *Seeing the Insane* – see above).

Riding, Laura: *Selected Poems: in five acts*, **Faber**, London, 1970.

Rimbaud,Arthur: *Collected Poems*, with an introduction and prose translations by Oliver Bernard, **Penguin Classics**, 1962, reprinted 1986.

RiviPre, Joan: *Womanliness as Masquerade*, **International Journal of Psychoanalysis**. Vol 10, page 376. This essay reprinted and included in *Formations of Fantasy*, edited by Victor Burgin, Donald James and Cora Kaplan, **Methuen**. London & New York, 1986.

Robbe-Grillet, Alain: *Last Year at Marienbad (L'Année Dernière à Marienbad)*, film-script written with Alain Resnais, trans. Howard, **Grove Press,** New York, 1962.

Rycroft, Charles:*Critical Dictionary of Psychoanalysis*, **Penguin**, London, 1995.

Sacks, Oliver: *The Man who Mistook his Wife for a hat*, **Picador**, London, 1986.

Schneemann, Carolee:*More than Meat Joy: performance works & selected writings*, Documentext, **McPherson & Co.**, Kingston, NY, 1997.
　　Carolee Schneemann: up to and including her limits, **New Museum of Contemporary Art**, New York, 1997.

Silliman, Ron: *The New Sentence*, **Roof Books**, New York, 1987.

Sophocles: *The Dramas of Sophocles*, trans. Young, Everyman Library, **J.M. Dent & Son**, London, 1928.

Sprinkle,Annie:*Love and Kisses from Annie Sprinkle*, Vols I & II, **Gates of Heck Inc**, New York, 1997.
　　Annie Sprinkle – Post Porn Modernist, **Torch Gallery**, and new edition by **Clies Press**, San Francisco, due 1998.

Stanislavsky, K.S.: *An Actor Prepares*, trans. Elizabeth Reynolds Hapgood, **Eyre Methuen**, London, 1980.

Šukvaković, Miško: *Neša Paripović: Autoportreti*, **Prometej**, Novi Sad, 1996.

Svevo, Italo: *The Confessions of Zeno,* **Penguin,** London, 1973.

Templeton, Fiona: *You: The City,* **Roof Books,** New York, 1990.

Virilio, Paul: *Speed and Politics: an essay on Dromology,* trans. Mark Polizzotti, Foreign Agents Series, **Semiotext(e),** New York, 1986.

Walter, Norman: *The Sexual Cycle of Human Warfare,* **The Mitre Press,** London, 1950.

Walwin, Jeni: Low Tide, Writings on Artists' Collaborations, **Black Dog Publishing Ltd,** London, 1998.

Wedekind, Frank: *Spring Awakening,* trans. Ted Hughes, **Faber,** London, 1995.

White, Allon: *The Uses of Obscurity,* **Routledge & Kegan Paul,** London, 1981

Wilden, Anthony: *System & Structure: essays in communication and exchange,* **Tavistock,** London, 1977.

Williamson, Aaron: *A Holythroat Symposium,* **Creation Books,** London, 1993

Winnicott, D.W.: *Playing and Reality,* **Routledge,** London, 1991.

Wittgenstein, Ludwig: *Tractatus Logico-Philosophicus,* **Routledge,** London, 1922.

Zizek, Slavoj: *Metastases of Enjoyment,* **Verso,** London, 1994.

INDEX

Other titles in the Contemporary Theatre Studies series:

Other titles in the Contemporary Theatre Studies series:

This book is part of a series. The publisher will accept continuation orders which may be cancelled at any time and which provide for automatic billing and shipping of each title in the series upon publication. Please write for details.